Julian More has written both book and lyrics for musicals *Expresso Bongo*, *Irma La Douce* and the award-winning *Songbook*. As a travel writer he has collaborated with his photographer-daughter, Carey More, on *Views from a French Farmhouse*, *A Taste of Provence* and *Impressions of the Seine*.

More About France

A Sentimental Journey

Julian More

PAN BOOKS
LONDON, SYDNEY AND AUCKLAND

First published 1992 by Jonathan Cape, London

This edition published 1993 by Pan Books Limited
a division of Pan Macmillan Publishers Limited
Cavaye Place London SW10 9PG
and Basingstoke

Associated companies throughout the world

ISBN 0 330 32736 4

A CIP catalogue record for this book is available from
the British Library

Printed in England by Clays Ltd, St Ives plc

Lyrics from *Irma La Douce* are quoted by arrangement with
Monty Norman, David Heneker, and Éditions Micro.

For Sheila

who appears as S in the book, sharer of the journey,
funder of ideas, reader of drafts
and provider of encouraging libations.

Le POUR, et le CONTRE se trouvent en chaque nation; there is a balance said he, of good and bad everywhere; and nothing but the knowing it is so can emancipate one half of the world from the prepossessions which it holds against the other – that the advantage of travel, as it regarded the *sçavoir vivre*, was by seeing a great deal both of men and manners; it taught us mutual toleration; and mutual toleration, concluded he, making a bow, taught us mutual love.

Laurence Sterne, A Sentimental Journey

Contents

Acknowledgments

If I thanked all the people in my France Past who have contributed to this book, it would need another book. So I must reluctantly limit gratitude to those in France Present for all kinds of help on my sentimental journey.

I could never have penetrated Euro Tunnel without William Coleman, nor had news of an old flame at the Hôtel d'Alsace without Guy-Louis Duboucheron, nor attended the village school of Bargemon without Monsieur Nicollet, its headmaster. La Famille Pic jogged my memory about a meal eaten thirty-three years ago. Edith Bounin-Knight comes top of the list of helpful Niçois, while Claire de Andia gave me an update on St-Tropez. I was entertained royally by International Distillers and Vintners at Château Loudenne and Anthony and Eva Barton at Château Langoa; by Mary Crook in the Loire Valley and the Mayor of Saulieu, Docteur Philippe Lavault and Madame Lavault. Not to mention Bernard Loiseau at the Côte d'Or.

Thanks also to Carey More for the jacket pictures, to Bruno Leroy, my agent Abner Stein, and the patient people at Jonathan Cape who supervised the journey's end and new beginning: Tom Maschler, Anne Newman, and Peter Dyer.

Julian More, 1992

I

Picardy, 1937

Getting to know a foreign country is like sex: the younger you begin, the longer you continue. And my chequered affair with France started when I was nine.

I shall never forget my first Channel crossing in 1937. Though the details are hazy, my memory is jogged by two photographs.

In the first, now faded black-and-white, my father and mother look happy on deckchairs on the primitive car ferry. My father, always a dashing dresser, wears a spotted bow-tie, matching silk handkerchief in his jacket pocket, plus-fours and white and brown co-respondent's shoes. My mother sports a racy, not quite French beret. Manfred, our Swiss au pair boy, also wears plus-fours, but Swiss-style – down to his ankles.

The second snap shows our family motor car suspended in mid-air, with Calais Gare Maritime in the background. A ship's funnel is all that is visible of the Dover-Calais car ferry; the rest hidden below the level of the quayside. The crane lifting the Vauxhall, with ropes attached to the four wheels, is also out of shot. But stepping off a ladder, the clean-cut, upright figure, in regimental raincoat and trilby hat, is none other than the ferry's owner, Colonel Stuart Townsend.

'Thank you, Colonel,' said my father, shaking Townsend's hand rather to his surprise. My father was prone to shake hands with Great Western Railway engine drivers who had delivered him safely to Paddington from Llanelli, our Welsh town, so I was used to it. 'Splendid trip.'

Pioneer of car ferries, Townsend had converted a World War I minesweeper *The Forde*, and his ferry, like me, was nine years old.

In 1937, Townsend still personally supervised the occasional crossing, especially when tricky transportation called for his officer-like qualities. On this particular day, a London to Switzerland tour bus had been perilously crane-loaded on to the deck at Dover, handled by a Kentish crew of eight. A similar crew of sturdy Calaisians now swung it safely shorewards. Despite the Colonel's cool command of the operation, the bus ended up in a ditch ten miles out of Calais. We found the unhurt passengers forlornly wondering how they would get to Switzerland.

We were headed for Switzerland too, but had no room for passengers. With all our clobber, the Vauxhall was a tight squeeze for myself, my mother, father, and Manfred, six-foot-six of Helvetic beefcake who took up most of the back seat. Compared to the stranded coach passengers I was privileged but failed to appreciate it with *him* next to me.

Manfred had been engaged as a kind of mobile crammer; I had missed a lot of school due to diphtheria, and in theory he would help me catch up. In fact, he ruined my hand-writing. 'In Switzerland, we do not allow left-handed writing,' he announced, making me draw a map and write the names of the villages round Lake Lucerne with my right hand. Naturally, as soon as I went to prep school, I returned to a left-handed script, from then on as illegible as a doctor's.

Early morning runs and a predilection for throwing me into the deep end of municipal swimming pools, shouting 'Schwimm! Schwimm!', were Manfred's further attempts to give me strength through joy. We stayed with his family in Switzerland; his father had a hunting-lodge and looked unfortunately like Adolf Hitler. But there any resemblance to their Nazi neighbours ended. They were kindly hosts: Manfred's pretty sister embarrassed me with an affectionate farewell, kissing me on both cheeks, and in front of my parents too. Brought up to single Anglo-Saxon pecks, I wasn't ready for the feel of lips even faintly lingering. In this family, it was a mystery where Manfred's regimental nature came from.

Perhaps I have the darker side of Manfred to thank for this book being about France and not Switzerland. To be fair, I do have memories beyond those boring Lake Lucerne villages, memories of proudly adding metal insignia to my alpenstock – 'Rigi', 'Matterhorn', 'Zermatt'; the taste of black cherry jam; the ratchety sound of mountain railways; walking the ice of the Rhône glacier . . .

But Switzerland is not France.

Nor do I remember my father quite so excited, at any moment of our Swiss holiday, as at the first glimpse of the Hôtel de Ville, tallest of Calais landmarks, its dotty neo-Flemish spire and ornate clock tower, like some Renaissance fairy castle dominating the town. For my father, it was a return to familiar ground. This was Flanders Field, where he had seen service in World War I. Where many comrades-in-arms had fallen. And where now we would see tanks still preserved on the battlefields, trenches as tourist attractions, and the Futurist monument to the Canadians at Vimy Ridge.

Sweet enemy attitudes die hard. Across what the British call the Strait of Dover and the French call Le Pas de Calais, a love-hate relationship has flourished for eight centuries – since Richard the Lionheart passed through on his way to a Crusade and English longbowmen routed the French army at nearby Crécy.

'Wogs begin at Calais,' announced Nancy Mitford's Uncle Matthew. 'Abroad is unutterably bloody, and all foreigners fiends.' Yet cross the Channel we must – by whatever means.

In 1785 Blanchard and Jeffries made the first balloon crossing of the Channel. In order to stay airborne for the 22-mile flight, they were forced to jettison all ballast from their wicker basket, and only just made it, their hairy descent through the trees of the Forest of Guines nearly ending in disaster.

Larkier first crossings, perpetuating the legend of British eccentricity, have been made on a plank of wood, by pedalo, parachute, windsurfer, astride a whisky bottle, and in a four-poster bed. And in 1975, thirty-two oarsmen rowed over in a *drakkar*, such as had not been seen in the Channel since the Danish invasion of France in the ninth century.

Our 1937 crossing seemed to me every bit as adventurous. And my father, a compulsive car-worrier, was forced to stop the car after less than a mile of tight-lipped *tenez la droite* driving. He thought he heard a noise from under the Vauxhall. While he did his usual round, gently kicking the tyres as though reassuring himself that the wheels were still there, my mother prepared our first picnic in France, its ingredients cautiously bought in Dover. By the next day, however, Hovis and meat loaf had confidently given way to baguette and garlic sausage, a smell with which the blue-smocked Calais porters, scuttering aboard our ferry in search of foot passengers, had seemed impregnated.

My father checked the oil and water, just in case. And my mother read to us from Great-Aunt Bessie's Baedeker, lent to her for the trip, about Rodin's *Burghers of Calais*, a monument a couple of minutes' walk from our picnic spot beneath the trees in a municipal park. It commemorated a most poignant incident in the Channel's turbulent history.

A notorious Calaisian pirate, Pédrogue, had been terrorising English merchant ships in their trade with nearby Flanders. In 1346, Edward III retaliated by blockading the French port. The siege lasted three years. Finally, weak with starvation, the Calaisians surrendered, and the English king agreed to pardon them on one condition: six of the most distinguished citizens must throw themselves upon his mercy. Six merchants duly volunteered to sacrifice personal riches, and, if necessary, their lives for the people. Whereupon, the English Queen Philippa, touched by their abject appearance, begged the King not to have them executed. The King consented; city and burghers were saved. And Calais became a British possession for 210 years.

Mary Tudor's dying words, Francis de Guise having reconquered the Calaisis for the French in 1558, were: 'If my heart were cut out, engraved upon it would be the name of Calais.'

Even from Great-Aunt Bessie's Baedeker, the burghers of Calais beat the villagers of Weggis (Lake Lucerne) any day. So I didn't moan too much when my mother, herself an artist, proposed we see Rodin's famous statue before pushing on to the first night stop at Amiens.

Standing in the gardens of the Town Hall the group of six figures sculptured in bronze, now covered in verdigris, is doubly dignified by that Disneyland folly in the background. Noble green faces of the burghers contrast with the droll face of the Town Hall's clock behind them; orange with a red sun in the middle, white hands, and blue numerals. The burghers are depicted as they paid obeisance to King Edward: wearing austere shifts, barefoot, carrying the keys of city and castle. Equally humble is the artist's name on the plaque. Of the five notables present at the 1895 inauguration the sculptor comes fifth, mentioned simply as Monsieur A. Rodin, Statuaire. He had worked ten years on it.

From *The Burghers of Calais*, it was a short drive to the beggars of Amiens, where we witnessed a savage settling of scores – the bringing of an apprentice beggarwoman into line outside the cathedral. The harsh realities of the present disturbed our cosy communion with the past, and the sound of slaps and punches stayed with me longer than the pealing of cathedral bells.

Amiens seemed at first such a genteel town. My father, a methodical man, travelled with a neat wallet of documents: passports, Automobile Association route to Switzerland, insurance vouchers in case of accident. From it, he now took his letter of hotel room confirmation at the Grand Hôtel de L'Univers. The desk clerk bowed and beamed. Never before had I been welcomed in such splendour. Though it was a tourist hotel, to me it seemed like the Ritz. Chandeliers glittered, plush carpets yielded to my gym-shoes. My room, shared with the dreaded Manfred stuffing various parts of himself with cotton wool, overlooked the trees of the Place René-Goblet, and late night car horns from the Rue Noyon woke me often. I did not care. I went to the window and looked out: France . . . I was in France.

France was life with the dull bits cut out – as Alfred Hitchcock once said about movies.

The bread in the dining-room tasted crustier. I had never seen bigger peaches, nor whiter napery. At breakfast, there was a faint, lingering smell of exotic sauces and black tobacco left over from dinner the night before. A grown-up dinner with me at it, like the French children at the next table. I was even given a taste of my father's wine.

Then a dull bit threatened. My mother suggested we do the cathedral, which was not exactly a nine-year-old's idea of fun. And if I was good, she promised, we would go afterwards to the Gare and look at the trains. I drew French trains and guillotines with an obsessive passion, using a set square to get the guillotine knife right. French trains I could be taken to; guillotines, even to satisfy a ghoulish brat like myself, were beyond my parents' scope.

Violence, however, was not far away.

From the far side of the cathedral square, my eyes travelled down the two Gothic towers, down the intricate façade with its ornate stone carvings, past the rose window, and, on reaching the three stone portals, became aware of a cluster of black figures at ground level. 'What are they?' I asked.

'Nuns, probably,' my mother replied casually.

'They look like crows.'

On approaching the cathedral entrance, I saw they were not nuns. Or crows. A whole gang of beggarwomen were waiting for us. They hovered, sullen and predatory. As we came nearer, they made a move, some limping professionally, others making the pathetic wheedling sounds learned in a tough school, all closing in for the kill.

'Nothing to be afraid of, old man,' said my father. He raised a masterful hand, smiling pleasantly. '*Après, après.*'

'*Après quoi?*' asked the cheeky young apprentice, bold and beautiful compared to the old crones behind her. She was my first Frenchwoman; even the poorest seemed sure of themselves.

'*Après nous avons fait la cathédrale,*' my father replied.

'*Mon p'tit cadeau avant . . .*' the girl teased, and another young beggarwoman gave a dirty cackle. An older woman shut her up.

Whereupon the burly Manfred, springing to the defence of his English family, strongly and silently strode in among the sinister flock. Astonished, and afraid of being trampled to death, the beggarwomen made way for us. We followed Manfred briskly towards the entrance, where lounged a group of toughs in scarves and rakish cloth caps with yellowed cigarettes dangling from their lips.

I have never been happier to be inside a church.

It was the biggest cathedral in France, my mother read out from her guidebook. The organ, she explained, was Flamboyant Gothic. And the description reminded me of another churchy word I'd read somewhere.

'What are gargoyles?'

'Little monsters.'

'Where?'

'Outside.'

'Like those beggarwomen . . .'

My mother, who was a socialist and feminist, was shocked and upset by them, too. But for different reasons. How could Léon Blum's Popular Front, the recent leftist government, have failed to get such *misérables* a better deal? She would have agreed with Laurence Sterne, encountering his first French beggars at Montreuil:

> Let no man say 'let them go to the devil' –
> tis a cruel journey to send a few miserables, and they
> have had sufferings enow without it . . .

To me, I'm ashamed to say, they were traumatic hags such as Smollett encountered in the Roman baths of Nîmes. My sheltered life had so far suffered no worse than diphtheria and Manfred.

We must have paid our respects to the cathedral's resplendent marble floor; the intricate wood carving of the choirstalls by a local rabbit-hutch-maker, with their superb tracery and images of thistles, oak-leaves and vines as well as biblical scenes; the baroque seventeenth-century altar piece, its sun's rays spurting out like a fountain of gold. But I remember none of it, obsessed as I was by the thought of those beggarwomen waiting for us outside.

We emerged to angry shouts. Mayhem had broken out among the beggarwomen and some of the Jean Gabins lurking in the portal had moved in for action. The apprentice was in deep trouble.

Remembering my father's promise, she defiantly broke away from the others and strode towards him with an avaricious grin. My father was prepared. Like Laurence Sterne, he had a handful of sous at the ready, giving one to the apprentice who was well ahead of the crones limping after her.

'*Dieu vous bénisse!*' the girl said provocatively to my father, and would have tried extracting the rest of the sous from him, had it not been for the creatures clawing at her from behind.

She shook them off and turned angrily, only to be set upon again by punching, grabbing and scratching hands. Their rage seemed out of all proportion to the girl's offence. She had merely been a little more enterprising than the others, and now here she was, arms flailing in self-defence, clogged feet aiming painful hacks, until two toughs pulled her roughly from the mêlée, smashing her against the cathedral wall, pinning her arms.

Meanwhile I had my own problems. With his usual interference, Manfred tried to pull me away from the ugly scene and I resisted, determined to see the outcome. I was rooting for the girl, and reckoned Manfred should defend her instead of pushing me around.

But nobody defended her. After a brief argument among the crones, a delegate was chosen to give the girl a sound slapping. While the men held her, a beefy bitch handed out the punishment. The slaps resounded round the cathedral square like firecrackers at a fête.

This was street justice, a settling of scores in which tourists had no part. After a few brave but futile protestations, my father looked around for a gendarme. There was none. As the slaps gave way to full-face punches and blood began to spurt from the girl's mouth, I was thankful to be rushed from the scene of her punishment.

For many nights, I was awoken in my strange hotel rooms not by traffic in the street but nightmares of gargoyles and fighting crows. And I never drew guillotines again.

In 1990 I returned to Amiens for the first time. By no means did I have any special fondness for the place, but such strong memories of it drew me ineluctably back to its cathedral square.

The cathedral itself, apart from the installation of new organ pipes in 1938, had not changed since I'd last seen it. What are a mere fifty-three years in eight centuries of existence? And the first thing that greeted me at the portal was the hand of a beggar.

It was the eternal return – '. . . no right to work, see. Got my accident pension, M'sieur, but it doesn't pay for the little pleasures . . .' Fumes of Pelforth beer with every syllable. 'Three years in hospital after a truck crash . . . two months in a coma . . .'

The beggar's face was scarred. He had a glass eye, wore a bright blue sweater and double-breasted tweed suit. When he took my coin, he took it with healthy disrespect. No show of grovelling

gratitude and God-bless-you-squire. And why am I calling him beggar? The *mot juste* nowadays is down-and-out or, at worst, derelict.

My childhood brush with the beggars of Amiens left its mark.
To this day I have a horror of street violence, and the mildest
stranger asking the way is a potential mugger. Charity, for me,
begins in the street: dropping a coin into a cap seems an essential
part of good karma, a form of protection. It's an indulgent hang-
up, I know. In a better world, there should not be bodies prone on
the pavements of Calcutta – nor, for that matter, homeless sleeping
rough on the Strand and Fifth Avenue, nor derelicts on the steps of
Amiens Cathedral.

And this return to Amiens, which I had avoided over the years,
was intended to exorcise old ghosts. Now, greeted by the derelict
with the glass eye, I wondered what had been the fate of the
apprentice beggarwoman, and found it hard to pursue the good
things Amiens was now said to offer.

The pious commentary of the Son et Lumière inside the cathedral seemed unrelated to the precarious lives outside: 'Man is a
cathedral. Each stone represents a man, and the whole is mankind
working towards spiritual good.'

But, as the light show came into action, the cathedral's architec-
tural marvels emerged stunningly from the darkness to speak for
themselves. High above, light focused on one feature, then cross-
faded to another in waves of colour; the tall pillars moved in and
out of shadow and revelation. Suddenly the concavity of the
vaulted ceiling changed in an optical illusion to a convex shape.
One moment, it was like being a bird inside a cage, looking at the
wires curving above; the next, I was outside the cage, looking at
the wires rounded on its top. In those moments a childlike
enchantment took over and I was lost in the cathedral's splendour.

Today's parents, bringing their nine-year-old on his first trip to
France could do worse than start with Picardy. Amiens, I discovered, had much to recommend it besides Son et Lumière – even a
permanent circus.

French towns possess their bricks-and-mortar circuses just as
they have their law courts and town hall. And the Circus of
Amiens, a nineteenth-century building which would have
delighted John Betjeman, contains 3,000 seats. Famous for its

trapeze acts, it now also houses a circus school. Its original construction in 1889 was highly experimental, using a metallic structure in the same year as the Eiffel Tower, which the novelist Jules
Verne, then a city councillor, maliciously referred to as 'a baby
with Amiens paternity'.

Amiens is full of Jules Verne: Boulevard Jules Verne; the Jules
Verne Memorial; and Jules Verne's tomb with a sculptured torso
reaching dramatically out of the ground in a last death-defying gesture before sinking into eternity. But try finding Jules Verne's
house . . .

'Who's he?' asked the boy on the bicycle.

'The author, Jules Verne . . .'

'Oh, him.' Turning to a girl with a pram (in the Boulevard Jules
Verne), 'Know where Jules Verne's house is?'

'Know where Jules Verne's house is?' she repeated to a bearded
man passing. An *intello* would surely know.

'Ah, yes. I believe it's . . .' The *intello* looked up and down the
road, tugged at his beard, '. . . on the corner of the Boulevard Jules
Verne.'

'M'sieur . . .' I said. 'This is the Boul . . .'

'I know, I know,' he said. 'Follow me.' We all followed him to
the junction with Rue Charles Dubois, where stood an imposing
Victorian mansion. '*Voilà, M'sieur* – the Jules Verne Documentation Centre. I must visit it myself some time.'

He would not be disappointed.

From its name, I had expected some stuffy literary shrine. Not a
bit of it. Greeted by a blonde *gardienne* in jeans, I was informed
briskly: 'The people of Amiens couldn't care less about Jules
Verne. The Office de Tourisme doesn't even put up signposts from
the railway station.'

And no one would hit this dull residential part of Amiens by
chance. The great adventure writer clearly didn't need the stimulus
of exotic surroundings to come up with *Around the World in Eighty
Days* and the other fifty-five extraordinary voyages written at
Amiens. Just quiet and calm – and there was plenty of that. As he
wrote to his son, Michel: 'On the wishes of my wife, I'm settling
in Amiens, a sensible town, law-abiding, of even temper, with a
friendly and well-read society.'

Jules clearly did not frequent the cathedral square.

My spirited *gardienne* showed me round a solid provincial town house perfectly suited to the Vernes' life-style. His wife Honorine used to hold weekly soirées. Jules could not abide the music, and retired to his office to work.

The office was also his bedroom. The lighting, the girl explained, had been kept purposely low to create a dawn effect. I gasped, as though intruding on privacy – I was suddenly aware of a man sitting in the study chair: a waxwork of Jules Verne starting the day's work at 5.30 a.m. Replicas, too, of the *Nautilus*, Captain Nemo's submarine, a model of the circus, and copies of Verne's sixty-seven novels and plays in all languages, memorabilia for children of all ages.

Apart from his writing, Councillor Verne worked tirelessly to provide amusements for the parents and children of Amiens – the circus, municipal theatre, street fairs and festivals.

And how he would have loved The Night of St-Leu on Midsummer Night!

I joined the rush of Amienois taking to the streets. This was the night of clowns, musicians, street artists, jugglers of all kinds, a pop-culture free-for-all filling the quaysides and corners, cafés and pedestrian precincts of St-Leu. Once, catching a glimpse of jugglers' clubs flying about against a background of the cathedral, I imagined myself at some medieval fair.

The St-Leu quarter was a revelation, worth the visit to Amiens even without street theatre. Below the cathedral, the River Somme feeds little streams which separate the old streets, making a secret canal zone. Between gaily painted two-storey houses, with their bright green or yellow doors, sky blue shutters, red brick or painted wood façades, bridges connect one side of the street with the other, backyards explode with geraniums and roses. Some call it the Amsterdam of Amiens, others the Venice of Amiens. I prefer the St-Leu of Amiens.

If St-Leu reminds me of anywhere, it's Bradford, Yorkshire, and Baltimore, Maryland. The same mix of races, the same determination to revive its run-down but architecturally worth-saving areas or buildings. Bradford has its Asians, Baltimore its Afro-Americans, and Amiens its North Africans.

'Have a tea, M'sieur! Very fresh, very good, very hot.' The old Moroccan offers me a glass of steaming, sweet mint-tea and a small coconut cake. The vast tent smells like a bazaar with its charcoal braziers and merguez sausages sizzling everywhere.

Seemingly the whole maghrébin population of Amiens has come to hear Cheb Khaled, Algerian innovator of the music called Rai, a fusion of traditional wedding and brothel songs with rock. Cheb is giving a free concert. During the long sound balance, whole families – women in head-scarves carrying babies, men sitting together, one or two holding hands – are filling the front benches.

A wild six-eight rhythm begins the concert.

Cheb's plaintive songs with rock guitars and Arab drums tell of dreams and disillusion, of women won and lost, of homesickness, classic maghreb themes with a new beat. The audience clap along. Suddenly a tiny girl in a flowered skirt does a belly dance among the musicians on stage; clearly she's not meant to be there. Cheb, smiling, lets her stay.

Dancing begins. Now maghrébin girls are in front of the band, performing arabesques around each other, hands clapping above their heads. An old white-haired Frenchman joins in, dancing gracefully alone, maybe dreaming of some faraway North African post he held or land he owned when most of North Africa was French. I lose sight of him among the dancers, as more and more pack the floor, clapping and chanting, loving the plangent song and ever-more intricate rhythms of the music.

Near by, round the Place du Don, St-Leu's centre, fairy lights festoon restored medieval houses and the cathedral is floodlit green behind. A juggling act, Pandora's Box, teach a lanky, six-foot girl how to ride a unicycle. As she struggles to stay on, they juggle dangerously, spinning clubs over her head, missing by millimetres. She enjoys it hugely.

On the Quai Parmentier, *marionettiste* Laurent Divine shows a group of children how his puppets work. To the sound of a Barbary organ, a miniature ballet holds their attention till some other act beckons, some wilder music ripples over the River Somme.

Looking for life without the dull bits, I found Amiens did indeed have many treats. But in all of today's Picardy the greatest excitement is, of course, Euro Tunnel, the first landlink between

Britain and France since the cavemen of Kent would cross by causeway on a day trip to Picardy, have a few draughts of rough mead, club a few Picardians for a lark and take home a maiden or two as souvenirs.

I began at the Euro Tunnel Information Centre at Sangatte, where the world's biggest building site has the world's best model railway. Children ooh and ah, as 100-mile-per-hour trains, passenger and car-carriers, speed from the spaghetti junction of Cheriton Terminal in Kent, plunge headlong below Shakespeare Cliff, disappear beneath a telescoped Channel, to emerge seconds later, weaving and whirling into the complex loop of the Coquelles Terminal in France. In 1993, the first real train will take thirty-five minutes, just over 30 miles of its journey underground; a Belgian granny, enthralled by the model train's journey, was heard to exclaim: '*Tiens*, that was quick. I never knew the Channel was so narrow.'

I was about to enter a world worthy of Jules Verne, and one that would stir the imagination of any nine-year-old. The tall, *soignée* young Euro Tunnel hostess assigned to me was hardly what I'd expected. Tiphane, she was called – a brunette with the name and long tresses of a fairytale Breton princess, and the practical directness of a Nanterre sociology student on a summer job.

'Your passport, please, M'sieur More,' Tiphane requested, with a these-bureaucrats-you-know smile of apology. Armed with my documentation, she led the way with a confident stride.

As we approached the main Euro Tunnel complex, a weird metallic sighing sound, carried on the off-shore breeze, drew my attention to the muddy hillock above Sangatte. Three million cubic metres of blue chalk, extracted from the French tunnel works, will be terraced into the foundations of one of the many projected Calais theme parks.

I asked Tiphane what the sound was.

'Like a sea-giant breathing?' So she was poetic, too. 'It's the pumping of liquid blue chalk from the tunnelling. It dries out behind a dike up there, to make that new hill the locals hate.'

'Well, it's not the most attractive hill in northern France.'

'One day', said the loyal Tiphane, 'it will be The Hanging Gardens of The City of Europe. Or something of the sort.'

The Sangatte locals also disapproved, no doubt, of having their small cemetery incorporated in the Euro Tunnel complex. Tiphane strode on, past the cemetery to Security Control, briefly flashed my credentials, and led the way up steps to what looked like a makeshift office block.

A long, empty corridor greeted us. Tiphane excused herself to fetch a key. A little embarrassed, she unlocked a room containing yellow boots, plastic coats, and hard hats for visitors. 'Regulations,' she apologised, helping me into my boots and coat, adjusting the strap of my hat.

Clad for action, Tiphane and I strode off to adventure. Now, with a mane of auburn hair falling from hard hat on to shiny plastic, she was my James Bond girl, and the long, anonymous corridor became a link to some secret and deadly underground operation. Doctor No-Man's Land.

She smiled enigmatically as I glanced through an open door. Miner's clothes were suspended from ceiling racks, rows and rows of them in menacing array, to be lowered and raised like men on a gibbet. 'We call that The Hanged Men's Room,' she said.

At the end of the corridor, Tiphane paused a moment. 'Are you ready for this?' asked her half-closed eyes. She flung open the door . . .

Oh my God!

Where were we? I blinked at the bright light. Suddenly, lo and behold, we were at the top of the shaft – a vast, cylindrical factory open to the skies. Above us, curved segments of reinforced concrete tunnel lining came floating past, carried by travelling crane from the nearby production unit, one every two and a half minutes, to be lowered into the shaft.

I peered over the parapet where, 213 feet below, a bonsai world of tiny workers and miniature rail tracks disappeared into the tunnel entrances. Earth trucks and service trains no bigger than the models I'd been watching less than an hour before, came and went.

The shaft, Tiphane told me, was big enough to contain the Arc de Triomphe.

I had stepped into an adventure movie set; one of those high-tech hideaways of world-class villains. The perfect decor, I thought, for James Bond Meets the Nibelungen. Dizzily I fol-

lowed Tiphane. 'Everything is electronically controlled,' she said
as we passed an Ops Room where men faced control panels and
screens as intently as air traffic controllers. In the Staff Information
Room, closed-circuit TV showed work at the face; charts indicated exact progress at precisely that moment, distances tunnelled
and completed.

We reached the lifts. Above them were the names of the five
Tunnel Boring Machines (TBMs): Brigitte, Europa, Catherine,
Virginie, Pascaline/Séverine. Ian Fleming inventions all. Why did
Pascaline need that alias Séverine? And just where was Tiphane
taking me?

Our lift was eerily silent. It didn't seem to be moving. Then
the doors slid open and a shockwave of sound enveloped us.
Nothing Wagnerian about this subterranean music, more Stock-
hausen, Berio or Cage. I followed Tiphane mechanically now,
like a faithful automaton, into a network of iron stairways and
footbridges.

One level below us were the tunnel entrances – two regular
train size, with a smaller service tunnel between – heading east up
the slope to the French exit at Coquelles and west down towards
England.

I found myself shaking with childlike excitement. For a brief,
ecstatic moment Euro Tunnel was my toy.

Tiphane yelled explanations, and her face flushed with the
effort. 'Watch that earth train. It will disgorge its load . . .' The
automated trucks were tipped simultaneously, and the blue chalk
from the face tumbled into a pit below. Water was added so it
became liquid, and could be pumped up top. 'Come, we will go
down to the tunnels. It is not really allowed, but I have a *copain*
who is foreman . . .'

It was like Clapham Junction at rush-hour down there. A little
yellow personnel transporter clattered in, and the fifty workers
returning from their eight-hour shift at the face couldn't come up
for air fast enough. They doubled past us to be first at the lifts.

A couple of them hesitated politely on a narrow bridge to let us
pass. I felt mean, delaying their exit. 'It's hot down there,' one of
them grinned. 'Forty degrees at the face.'

'A permanent sauna,' added his friend.

We passed a control box, where a man pressed buttons and watched screens. 'He manages all the train movements by computer,' Tiphane yelled. 'Sometimes it breaks down and he just shouts and waves his hands.'

She had to be exaggerating. In such a model of technological efficiency, how could anything break down? 'And what will happen when a TGV breaks down or, God forbid, there's an accident?' I asked, voicing the doubts of millions.

'Emergency exits join the service tunnel, every 410 yards.'

'So if I was in my car,' I shouted, 'travelling in an enclosed car-carrier and the train broke down, I'd have to get out of my car, leave the train, walk maybe 205 yards?'

'And be rescued in the service tunnel.'

Hijacking by terrorists and bomb explosions were also high on my list of awkward questions, but this was neither the moment, nor Tiphane the person to allay the fears of someone scared by a stranger asking the way in the street.

We were looking down one of the brightly lit tunnels towards England. Tiphane's *copain* the foreman inspired confidence, showing off his three tunnels with the pride of a master. Somewhere, several tubed miles down that brightly lit tunnel, a giant earthworm pushed its way towards England.

Little did Thomé de Gamond know what he'd started. After the first murmurings about a Channel Tunnel in 1751, along came this French doctor of law and medicine, hydrographer and geologist extraordinaire. De Gamond made primitive dives in 1833 off the chalk cliffs of Boulogne, wearing ten pig bladders, weighed down by lead weights, ears and nostrils stuffed with cotton soaked in butter, and mouth filled with olive oil. Many and crazy were his tunnel schemes, but his geological findings were crucial to all subsequent developments, including today's trajectory.

The British had the easier dig and the greater distance to tunnel through dry blue chalk all along their 20 miles; the French 12 miles were tougher going – some of them through permeable grey and white chalk using special drilling equipment to cope with the water.

Those French TBMs with Bond-lady names were more like submarines than earthworms. Behind her, Europa drew a 304-yard back-up train, an autonomous production unit: transformers and hydraulic system; excavation equipment; automated placing of concrete lining segments; rail-track laying; ventilation; even a canteen for the fifty-strong face team.

The drill worked on the principle of a slow-speed, superpowerful kitchen mixer. Japanese-designed, the drill heads could adopt open mode in dry sections or closed mode in wet sections, operated by highly sophisticated controls in the driver's cabin.

The driver eased Europa forward, keeping her on course by laser beam and computer. It was high-precision work, following the gentle undulations and curves of her predetermined passage. The margin of error was a mere millimetre per kilometre. At the rate of twelve centimetres a minute, she ploughed calmly on towards England, and you'd hardly know there were other men back there, sweating and striving, keeping up with the relentless moving factory as Europa left a completed tunnel in her wake.

Every few minutes, a polished curved surface of naked blue clay emerged. To this, Europa's hydraulic rams offered up curved segments of reinforced concrete for the men to fix in place, the largest weighing eight tonnes; it took a mere fifteen minutes to fix all six segments of a completed lining ring. Fifteen minutes when human error − a step wrong, a hand mistiming − and you could be crushed to death.

'This is my last job as a hostess,' Tiphane confided, as we said goodbye. 'Tomorrow, it's back to Nanterre and studying. But showing you our tunnel has been an end for me *en beauté*.'

I didn't know what I'd done to deserve such a compliment. My questions had been averagely unintelligent, being a slow grasper of high- or even middle-tech. Mostly, I had followed my yellow-clad guide like an obedient zombie, dazed at the fine madness that is Euro Tunnel.

We have come quite a way since that old converted minesweeper *The Forde* chugged across the Channel under the command of Colonel Stuart Townsend in 1937. But that was my first French connection, and I shall always remember it with affection.

Paris St-Germain-des-Prés, 1948

Every young man of taste and discrimination goes to Paris for the first time, not for the *Mona Lisa* but for a touch of *tendresse*, and I was no exception.

Demobilised from National Service in 1948, I used my government grant to visit French relations in a bourgeois apartment on Avenue de la Grande Armée. Though the bawdy of the barrack room had helped to loosen me up a little, I was at twenty, comparable in maturity to a fifteen-year-old today. English public school had taken its toll on my libido, which lurked in its shell like a retarded snail. It needed liberating, as Paris herself had so recently been. An existential problem easily soluble in the City of Light at that time. Or so I imagined.

'Why do women stare at me in the cafés?' I asked my cousin Bernard, oil executive, devout Catholic and very proper. Also, surprisingly worldly despite the beret he wore on Saturday.

'Not just girls, *mon vieux.*'

So he had noticed. Everyone stared at me. I couldn't fool Bernard. Was it my British warm, the kind of ex-Army officer's overcoat which was rapidly becoming fashionable among the British criminal classes?

'I must tell you, Julian. In all confidence.' Bernard lowered his voice and took a fortifying nip of cognac. 'You look Boche.'

'Boche?!'

'Underneath the British warm.' Nonplussed I looked down at

my bespoke lovat tweed demob' suit by Hawkes of Savile Row, the very essence of Englishness. 'Your suit is exactly the green of a Wehrmacht uniform.'

I was ashamed of my insensitivity. Four years after the Occupation, not even a German went around Paris looking German. And the uniform of the Left Bank was bobby sox, check shirts, and baggy trousers worn with braces (jeans were still far off in the future). The suit remained on its hanger for the rest of my stay.

Somewhere over on the Left Bank rampaged the liberating life of the existentialists. My liberation. The life I was longing to taste, in spite of my conventional appearance and timidity.

'What is your view of Jean-Paul Sartre?' I asked Bernard hopefully. Everyone had one. I supposed Bernard must.

'*Il est fou!*' Bernard pronounced, opening *La Croix*, the militant Catholic newspaper. 'A socialist madman.'

'In my day at the Sorbonne,' added Reine, his otherwise most *sympa* wife, 'it was not necessary to have *le boogie-woogie* playing full blast to discuss philosophy.'

No philosophy was discussed that night – or any other in the Leleu home. Chat was doggedly domestic. With my desire for a little wild living, I didn't feel at ease with my kindly, all-too-respectable French relations. The Leleus were connected to my mother's side of the family via a former French Minister of War, André Maginot. And my mother's maiden name was Lyne, poor thing. What terrible jokes she had to put up with, thanks to that flimsy fortification! The Maginot Line was not a French connection to mention around Paris in the 1940s. Nor have I done so at any time since. Come to think of it, I don't remember the Leleus mentioning André Maginot, either.

Bernard's mother owned the house, so the Leleus had a spacious apartment; French property ads would have called it *grand standing*. It was just five minutes' walk from the Étoile, where traffic hurtled round the Arc de Triomphe, while horns squeaked and gendarmes in capes brandished batons and blew whistles like a scene from *An American in Paris*. The Leleus had no car; they couldn't afford the black-market petrol. Reine and the two little girls, Martine and Blandine, went everywhere by bus. Bernard walked to his office a couple of miles away, eating his breakfast *tartine* as he went.

Bernard's energy was boundless. It explained why the French had already rebuilt their war-shattered railways and ports, and got rid of rationing (except butter, milk, and some sweets). Bernard invited me, as a paying guest, to a business lunch at La Reine Pédauque, a medium-priced restaurant near the Gare St-Lazare. While he talked non-stop with his business colleagues, I quietly spent two-and-a-half hours enjoying oysters and white Burgundy, *omelette paysanne*, steak and red Burgundy, chocolate ice-cream, coffee and armagnac. My share of the bill was two pounds, a sum that made quite a hole in my government grant. But I thought of England and post-war austerity and frugal restaurant meals and how lucky I was to be here.

Then I thought of the Left Bank and Jean-Paul Sartre, and how much luckier I could be.

Bernard's working day began at eight-thirty and lasted twelve hours albeit including a two-hour lunch break. By Friday he was exhausted but he always found time to take me sight-seeing on Saturdays. He was informative and good company – up to a point. He would show me the machine-gun bullet marks of the Liberation on the Palais de Justice, and where Goering liked to lunch. And also where the prettiest prostitutes used to be found.

'Used to be?' I reiterated a little too hastily. 'Where are they now?'

'They have gone,' Bernard replied with a shrug. 'Too many amateurs, thanks to Sartre and friends. There is not the demand there was.'

Why on earth not, I wondered? I couldn't believe that. Not from what I'd heard about Paris from my Uncle Raymond, the family raver from Birmingham. 'What about Montmartre?' I suggested. And invited him to accompany me to the Folies-Bergère.

Bernard looked at me pityingly. 'Those days are over for me. The opera, perhaps.'

So I went to the Folies alone. I liked Josephine Baker, the American coffee-coloured star, warbling '*J'ai deux amours, mon pays-ee et Paree*'. By then in her forties, old enough to be my mother, she was still looking terrific in a modicum of baubles,

bangles, and beads, shaking up a storm. Though not for the finale –
a religioso set-piece with La Josephine as a stained-glass madonna,
to the music of *Ave Maria*. After the show, a man furtively waylaid
me in the foyer, murmuring: 'You want exhibition of love, *jeune
homme?*' Not, I decided, if he were one of the exhibits. Anyway, I
was not interested in spectator sports; I wanted to be a player.

Day after day went by. I did Les Invalides with a group of Welsh
miners. I saw Louis Jouvet in *Knock*. I tramped along the Seine
from Trocadéro to the Ile St-Louis, and made myself sick on
chocolate cakes at the Marquise de Sévigné Salon de Thé. I
traipsed out to Versailles, still dilapidated after the war years. I went
to Gounod's *Faust* at the opera. I even heard a Jesuit priest, former
prisoner in Buchenwald, at an anti-Communist rally outside Notre
Dame, sounding hellfire and damnation against corruption in high
places which could be fodder for the Communist cause.

Corruption in low places, however, continued to elude me. But
I threw myself dutifully into Leleu family life. I went to Martine's
First Communion. The little girls looked sweet in their white veils
and blue rosettes, and we all posed for endless photographs.

I went with Bernard to lunch with his eighty-three-year-old
mother, who lived in a hotel at St-Germain-en-Laye. An English
guest, a peer of the realm to boot, over for some horsey event at
Maisons-Laffitte, had quibbled about his bill, unqualified cad's
behaviour in the view of Bernard's mother. '*Ça ne se fait pas*,' she
muttered. The central heating was so hot, Bernard had an attack of
asthma. After lunch, he and I both fell asleep, to be awoken by his
mother still in full monologue: '*Je me suis trompée*, he was only a Sir,
not a Milord . . . even worse . . .'

St-Germain-en-Laye was not St-Germain-des-Prés. And yet
who, at twenty, likes to sit in a night spot alone? Theatres, operas,
salons de thé, fine. But a smoke-filled, jazz-jumping cellar without
a girl or a *copain* or two . . . what kind of existence is that?

Every French bourgeois family has its black sheep, and the
Leleus had Michel. One day Michel – destined to be boss of a perfume business if he didn't go to prison – blew into the flat like a
refreshing whiff of Sin. '*C'est un mauvais garçon*,' warned Reine
darkly.

Michel and Bernard instantly started an argument about the role

of religion in politics. Michel, a staunch Gaullist, attacked *La Croix*
for being too political a newspaper; it was not the Church's job to
meddle in politics. Bernard yelled that the Popes were the true
champions of the people; since 1884, their Holinesses had tried to
persuade bosses to give their workers a share of the profits.

'With ten per cent for the Pope!' Michel scoffed. Destined for *le
patronat* though he was, Michel was in Bernard's view a triple-A
man: amoral, atheistic, and anarchic.

'Michel will take Julian to St-Germain-des-Prés!' Bernard
teased. 'Won't you, Michel?' In their milieu it was like suggesting
he take me to a sado-masochistic brothel.

Michel, though he also thought Sartre was *fou*, said: 'Willingly,'
and kindly arranged to look after me on the following Saturday.

Unmarried and moneyed, he could afford a car: a vintage
Citroën. When he picked me up, I was surprised to see two girls in
the back. Even more surprised when one of them was introduced
as his fiancée, Pierrette. The other girl was the fiancée of Freddie
Boyer, another *mauvais garçon de bonne famille*, who occupied the
passenger seat. I shook hands with everyone, and was crammed
between the two fiancées, who smelled even better than Michel.

On the roof rack was a kitchen stove, a marble slab, and a card
table. 'For Fred's fishing hut,' Michel explained. In spite of the
load, he managed to coax the pre-war heap into its top speed
before we'd even reached the Porte de Maillot. At the first *rond-
point* taken at the speed of the Devil's Elbow at Monte Carlo, I
heard the kitchen stove sliding above me. Pierrette gripped my
knee.

False hopes. In early spring sunshine, the two couples cuddled
and kissed by the Seine on the Ile de Chatou. Freddie's fishing hut
was a charming shack straight out of an Impressionist painting,
with its own pontoon and boat. I went rowing with Pierrette; she
played scratchy Charles Trenet records on an ancient gramophone.
Then, back to the fishing hut where Freddie, Michel, and the
other fiancée had begun preparing lunch on the newly-installed
kitchen stove. But before lunch, there was further kissing and cuddling. I felt more and more *de trop*.

After an afternoon of it, with me disc-jockeying Charles Trenet,
back we went to Paris for cakes and champagne at Pierrette's luxury

bedsit. My hopes rose again. The double bed seemed big enough for five, the coverlet was existentially stained. Maybe I would arrive at St-Germain-des-Prés knowing my friends a lot better.

More kissing and cuddling. Outside, the red roof-tiles were deepening in the setting sun. 'Julian,' Michel murmured between kisses, 'we are all a little tired. You will excuse me and my friends if . . .'

He did not have to finish the sentence. I thanked them all for a wonderful day. The fiancées uncurled from the bed sufficiently to shake my hand. Freddie stood up with a slight stoop and also shook my hand. Michel couldn't even get that far, and gave a weary wave from the bed.

That very Saturday night, I did what any twenty-year-old with balls would do in Paris in 1948. And what I should have done my first night there. Without a second thought, with a refreshing breeze blowing through my hair as I stood on the open-air platform of a bus crossing the Pont de la Concorde, I headed for freedom. Alone.

'One must take a gamble,' wrote Jean-Paul Sartre. 'After the death of war, man is left naked, without illusions, abandoned to his own resources and finally understanding he has nothing more to rely on but himself.'

Existentialists were the first of the Me people after the war, forerunners of the Beatniks, Flower Power, and other seekers of alternative ways over the past forty years. As a twenty-year-old, I had an urge to be Me too, to find out more about myself if it killed me. There were people my age in St-Germain-des-Prés, all trying it, and I longed to be with them, to let go a bit, and shed the straitjacket of my British warm.

Well, that's being too analytical, with the pretentiousness of hindsight. I was primarily there, let's face it, for *les bopettes* and *le boogie*.

There was hardly room to write 'Søren Aabye Kierkegaard', father of existentialism, on the walls of the tiny vaulted cellar of Le Club St-Germain in Rue St-Benoit. A boy in a clean white shirt was twirling a girl round his head, her long black skirt flying up to reveal marble white legs and pristine panties. The couple looked scrubbed and innocent, as did the *copains* watching their acrobatics and snapping fingers to the bebop. It was the first time, outside costume drama, that I'd seen men with long hair tumbling over the fur collars of their leather blousons.

I eased my way shyly through the crush of people to an empty corner table, proud of my membership card made out to J.MORI. I ordered pineapple juice, the cheapest drink available. The waiter told me that Charlie Parker, Coleman Hawkins, Max Roach were all habitués of the club.

St-Germain-des-Prés had become the meeting place of black and white. Mixed couples were everywhere, especially at the Hôtel Louisiane, that timeless hostelry, later featured in the jazz movie *Around Midnight*. White and black dancers jived at Mark Doenitz's Vieux-Colombier; white Claude Luter was succeeded as band-leader by black Sidney Bechet, and they often recorded together. One of my new Left Bank friends, facing a lonely Christmas, found himself cooking turkey for Louis Armstrong and Duke Ellington, complete with managers, wives, girlfriends, children, and assorted hangers-on. The carols were followed by a jam session. With its classlessness and racial freedom, it was excitingly different from England's drab post-war cultural conformity.

Next night, I returned to the club, already feeling an habitué myself, flashing my membership card with new confidence. 'Bonsoir, M'sieur Mori,' said the man on the door.

Once seated I spotted a face, two tables away, almost within touching distance. Could it be? Yes, it could . . . the Duke! He was by himself, too. Dare I approach? Too corny to ask for an autograph here. I swigged pineapple juice, mentally working on an opening line. 'Mr Ellington, you don't know me, but . . .' Shit, if only I could have afforded a Scotch! The pineapple juice just wasn't inspiring me.

While I was busy missing my chance, dancers moved respectfully out of the way to let through a party of new arrivals. Among them was a short man with heavy-rimmed glasses and a magnified squint, a cerebral Cyclops, a mythic figure without lookalikes. I couldn't wait to tell Cousin Bernard . . . Jean-Paul Sartre and Duke Ellington – both in one night!

To my astonishment, Sartre's party joined the Duke. Sartre and he greeted each other like old friends. How different from Forties

England with its stiff cultural barriers. I simply couldn't imagine a philosopher joining a jazzman's table – not even Bertrand Russell.

Now that Sartre was present and with the band playing 'Don't Get Around Much Any More' in the Duke's honour, I decided I wasn't getting around much, either. I had come here for liberation not hero-worship.

One very beautiful, very mournful girl, swathed in black, sat at a table alone. She stared and stared at nothing in particular. With Sartre and the Duke to stare at, not more than a few feet away, she must either be myopic or stupid or both. Or was I being unfair? Perhaps her mind was elsewhere. I tried to imagine what made her so sad. Bitter memories of wartime Paris? The shadow of the atom bomb? Genocide and holocaust so comparatively recent? Or perhaps she just couldn't pay the rent. I fantasised about taking her to the Hôtel Louisiane. A girl so beautiful should not be alone and looking so unhappy. I wrote a note and gave it to the waiter. He took it to the girl. My mouth was dry with fear, my face set in a rictus of existential availability.

The girl read the note, turned in my direction. With a wan smile, she shook her head, brushing a wisp of long black hair off her forehead. A few minutes later a Right-Bank boulevardier, grey-templed, business-suited and old enough to be her grandfather, was shrugging apologies, bowing low over her limply proffered hand.

I was undeterred. I had found my spiritual stomping ground, and here I would stomp until it was time to leave Paris – day and night, night and day in Sartre's green acre around that solid Romanesque 'factory for prayers' as Boris Vian called the Church of St-Germain-des-Prés. If God was dead, Sartre was filling in nicely.

Poet Léo Larguier said that the very name St-Germain-des-Prés made him think of a village in deepest France 'with the ruins of a famous abbey, meadows, fine trees, and spring water'. In fact, the focal part of St-Germain 'village' had its origins in just such a setting.

Forty-two thousand acres of meadow had surrounded the Benedictine abbey. A thirteenth-century woodcut shows the enormous fortifications, the land clear to the banks of the Seine, the Palace of the Louvre across the river, and the bucolic hill of Montmartre in the background. The quartier retained its village charm thanks to the surrounding properties of the nobility: in the Rue de Varenne, great houses like the Hôtel de Broglie and Hôtel Matignon; the Carrefour de L'Odéon, once part of the house grounds of the Condé family; between the Seine and the Church, the park of the Rochefoucault-Liancourts. The proximity to the Sorbonne and the arrival of publishing houses like Flammarion and Hachette in the Twenties attracted intellectuals. They loved the village atmosphere of bookshops and artshops in narrow streets and corner cafés where new ideas could be tossed around and old philosophers tossed out over a *p'tit rouge*.

During the Occupation, unknowns continued to keep the literary spirit of France alive, publishing clandestine reviews, living in little 'underground' hotels. Simone de Beauvoir at the Louisiane, playwrights Arthur Adamov and Jacques Audiberti at the Madison found their hotel rooms too cramped to work in. Cafés like Le Flore and Les Deux Magots became their workshops.

Above all, St-Germain-des-Prés was a place of much-needed laughter, a release of tension after the privations of the Occupation. The cinéastes came. The actors came. The bums, the beards, and the bourgeois came. The journalists came. The models and photographers came. And naturally, the young came.

Straight from my peacetime military service in Britain, and never having experienced the challenge of German occupation, I was dazed by the explosion of vitality. Talents were multi-faceted: Camus, Prévert, Genet . . .

I read Albert Camus' 1947 novel *The Plague*; an existentialist, I discovered, could also be a keen footballer. Poets wrote song lyrics; Jacques Prévert's 'Autumn Leaves' was to become a classic. And Jean Genet turned from a life of crime to write exquisitely subversive books (*Our Lady of The Flowers* and *The Thieves' Journal*) and plays (*The Maids* and *The Balcony*).

I discovered that the *caves* and cafés were the most accessible way of feeling part of the scene. I would spin out a coffee or beer for hours. And just watch. And get into conversation. You made a friend for life at six o'clock at night, and never saw them again after six o'clock next morning. Like Suzanne, a gallery owner's wife (or so she said), whose old man had just gone to New York with a pretty tachist painter he was trying to promote. The painter, Suzanne added, was male.

'What's a young man like you doing at Le Tabou alone?' she asked. I bought her another coffee, and told her a few lies. 'Normally I hate to go out alone,' Suzanne continued. 'But the apartment was getting me down.'

It had the reverse effect on me. Suzanne, a woman of a certain age, uncertain of her future, drifted effortlessly towards a night of uncommitted love. In return, she released my libido from its shell.

The Leleu apartment had creaky floors. My returns, shoes off in the hall, squeak-squeak on tiptoe to my room, were a dawn chorus to rival the birds. But they were never questioned. My billet with the Leleus required the occasional dinner at home out of courtesy, then the kindly Bernard would say: 'Julian is looking at his watch again.' And I was released. For all their conventions, they were most tolerant about my night-owling. And though I left Paris still with my British warm, it no longer felt like a straitjacket.

Over the years I returned to St-Germain-des-Prés as often as I could. And I was happiest of all in the theatre.

In the early Fifties, the cabaret acts and plays reflected the break with the past; they had nothing in common with the declamatory staginess of French classical theatre, old *Britannicus* banging on at the Odéon. Their style was total theatre on a cabaret scale: a synthesis of poetic mime, dance, circus, music hall, improvisation, violence and comedy.

It was my first experience of 'Off' theatre. At the Tabou, I saw the Frères-Jacques, with their dazzling mime, song and dance act. At the Rose Rouge, I heard Juliette Gréco. '*Je suis comme je suis*,' she sang, and I very much liked the way she was. Little did I know that ten years later I would get to know her for a brief but enchanting time in London.

What struck me most was her shyness. I just didn't believe that anyone who had grown up with the existentialist greats could be so quiet and unassuming. At odds with her femme fatale image: black clothes, musky perfume, and ambiguous, throaty laugh. The antithesis of showbiz, Gréco used her hands while she talked with the same expressive delicacy as she did when she sang. She first encountered Sartre at a dancehall, and was really bored by the idea of meeting him because it meant she had to stop dancing. She did not know then what it would lead to: close friendship, advice on all manner of things, and, more surprisingly, songs. Later Sartre wrote lyrics for Gréco; so did Simone de Beauvoir.

'They were generous people,' she told me. 'I never said much when they were around, just observed and listened.'

Like all creators of sure talent, she would often put herself down. 'Eartha Kitt's much more interesting than me,' or 'I really don't much like the way I look.' Her lover at the time was Hollywood producer Darryl Zanuck who launched her on a not very successful movie career out of which came one good thing. 'My new nose changed my life.' Many regretted the passing of her old nose; as French builders say about a house's charming defect, '*C'est son joli . . .*' 'But', she said, 'I could forget my nose for a change. It was wonderful to be free of it.'

Juliette Gréco, as a bewitching singer of subtle songs, has the staying power of French women. Her public is young again: in her mid-sixties, she was singing songs by the French rock group Négresses Vertes and by Françoise Sagan, bridging the years with characteristic daring. With the loyalty of French fans to their *Variétées* stars, in 1991 they welcomed her back to the Olympia Music Hall. No wonder she has survived – lovers, husbands, and a suicide attempt. Her existence, Gréco says (still loyal to the word), 'is miraculous'.

St-Germain-des-Prés always acted like an injection of adrenalin. As a writer of musicals, song lyrics, and screenplays, I began to have professional reasons for returning. And I often stayed at the Hôtel Alsace, rivalled only by the Louisiane for eccentric ambience.

At number 13, Rue des Beaux-Arts, there was a late eighteenth-century *pavillon d'amour* built over the vaults. At the beginning of the nineteenth century, six floors were added around the courtyard and eventually it became the Hôtel d'Allemagne. Not for long, however. The Franco-Prussian War of 1870 led to its name being changed to the Hôtel d'Alsace, where a Frenchman could stay without being reminded of the first of the German occupations.

The short street was filled with celebrities – Gérard de Nerval, Jean-Baptiste Corot, and Prosper Mérimée, author of the book on which Bizet's *Carmen* was based. And finally, to the Alsace came the exiled Oscar Wilde. It was his last home, far from Albion at its most perfidious.

Wilde was dying and broke when he arrived in 1899. Jean Dupoirier, then manager of the Alsace, was the epitome of kindness, settling Wilde's debts at another hotel where the owner had threatened to confiscate his goods, and installing him as comfortably as possible at the Alsace. Officially a tenth-grade hotel, Dupoirier upgraded it for Wilde, bringing him breakfast in bed at eleven, lunch at two, and a supply of his favourite cognac. Thanks to Dupoirier's hospitality, Wilde could justifiably claim: 'I am dying beyond my means.' Apart from visits from friends and doctors, and outings to cafés for absinthe, Dupoirier and the Alsace were all he could depend on. And, after his death in 1900 from an abscess in the ear, it was Dupoirier who laid him out – by all accounts, a most gruesome task.

Once I stayed in the Oscar Wilde room. Hung with memorabilia such as his last laundry list, it was not the jolliest of Left Bank lodgings. Other times I was happier with the sagging beds of tattier rooms, cleaned by the one *femme de chambre*, stout and stalwart Juliette.

The exceptional quality of the Alsace, inherited from Dupoirier, was its friendliness. Old Madame Gelli, the next proprietor, carried this on, working till the day she died. The hotel was bought by its present owner, Guy-Louis Duboucheron, in 1964.

Duboucheron has a special touch. Former actor, male model, and social butterfly, he filled the drawing-room with antiques, many of them the same Directoire period as the exterior; and had a huge round table put in the dining-room, where guests shared the *table d'hôte* as though at a private house party. Those wanting privacy could go to the bistrot on the corner of the Rue Bonaparte; at the hotel's round table, conviviality was expected of the guests.

Duboucheron's sister made a charming hostess, holding court in the tiny office to the right of the entrance hall, never forgetting a telephone message, attentive to one's bottle of Perrier after a heavy night out and always clear about what new show, movie, or exhibition one should see – even who one should see it with.

'M'sieur More,' she confided. 'There's a delightful young Swedish countess I'd like you to meet . . .' Alone in Paris, doing a little light modelling to pay her way. She sounded mysterious. I was intrigued.

The Swedish countess was a vision – without any of the clichéd Nordic features one associates with Scandinavian models. She was auburn-haired, not blonde. Her face was pale as Gréco's, not florid. Her eyes were almond as an oriental's, not ice blue. She wore no wedding ring; I was even more intrigued.

I had one more night in Paris. And a dinner appointment I could not cancel. Astrid said it didn't matter, she was tired after a heavy day in front of the camera lens. Couldn't we meet for lunch tomorrow, she suggested? I had another appointment I decided to cancel. At one o'clock, I was waiting for Astrid at the Alsace. At two o'clock I was still waiting. While I was munching a sandwich around two-thirty, Astrid arrived, profuse with apologies; her photographic session had run late and the photographer's phone was out of order. And now precious minutes were ticking away to my plane.

We settled for an early tea in the bibelot-filled drawing-room. We would both be back in Paris; we would surely meet again on another trip. The tea arrived, and while we chatted, my Louis XVI chair shifted uneasily beneath me. I heard a woody snap, and began a slow, undignified descent floorwards. Before I could get up, the whole chair floundered and my foot shot up, sending table and tea things flying. Astrid's merciless laughter brought Monsieur Duboucheron and his sister over at the double. They were less amused but, with the discretion of superb hoteliers, never once mentioned the broken antiques. That's the kind of hotel it was.

Scene: L'Hôtel as L'Alsace has now become – one of the most expensive hotels in Paris. Time: 1989. In the restaurant bar, a bored young man fiddles with his Filofax, eyeing a plumpish single

lady of Iranian appearance, expensively dressed, ravishingly jewel-
led, sipping a *coupe de champagne*. I am with that very same Guy-
Louis Duboucheron who, years before, had had the grace not to
put the smashed chair, table and tea things on my bill. He wears a
permanent tan, a bright green shirt open far enough down to
reveal all three of his gold medallions on chains. A Sixties man still.
Charming smiles and impeccable guest-care, eyes darting this way
and that as we talk.

'Of course, I remember your Swedish countess! A beautiful
girl.'

'What happened to her?' I asked.

Duboucheron sighed, wagging his head. 'Such beautiful parents.
Her father, so handsome. Her mother, so . . .'

'But what happened?'

'She married a hippie. There was some trouble with drugs, I
believe. Apparently, she came to no good in the Camargue. I
never heard of her again.'

Looking around the hotel as it now is, I was not surprised.
Hardly the place for wilting Flower Power.

The new decor was Designer Flamboyant: a tree-trunk from the
old courtyard adorned the hotel's gastronomic restaurant-cum-
winter-garden; a fountain sprayed water into a flowery shell; a
tinkling Piano-Bar piano accompanied the tinkling water; a curious alligator made of painted papier-maché, emerged from a
Rousseau-esque mini forest of exotic ferns and potted palms; rustic
brass lamps hung by chains from the vaulted ceiling; a cosy, red
glow suffused the tables.

Flush-looking jetsetters dined by candlelight on steamed vegetables with coriander, and lamb cutlets cooked in cider vinegar,
praised by Gault-Millau for their lack of pretension. As unpreten-
tious as the vegetable soup of the Alsace's *table d'hôte*?

'I wanted to keep the personality of the old hotel,' Duboucheron said. 'Combined with the luxury of the big palaces around
the Champs-Elysées. I just hated how unfriendly they are. The
French are so inhospitable – obsequious smiles but no warmth.
And service? Forget it. Horrid little bits of soap. If you want a
decent size, you have to bring your own!'

The facelift began in 1966. It took two years to restyle: to lighten up the Oscar Wilde rooms, bring Mistinguett's art deco furniture from her house in Bougival, and colour the Cardinal's Room purple and violet for the likes of Barbra Streisand or Robert de Niro. 'I only have film stars when they're on holiday,' Duboucheron added. 'There's no room for press conferences here.'

'And the name L'Hôtel? Your idea?'

'Of course!' Duboucheron chuckled at the cheek of it. 'It was, after all, going to be *the* hotel. And, I hope, still is. Why be modest when there's nothing to be modest about? But it was awful at first – before the taxi-drivers knew us. Guests would ask for L'Hôtel. "Which hotel?" "The hotel." "There's two thousand hotels in Paris, M'sieur" If they didn't know the address, they'd probably end up staying at the Crillon, poor things!'

With rates of between one and three hundred pounds a night, bed-and-breakfast, it's no longer the writer's snip the Alsace used to be. But then neither is St-Germain-des-Prés, and L'Hôtel fits the current mood of style-without-content. A dated amalgam of last year's trends, appealing to rich outsiders who just love all those cute little boutiques and fun art galleries and overpriced bistrots.

But I know people who live in the *quartier* and still feel at home there. They turn a blind eye to the passing trade, as they head for their old haunts. Beyond Le Shopping and Le Fast Food, beyond Le Drugstore where the Royal St-Germain used to be, I found vestiges of my old stomping ground.

Across the boulevard from Le Drug, next to Les Deux Magots is La Hune which shares honours as the best bookshop for the arts in Paris with the new one at the Louvre. At nine-thirty on a cold January evening, browsers were browsing and a small line of book-buyers had formed at the cash counter. Had I been looking for a book on pre-Columbian Chilean art, there was a choice of four.

I used to love a late night beer at Le Flore, so wandered the few steps up the boulevard to check it out. I had seen someone wearing a 'Flore' T-shirt, and feared a brisk trade in hamburgers on paper serviettes with a picture of Sartre. I was wrong. Exclusively gay now, rumour had it, straights feel frozen out. Wrong again: heterosexual couples as well as gay exchanged intimacies on the red leather banquettes. The waiters were as grumpy as ever. The upstairs saloon was still the quietest place in town for a café meet-ing. And clients were still requested not to smoke joints on the premises: 'The odour of certain tobaccos of the perfumed type upsets the majority of our clients,' reads the notice.

But the village life, not surprisingly, has gone. High rents have priced out many colourful locals, and streets have taken on the international anonymity of big city tourism. It is hard to find a French restaurant sometimes. In the short stretch of Rue Princesse's sixteenth- and seventeenth-century houses, I had a choice of the Yakatori (Japanese), the Ristorante Italiano, the Bedford Arms Pub, Le Palanquin (Specialités Vietnamiennes), the Mexican Bar Cantina, the American Restaurant, the Birdland Bar and, just to show it was Paris after all, Chez Tony serving *tripes maisons*.

Enclaves of the past, however, were few, and haunting as attics full of old dolls and stuffed animals. It was appropriate that the Rue du Bac still has a taxidermist where I once got a new glass eye for the Pooh Bear given to me in my second year. 'Don't be embar-rassed, M'sieur,' the man had said as he found a match for Pooh's remaining eye. 'Many of our customers have older bears than yours.'

Then they too would remember the heyday of Left-Bank jazz. What of it now? Still flourishing in basement and bar, sounds float-ing from cellar grilles where bag ladies sleep for warmth.

At number 13, Rue St-Benoit, Le Club St-Germain had long since become Le Bilboquet. Today's young were at Le Palace and Les Bains, discoing. Here, affluent wrinklies were eating and drinking, as a man in a blue blazer ushered me to the bar. Now it was all red flock wallpaper and mock art nouveau globe lamps. The barman served me a generous splash of Glenlivet, and said I was lucky to find a place at the bar. Long gone were the bebop and New Orleans of the old club. A cerebral trio of piano, bass, and drums swung for its fans, who listened as intensely as would exis-tentialist students to Professor Sartre.

The jazzman's hotel, the Louisiane, was still there – with food available on the doorstep from the Rue de Seine market. Round the corner in Rue de Buci, a queue had formed at a kiosk serving delicious takeaway dishes: venison stew with spinach for 22f., fillet of skate in a caper sauce for 19.50f.

Life in St-Germain-des-Prés can still be enjoyable on a smallish bundle of francs. First, leave your credit cards at home and the boutiques and bistrots to the tourists. Then, take a room at the Louisiane, drift down the galleries of Rue de Seine, spin out a rum punch at La Rhumerie, take in a movie in Place de l'Odéon, or just potter around the familiar strollable streets near the church of St-Germain-des-Prés, where echoes of Boris Vian's 'Rive Gauche' can still be heard:

> At St-Germain-des-Prés
> By night and by day,
> They wend their way,
> Those loonies at play,
> Drinking new Beaujolais
> In a bistrot's mirrored hall,
> Where they gawp at all
> Who pay a call
> On their café,
> Like them, drowning their cares,
> But not in the fountain's waterfall
> In front of the factory for prayers.

3

Gulf of Morbihan, 1951

Ile aux Moines – Monks' Island – may sound an odd place for a honeymoon, but that was where I spent mine.

In 1951 young marrieds could not be choosy. There were no luxury loveboats, no packages to Polynesia with a courtesy bottle of champagne waiting under the bridal bamboo. Funds for abroad were restricted – by one's bank manager and His Majesty's Treasury with equal austerity. The twenty-five pound travel allowance would just about see S and me through ten days of off-the-beaten-track Brittany.

Short distance, long haul. BEA hop from Northolt to Dinard, overnight stop at St-Malo; cross-country steam train through the 'mountains', as Bretons call their rolling hillocks; two sweaty changes of train; an hour or so's wait in Vannes, and another hour's ferry ride to Ile aux Moines. The journey from London took roughly as long as it now takes to Waikiki Beach.

Our ferry boat's Captain Rozo, an islander himself, filled us in: 'Originally called Izenah (Pearl of the Gulf), the island changed its name to Ile aux Moines, when King Erispoe of Brittany gave it to the monks of the Abbey of Redon in 854. They never lived there but screwed the local fishermen and peasants rotten for rent; you'd think we'd have called it Pearl of the Gulf again when the French Revolution changed fief to commune. But, oh no, those absentee monks had instilled us with a proper fear of God.'

Pearl of the Gulf, conjuring up images of Dorothy Lamour in a sarong, sounded more fun for a honeymoon than Monks' Island.

But the friend who recommended it promised us sunny skies and romantic beaches. Not to mention candlelit dinners, electric light being frequently on the blink in summer storms.

Our ferry from Vannes puttered through the Gulf of Morbihan (*mor-bihan* – small sea, as opposed to *mor-vraz* – big sea) on Brittany's Atlantic coast. Coming from the Continent, as the islanders call the French mainland, the Gulf seemed like another planet. Here, drifting peacefully, we entered a Chinese painting of islands and water, shifting and changing in luminous heat-haze. Now a larger island with trees and a house and a landing stage floated by, and a smaller one appeared beyond it, bare but for a flock of sheep; now a stretch of open water had sailboats becalmed against a scattering of mauve rocky shapes; now a group of pine trees were silhouetted against the misty sun.

All forty-six islands were privately owned except for Ile d'Arz and Ile aux Moines. We chose the larger – 137 acres, 4 miles long – so we could get away from the August crowds. We need not have worried. Shaped like an indolent sea monster, its head, tail, long body and disparate members were sprawled across the water in eternal siesta. It was as peaceful as a South Pacific atoll.

Our ferry had the proper island feel about it, the excitement of leaving Piraeus for Míkonos, or Barcelona for Ibiza. On a smaller scale, of course: beginning with a narrow channel from the inland port of Vannes, country church bells distantly chiming, and, as we headed out into the Gulf, plovers rising from silk-calm waters.

A dreamlike passage in the shimmer of a summer's afternoon was only slightly marred by Captain Rozo's relentlessly larky commentary: 'Vannes is named for the Venetians, who occupied the city in the first century BC. And when Julius Caesar conquered them in a sea-battle in the Gulf of Morbihan, who was his Lieutenant, *messieurs, 'dames?* None other than Brutus – yes, he of the Ides of March. You have learned – from Shakespeare, perhaps – that Caesar was assassinated in Rome. But it is possible that the assassination plot took place here on Ile aux Moines, with rebellious Brutus involved. And that's why, many many years later, the islanders were convinced that the body of the Roman Emperor lay buried somewhere on the island in a golden coffin . . .'

And so on. Mixing myth and mirth, the Captain regaled us with potted legends in the Breton manner. Legends of ghostly white ladies walking on the water; of a drowning damsel's last, melodious song to her lover that rose from the depths long after her death; of terrible galleys that put briefly into port, carrying their crew of evil-doers, condemned to sail the world like criminal Flying Dutchmen for eternity.

Celtic mists, instead of Breton haze, would have better suited the Captain's dark stories. But names on my large-scale map, hastily purchased in Vannes, conjured up Prospero's island rather than the Outer Hebrides, with names like the Wood of Love and the Wood of Sighs. Just the place for a honeymoon.

We were greeted by a vista of whitewashed, rose-festooned cottages clustered on a small woody hill. The village was small, but the locals grandly called it Le Bourg, meaning small market-town. Below, a few fishing boats and sailcraft were moored along the waterfront. And the hotel was a short walk from the jetty.

The Hôtel de la Brise, though not a breath of breeze stirred on its terrace that midge-heavy afternoon, looked perfect. A family hotel right on the waterfront with a view of the bay from every room.

'All the rooms in the hotel are full,' said Madame Corno with a welcoming smile.

'But we've booked !'

My tweed honeymoon suit jacket was slung over my shoulder, and I felt damp patches in the pits of my shirt. A crisis loomed. I must try to look cooler than I felt.

I peered over Madame Corno's shoulder at the room list; she was keeping it a closed book.

'*Il y a peut-être une petite erreur, Madame,*' I suggested and sweated some more. The weather was too hot for Brittany. Even in August.

'Tell her we're on our honeymoon,' S hissed.

'We decided not to book as a honeymoon couple!'

'Let's be corny if it gets us a room.'

'*Madame, c'est notre . . . miel de . . .*' The French for honeymoon escaped me. Honey of moon or moon of honey?

'You are in the annexe, M'sieur More,' cut in Madame Corno. 'You will find it most agreeable.'

And we did.

A narrow path led through the pine trees to a beach with the Proustian sound of French children at play. We followed the path to a solid, Victorian house shuttered against the afternoon sun. Better than the harbour, the view from our floorboard-creaking, faded-wallpapered, trough-mattressed room stretched gloriously towards the mouth of the Gulf, tantalisingly hidden by a crop of little islands.

Our view combined cultural stimulus from distant Stone Age megaliths with their unsolved mysteries, and sybaritic pleasures in young, brown bodies supine upon the sand immediately below. Ozone and Ambre Solaire wafted upwards with the heat. We tore off honeymoon gladrags, and, full of the joys of safe arrival and a roof over our heads, instantly fell asleep.

After this much-needed siesta, I was awoken by a dive-bomber mosquito to inhale a muddy smell. The tide had gone out. On the shiny mudbanks, women were planting sticks, marking the holes made by the antennae of clams, places where they would congregate in cloudier weather and be collected.

Where there's mud, there are oysters. And the oysters of Ile aux Moines were world-famous. The Hôtel de la Brise, being the only one of any standing, boasted some of the best, and we would start both lunch and dinner with half a dozen fat *huîtres creuses* (belly oysters) every day, included in the *en pension* price.

Oysters have eccentric breeding habits. They alternate their sex – laying and fertilizing the eggs one breeding cycle, taking it easy the next. But the oyster's predilection for swinging both ways had no bad effect on our honeymoon. To S and me, their reputation for aphrodisiac qualities seemed wholly justified.

Perhaps that's why they've survived so long. Celts and Romans guzzled *belons* by the dozen. And Guy de Maupassant, a Norman for whom the oysters were a daily fix, described them sensually in *Bel-Ami* as 'pretty and plump, little ears enclosed in shells, and melting between palate and tongue like salt candy'.

And there were other shellfish . . .

Every morning, at breakfast on the hotel terrace Madame Corno's son-in-law chef, Monsieur Le Sâout, let loose relays of freshly caught lobsters. Across the tiled surface they scuttled, while we laid bets on the winners and ate them for lunch.

To us, lobster was an exotic rarity. We learned from Monsieur
Le Sâout that *langouste à l'armoricaine* had nothing really Breton
about it, although the ancient Gallic name for the North Britanny
coast was Armor ('close to the sea'). In fact, *à l'armoricaine* is a corruption of *à l'américaine*, the culinary invention of a chef called
Fraisse who worked for a time in Chicago. Fraisse came from Sète:
his famous seafood sauce is neither Breton nor American in taste
but totally meridional – a mix of shallots, tomatoes, cognac, olive
oil, and white wine. Breton legend, we had already learned from
Captain Rozo, was to be taken with a large pinch of sea-salt.

More and more shellfish became our daily fare – *palourdes farcies,
grillées ou natures* (local clams, stuffed, grilled, or raw), prawns,
shrimps, scallops, and crab. All of which were of fishing-boat
freshness. We had never seen or dreamed of such crustaceous
abundance.

In England, oysters were only eaten when there's an R in the
month, never in August. In France, no such caution. And no one
seemed to suffer from it. Certainly not on Ile aux Moines. Shellfish
held no fears for us. We continued to crack, pick, gouge, suck, and
plunge our scarred fingers into lemon-water finger bowls.

But even on honeymoons, good things must come to an end.

We would work our binges off on the beach. But it was really
too hot for any serious exercise. Liberally smeared with Ambre
Solaire against the dogday sun, I would flop into the water, essay a
lethargic stroke or two, pant back up the few yards to our beach
umbrella, collapse towards my laid-out beach towel – and miss.

There is nothing worse than falling on hot sand, covered in
Ambre Solaire and beaded with salt water. I was patched with as
many sandy islands as the Gulf of Morbihan. I began to itch all
over.

'What are those spots?' S asked apprehensively, as we went to
bed that night.

'Prickly heat,' I said. 'I used to get it between my fingers from
too many strawberries.'

'You can get it from too much shellfish, too.'

'All over the body?!'

'In this heat . . .'

'Now she tells me.'

'I thought we were immunised by now.'

'We should have had a course of shellfish in London before coming.'

S gently bathed me with a cold sponge. It felt like a nail brush. 'We'll find a lotion tomorrow.'

But what about tonight? Our trough of a bed, normally welcome, was now an instrument of torture. I was reminded of the old joke: how do porcupines make love? Very carefully.

Next morning, at breakfast, S restrained me from kicking a lobster across the floor. At lunch, I chose tomato salad as a starter, and steamed sole to follow. At dinner, I refused the stuffed crab with a hostile grunt. Monsieur Le Sâout and Madame Corno began to look at me very strangely.

'*Il a une crise de peau!*' S explained to Madame Corno. My 'skin crisis' made her look at me even more strangely. '*À cause de la chaleur et des crustacés.*'

'*Ah, oui.*' Madame Corno managed a wary smile, gave instructions about how to find the pharmacy, and moved away sharply. There was no telling what pox this Englishman had brought to her hotel.

We bought cooling unguents. My body became a hideous patchwork of pink calamine lotion and flaky brown-and-white skin. For two days, I was off shellfish, sun and sex. For two nights, unable to sleep and a menace to poor S, I crept furtively out of the hotel annexe, and walked alone on the beach to cool down, safe in the knowledge that nobody would see me at that hour.

The third night, however, I was discovered leaving the annexe by a young French couple, arms round each other, returning at nearly one in the morning from God knows what revelry. Ile aux Moines hardly had a bar, let alone a nightclub.

'*Bonne nuit,*' I muttered in passing.

'*Bonne nuit, M'sieur More.*' Christ, how did they know my name? '*Et comment va Madame More?*' Paranoia set in. We were already notorious – the British honeymoon couple whose marriage was *raté* before it had begun, the husband who went raving on the beach at night to expiate some terrible shame. I was letting down the whole British male sex, perpetuating a myth the French love to believe.

Lorenza & John
7/3 Elizabeth Bay Cres
Elizabeth Bay
NSW 2011
AUSTRALIA

PARIS ET SES MERVEILLES...
Montmartre, la place du Tertre et les coupoles du
Sacré-Coeur

Editions "GUY" - PARIS
8, 40, Avenue Henri - Barbusse - 94200 IVRY SUR-SEINE
Imprimé en U. E. - Reproduction interdite

1811 Dear Lorenza & John couldn't go anywhere
in Paris without thinking of you two, wondering
who could've dreamed it were so many things too.
Here I esp the Louvre but maybe we had
seen more of the countryside. Went
for a Champagne tour that was
best place in Europe was Prague
I loved the Atmosphere & all
the buildings — So beautiful,
so was Florence/Sienna but
we kind of overdosed on Church
historical buildings & bread &
cheese (Teri refuses to eat
anymore). London now is actually

hot & sunny but after 5 wks we're
now apartment, can't you get
one big enough for 6 of us —
Lorenza had work on the
just heard Great News — Lorenza had
YAEH !!! Had a lovely chat with your mum
radio   Love Kasia & Teri
                              will visit end 4 ...

LA PLACE DU TERTRE

To avoid the curious gaze of the other guests, we ate our meals in dark corners and very late. French holidaymakers were always at their tables on the dot of midday and at seven-thirty. The kinder ones looked pityingly at S, and Madame Corno asked discreetly after my health, persistently checking our leaving date. The great actor, Louis Jouvet, was expected in two days. Unfortunately (for the Cornos and Louis Jouvet) the poxy English honeymooner would still be there.

In an attempt not to let my problems spoil our otherwise enjoyable honeymoon, we took walks in the cool of early morning and late evening.

We walked to the cemetery – not to check out a place for me, but on the recommendation of Captain Rozo whose ancestors were buried there. Behind its high wall and vast ferns – a lizard's paradise – we found Rozos, Daniels and Bevens – sea captains all, their plaques bearing witness to early deaths, some in faraway places like Tonkin. Sea captains were the island's aristocracy, employing the peasants as their sailors.

At the procession of the island's patron saint on 15 August, the captains are remembered by the 'Patrician Ladies of the Gulf', the young girls in elegant white lace and black costumes who carry the saint.

In the gardens of Ile aux Moines, glimpsed on our walks down lanes between banks of wild flowers, old women still wore white coiffes on their heads to keep off the sun. Among the hydrangeas and hollyhocks, their delicate appearance belied their strength. In the last century, women of the Gulf fished with the men. Both fishermen and fishing-boat were called Sinagot, and the saying goes: 'The Sinagot in clogs puts his daughter to the oars.'

A couple of these daughters, now venerable ancients, were speaking Breton. And I was reminded of my childhood in Wales; a Breton onion-seller visited our home once a month, in blue smock and cap, strings of onions over his shoulders and festooning his bicycle. Wales held no fears for him; he could communicate with the people, as much of their language was the same as his own. In both Breton and Welsh 'Aber' means estuary, so you find Aber Benoit in Brittany, Aberystwyth in Wales.

Once my prickly heat had gone, our honeymoon returned to

normal, and my minor setback was eclipsed by a genuine tragedy.

One evening, on our way to dinner, we found Madame Corno in tears, her son-in-law comforting her. A mood of reverential silence pervaded the dining-room; the clatter of cutlery, the cracking of shells, and the splash of mineral water and wine were, for once, louder than voices. Even the children were quiet.

We made our way to our table where our bottle of Gros Plant du Pays Nantais was waiting in its ice-bucket. Tonight, instead of Madame Corno, it was Monsieur Le Sâout who took my non-shellfish order.

'A sad day, indeed,' sighed Monsieur Le Sâout. 'Monsieur Louis Jouvet will not be coming to us this year.'

The great actor had died suddenly. Jouvet was something of a national hero, and the whole place was in mourning. I could understand why. At our school cinema club I had relished his masterly gangster performance in *Hôtel du Nord*, and I had also been lucky enough once to see him on the Paris stage.

By the time S and I were once again on that endless steam-train journey, chugging back north through the parched, gold-stubbled Breton countryside, my petty ailment seemed insignificant.

'The TGV-Atlantique has just reached its cruising speed of 180 mph.'

This astonishing fact is proudly announced over the high-speed train's public address system. We are suitably impressed. The flat, dull plain between Paris and Le Mans is flashing past, and the poor man's Concorde whisks us to Brittany in a mere three hours.

Suitably marine coloured in green and blue (as opposed to the orange-and-grey of the southbound TGV to Nice), the train has playrooms for children and telephones for businessmen. The bar sells *Elle* and *Paris-Match*. As usual, Princess Caroline of Monaco is on the cover of one, Princess Stephanie on the other. Second Class offers cramped seats with footrests for dwarfs. First Class has cosy-looking orange table lamps in airy, comfortable compartments for four – just right for groups of Japanese looking for a bit of Brittany to add to their French property folios. As TGV fare is French gastronomy at its most plastic, we had timed our journey from Paris to Vannes between meals.

I didn't remember Vannes at all from our honeymoon. And certainly not Le Sinagot where we now lunched. Just beyond the Porte St-Vincent, a medieval gate named after the city's Spanish patron saint, Vincent Ferrier, the restaurant-bar was full by twelve-fifteen. Not knowing where to eat, we had followed a cluster of regulars already at the door on the dot of midday – a sure way of discovering good food in a French provincial town.

Our sixty-franc menu began with six juicy Gulf of Morbihan belly oysters, as pure-tasting as ever in spite of the doomwatchers. In recent years, Breton conchyculture has suffered economic crises, wacky weather conditions upsetting the delicate environmental balance; and oyster larvae on the natural banks between Ile aux Moines and Ile d'Arz have been destroyed by the ugly sister parasites, Marteila and Bonamia.

This return to the land of my first oysters reminded me why I couldn't remember Vannes. Encumbered with honeymoon luggage, we had seen nothing of it. Now, thirty-nine years later, travelling light, we cased the town before catching the ferry to Ile aux Moines. A town for all ages and of all centuries, well worth casing. We did the ramparts, the moat, the medieval wash-house; and, between two half-timbered houses of the Place Henri IV, glimpsed the nineteenth-century storefront now housing Burton's the British Bespoke Tailor. Doves cooed above the Carnaby Boutique. Carousel horses, lions, and tigers lay surrealistically near the cathedral, waiting to be assembled on to a magnificently restored seventeenth-century roundabout, lights flashing against a backdrop of provincial park greenery. Later, a steam organ's music drew the children of Vannes in crowds.

France often seems inhabited either by the very old or very young. Saturday evening, the Place Gambetta – a noble crescent of houses, cafés and hotels on the port's waterfront – was jumping with post-Bac' students, releasing exam stress over a *panaché* or Kronenbourg beer or with a mighty rev of Yamahas, while riders in helmets and bareheaded pillion girls chatted with *copains* at roadside café tables. Incongruously, a group of arthritic, floppy-hatted British gentlefolk, tapping rubber-ended walking-sticks on the cobblestones, sought the sanctuary of a postcard shop.

Next day, at the maritime station, coachloads of French ancients tottered to our island ferry. From the nearby, high-tech aquarium, a line of infants, in the charge of sweating, harassed schoolteachers, were babbling about a Nile crocodile alleged to have been fished out of the Paris sewers. How had it got there, they wondered? There were many wild theories. A young teacher joked that a visiting Egyptian princess had probably flushed a pet baby croc down *les toilettes* by mistake.

Packed to capacity with young and old, our ferry looked like a refugee ship; there was hardly room for our two overnight bags on deck. As the hooter blew, S and I began to wonder if this was all a ghastly mistake. It is dangerous to revisit any place you've loved with a person you still love. A honeymoon island, most of all . . .

The Gulf of Morbihan's mainland had sprouted many white, prosperous second homes nestling in a continuous fringe of woods while yacht marinas overflowed from the creeks and inlets. We imagined the Hôtel de la Brise would now have a high-rise annexe and a Sinagot Bar with faded photographs of regattas, tastefully draped fishing nets, and waitresses in Breton costume saying 'Have a nice day!' like the girl at the Tourist Office in Vannes.

The jetty of Ile aux Moines was a mass of wheelchairs, their occupants waiting for the return ferry. Our own oldies trooped off to let the others on, followed by the babbling infants, and, noses twitching at the smell of frying galettes, headed for Le Cap Horn Crêperie and the souvenir shop.

Further along the waterfront, where once lobsters had danced on the terrace of the Hôtel de la Brise, another souvenir shop flaunted cheap and nasty Breton plates, ornate kitsch barometers and clothes brushes. The hotel had gone; its building now housed holiday apartments. On the porch, I asked an old lady if she remembered the hotel. 'No, M'sieur, I only moved here last year.' But she did know our annexe; that had become a Maison de Jeunesse. A children's holiday camp seemed like putting it to good use, but she didn't agree. 'We have enough young people with the daytrippers!'

When it comes to decibels it's a moot point whether French infants or old folk score highest. The two were in competition on

the waterfront. As we climbed the vaguely familiar hill to Le
Bourg, a merciful silence descended. Only a very few souls young
or old ventured further than the waterfront road. Blue-shuttered,
whitewashed, thatched cottages announced their age with stone-
carved numerals – 1720, 1660. Little gardens overflowed with
camellias, buddleia, genista, and roses. The air was heavy with lime
blossom. Tamarisk, mimosa and palm trees bore witness to the
micro climate, protected by the warmth of the all-pervading sea.

As an overnight stop, the seedy Hôtel-Bar de l'Ile held no
romance for us. But it was the only hotel. So we decided to look
for a *Chambre d'Hôte*, that increasingly popular and good French
equivalent of a B & B.

S stopped the first person she met in the street. Madame Béllego
had just what we wanted. White-haired and florid, wearing baggy
bermudas, she led us to a building, through a dilapidated hallway,
past a sail wrapped round a mast on the floor. Upstairs, the holiday
let was stuffed with family furniture – huge Breton dresser and
Venetian chandelier; four rooms for twenty pounds a night. Plus a
view from the living-room across the harbour to Port-Blanc on
the mainland.

The Béllegos were people of property. She had inherited the
Port-Blanc ferry from her late husband, Captain Béllego, though it
wasn't doing such good business since they banned tourist cars
from the island. And her cousin Maurice Béllego ran the only
decent restaurant, La Désirade, where the sea urchins were as fresh
as ever.

Ile aux Moines had become a daytripper's island in all but peak
holiday times. In high summer the island's population swelled
from 650 to 2,000 mostly in second homes or holiday lets like
Madame Béllego's.

But the island itself still had much Celtic magic. We rented
bicycles. Mine had brakes like a banshee's wail. Wheels shrieking,
I stopped on gentle hills to catch nostalgic whiffs of the Wales of
my childhood – warm ferns and bracken and gorse; hydrangeas,
honeysuckle, and fuchsias overflowing from gardens into hedge-
rows.

There was no traffic, except for the occasional truck headed for
a boatyard or thatched limestone cottage.

We paused at Penhap, the island's most southerly bay. A slipway sloped into clear, green water. We studied our map, trying to locate nearby megalithic sites.

Over the years, megaliths – stone monuments of the neolithic period (4000–1800BC in Brittany) – have been disappearing, their stones used by islanders for building houses. Few Bretons, according to an archaeologist at the museum in Vannes, give a damn about their old stone burial grounds. Most are not even intrigued by the mystery of the rock formations. Telling us about them, she managed to pass on some of her own enthusiasm, eager that we should know what the key Breton words meant:

Menhir – a long stone (*men* – stone, *hir* – long) placed upright in the earth. Pottery found near them, impossible to say for certain what religion, because there is no writing on them.

Cromlech – semicircles of *menhirs* facing west. Orientation towards setting sun suggests sun worship. Also in rows aligned towards moon or sun. To attract magnetic forces? Celtic mystery.

Dolmen – one stone placed across two others, table-fashion, covered by an earth tumulus, making a burial place. Sometimes several stones forming alley or a network of corridors leading to communal burial chambers.

The Dolmen of Nioul was hard to find, even when we located it on our map. The lane was suddenly barred by a rusty gate. *Chemin Privé*. Beyond the gate, a tacky farmyard with a beat-up tractor and a few mangy chickens pecking about among the debris. Sad pine trees had branches ripped off by the 1988 hurricane, and whole trees were a-tilt, root-masses in the air. I explored. The farmhouse itself was in the process of being repaired; perhaps a tree had fallen on the roof. No one about, in spite of a smoking chimney. It was a grim dump. A dog began barking. Then another. And another. And suddenly no fewer than five were upon me. I know better than to cross one French farm dog, let alone five. A chow snapped viciously at my hand. I fast-walked, pretending not to be scared, to the gate where S had wisely stayed with the bicycles.

So we never made it to the Dolmen de Nioul. At the Dolmen de Penhap, however, we were luckier. Just off the island's main lane, near a Celtic Cross, we heard young voices. Old stones need celebrating by human presence, or they're dead as the dullest museum. And these Breton schoolchildren touched them excitedly, photographing each other clambering over them, making contact with them as though engaged upon some ancient rite of ancestor-worship.

Their prof watched the spontaneous celebration without comment, letting his students discover the questions for themselves. Here, at Penhap, nobody expects to find answers, but the pull is strong towards the eternal mystery.

'A disgrace, M'sieur,' commented the prof on the barring of Pointe de Nioul by the farm. There was complicity from him and his students, a willingness to share their rite with strangers. They told us about a magnificent Dolmen on the neighbouring Ile d'Arz, among the pine trees at Pointe de Liouse. Over the years, the roof stone had slipped off, and there were plans to restore it. We could walk, they said, round the whole island in less than a day.

Unfortunately, we'd only left time for Ile aux Moines. As our ferry back to Vannes put in at Ile d'Arz, the saltings were alive with herons and skylarks, salt pasture lambs were eating on lush, buttercup-filled meadows. The island was flat and rural, few trees. There was a small, new-looking hotel, white and pristine, near the jetty with the inevitable Muzak playing.

As our ferry was preparing to leave, a launch chugged in from Conleau. It disgorged a wedding party somewhat the worse for wear from a banquet on the Continent.

The bride teetered along the jetty in fragile gold shoes. She wore a big white hat, jacket and tight skirt. Her bridesmaids were more comfortably dressed in white bermudas. They carried bouquets. Other relatives carried the presents. The bridegroom, struggling with a heavy suitcase, wore an electric blue suit with evening shirt and white bow-tie. With much ribald laughter and kissing, the wedding party took leave of the happy couple, piling them with presents, and boarded the launch which was giving an urgent departure toot. The laden couple made unsteadily for the hotel.

Our ferry's captain seemed to be enjoying the spectacle, and let the smaller boat leave first. Then we too left. The sun had nearly set. Across the water, on the tiny Ile de Dronec, egrets returning to their roosts speckled the dark tall trees with white. As a final set-piece to send us on our way, the sun's red disc went down between a gap in the trees over Ile aux Moines. The water turned mauve, and ripples began dancing on it.

4

Paris Montmartre, 1956

In *Quiet Days in Clichy* Henry Miller wrote of Montmartre: 'Sex is not romantic, particularly when commercialised, but it does create an aroma, pungent and nostalgic, which is far more glamorous and seductive than the most brilliantly illuminated Gay White Way. In fact it is obvious that the sexual life flourishes in a dim, murky light: it is at home in the chiaroscuro and not in the glare of the neon light.'

That same year *Irma La Douce*, an intimate musical on the same subject, opened at the tiny Théâtre Gramont near the Paris Stock Exchange. The musical's heroine was a Montmartre *poule* with a Louis d'Or for a heart, and in adapting it for the Peter Brook production, I and my colleagues, Monty Norman and David Heneker, spent many illuminating hours of research on the Miller beat.

> This is the Paris that blossoms at night
> Hiding in whispers away from the light.
> This is the Paris that turns in its sleep
> Up on the hill where the sad gutters weep.
>
> The shunting of a train,
> A lamp-post in the rain,
> The street girl's sad refrain
> Known as the Valse Milieu.

Although Irma's milieu of pimps and prostitutes was more romanticised than Henry Miller's, it too lived in the shadows, taking its sights and sounds from the realism of north Paris railway stations and *bal musette* accordions rather than from the ooh-la-la brashness of Gay Paree and Pigalle. Its comedy was back-street not boulevard, its humour blending the absurd logic of a Feydeau farce with the Parisian underworld cynicism of Jean Gabin and Arletty. Yet love conquered all, as it had to in hit musicals of the Fifties.

The original French production was like a Café-Concert: squeeze-box, trombone, banjo and drums for band; drapes and cut-outs for sets; a stocky, peasanty Irma sung by Colette Renard with a voice that wrenched every bit of street-gut emotion from the music of Marguerite Monnot, composer of Edith Piaf's 'Poor People of Paris'.

I saw the show many times at the Gramont, taking copious notes and wondering how to render choice phrases of Parisian underworld argot like *roploplos à la Milo* – breasts like the Venus de Milo's – into English as charmingly onomatopoeic. *Des coups d'reins pris dans l'bassin*, I was assured by the late Baroness Moura Budberg, an expert in Parisian slang, meant literally 'blows of the buttocks taken in the pelvis'; hardly suitable for a West End still bedevilled by the Lord Chamberlain's censorship.

'This is a love story, a fairy tale,' director Peter Brook insisted. 'The language must be charming and funny, not out to shock explicitly. We're not doing Genet.' Peter also produced Jean Genet's first production of *Le Balcon* in Paris and riot police attended the first night.

We and the French writers had many after-show conferences at a nearby restaurant, Aux Lyonnais in Rue St-Marc. I was very much in awe of the original author, Alexandre Breffort, an erudite, grey-faced man much older than us, more like a French Academician than the taxi-driver he had once been.

'*C'est très Shakespeare!*' Breffort kept saying of his text. The hero was named Nestor after a character in *Troilus and Cressida*. 'You will know how to translate "To be or not to be", Julian . . .'

> To be or not to be,
> *Le Grisbi, c'est l'oseille:*
> *Ret'nez c'qu'on vous conseille*
> *Et pas touche au grisbi!*

went Breffort's lyric, but there was no way 'To Be Or Not To Be' would give any feeling of the Montmartre underworld in English. Instead, we kept the French slang for money.

> Le Grisbi is Le Root
> Of Le Evil in man,
> So gather in the fruit,
> Grab as much as you can.

So sang our pimps, owing more to Brecht than Shakespeare. But no matter. Peter had given us a free hand, which he guided skilfully beyond any objections Breffort might have. 'You know your public,' Breffort conceded, doubtfully, and later became a tax exile in Switzerland on the proceeds.

Evenings at Aux Lyonnais were long and libant. Though the Théatre Gramont succumbed to property developers' bulldozers some twenty years ago, the restaurant still thrives – with what looks like, but can't be, the same rubicund waitresses in black dresses and crisp, white aprons, bustling about with *grosse quenelle comme à Lyon* and *cassoulet lyonnais*. The same dado of red, green, and white ceramic tiling, big mirrors, and potted palms make it still the kind of bistrot where projects are born and bottles killed.

Over huge, juicy *entrecôtes* smothered with onions and washed down with Juliénas or Chiroubles, we would listen to Breffort's memories of taxi-driving in Montmartre, tales of the *poules* and *mecs* he loved. They seemed much more relevant than discussions of Shakespeare or Brecht. It was an excellent briefing for my fieldwork.

> *Il court, il court,*
> *L'bel amour*
> *Sur le vieux Pont Caulaincourt.*

To the old Caulaincourt bridge I went – to check out how much *bel amour* flowed there. Disappointingly, the bridge had no water running under it, although Montmartre was officially known as a port. It had once been the scene of naval ship-building, though far from water, and was granted port status with its own branch of the Union Maritime in 1912. Its only 'boat' was *Le Bateau-Lavoir* (using the name for the old Seine laundry-boats), a

small wooden building of artists' studios. The hill of Montmartre
was an island, its symbolic port a haven for lost souls from near and
far; Van Gogh sailed in from Holland, Modigliani from Italy, and
Picasso from Spain. And very quickly they found themselves at
home, thanks to its bracing air and Irmas Les Douces.

The *poules* of the port, like mannequins in slow motion on
a bleak catwalk, paraded the road-bridge's pavements. Iron-
structured, it spanned the Montmartre cemetery. With so many
celebrities near by, the girls were in good company: Emile Zola
who, during the German Occupation of 1870, watched a balloon
take off from the slopes of La Butte, carrying Léon Gambetta to
Tours to found the Resistance; Edgar Degas, who discovered
models for his ballerinas at the Montmartre Ballet School; Hector
Berlioz, who tried numbers out on Chopin and Lizst in his precipitous Mont-Cenis flat; not to mention Fragonard, Dumas,
Stendhal, Offenbach and others in the pantheon.

I do not mean to be sidetracked from Montmartre low life by
cultural high life. But the two are necessarily linked. Its development from village to suburb to tourist attraction involved whores
and highbrows, pimps and poets alike. The fresh, clean country air
was inevitably tempered with cheap scent, oil paint and hashish.

Mid-nineteenth century Montmartre had windmills, gardens,
and vineyards in abundance; now only two windmills (inactive)
and one token vineyard remain. Gérard de Nerval came there to
study its countryside: '. . . silent lanes bordered by cottages, granges
and thickly wooded gardens, green shelves cut into cliffs with
springs filtering through the clay . . .'

With the artists came the girls. Like Degas, Renoir preferred
natural femininity to that of professional models. He found it
among the ambitious florists and shopgirls from Printemps who
spent their Sundays at the Moulin de la Galette, looking for a rich
lover to keep them in caviar.

Further down the social scale, prostitutes inspired Toulouse-
Lautrec, Degas, Rops, and others. The whorehouses of Paris were
a sexual paradise – for the men. From Le Grand Chabanais, where
Edward VII had a specially designed love-seat for his acrobatics (he
was a stout chap) to the Sphinx, whose pleasures were far from
enigmatic, these luxurious *maisons closes* provided every fantasy

imaginable. But for the girls, life was no fantasy: on duty twenty-four hours around the clock, in a suffocating prison from which the only escape was drugs, suicide or, only very occasionally, marriage to a client.

By the time we met Irma, brothels had been officially closed for more than ten years (1946). The girls on the Pont Caulaincourt, though at the mercy of their *mecs*, did not regret the passing of the good old days. At least, not the ones I spoke to. And, although we were working on a fairytale, I wanted to know more of their reality.

The girls were much rougher than our Irma, hardened as they were by the tourist trade. Some even addressed me in my own tongue – with brassy Parisian panache. 'You English? I make you grand standing!' 'You wan' I smoke the pipe, ainh?' 'I give you a good correction, ok?' 'My cat she jump for you, chéri!' Hardly dialogue for our show, which began with the line: 'Don't worry, it's quite suitable for the children.'

I went in search of sweetness, albeit with a bitter leavening – from Place de Clichy where Henry Miller had found sex at the Café Wepler, to Place Pigalle where I hoped to find it now. The pavement seemed to float under my feet. Bars and cafés drifted by. And catching the eye of a girl, alone at a table, I felt a pang of lust. Her face stayed with me a second or so, then joined my ragbag of missed opportunities.

The night was just beginning.

I drifted, happily breathing the smells of shellfish from the *huitrières*, black tobacco, and the damp, night air of the boulevard. It was cold, a night for onion soup. The lights were glamorously garish, and suddenly there were the Moulin Rouge's neon windmill and Sacré Coeur floodlit on its hill and more eyes of more girls lubriciously available. The Boulevard de Cliché . . .

I longed to find something unfamiliar, unliterary. Something real.

Alexandre Breffort had told me you could still find clandestine brothels, if you knew where to look. Just ask a taxi-driver. So I asked Breffort. 'I've retired,' he replied reticently.

'*Où est le bordel le plus proche?*' The taxi-driver at the rank on Place Pigalle had pebble glasses and the look of a wise night-owl.

'What is your speciality, M'sieur?' he asked.

'Speciality?'

'Do you like . . .?' He put his hand out and whacked it with an invisible switch. Then he made several more SM gestures and sounds to which I did not respond. He seemed surprised. 'You are an Englishman, aren't you?' I said yes, but no nanny had ever spanked me with the bristle side of the hairbrush. So various paedophiliac and scatalogical alternatives were proposed; again I declined. Lolita, I said, could piss in a pot, and duck-fucking was out, because I was scared of birds.

'What is it you want?' he asked wearily.

'Just straight sex.'

'*Ça alors!*' exclaimed the taxi-driver.

This was all done with perfect matter-of-factness. He drove me very slowly, with his meter clocking up the night-rate francs, the long way round into Rue de Douai, a two-minute walk. Brothels were now housed in back-street hotels and taxi-drivers knew which were for sleeping and which for business. 'Hotel de Douai', it announced, in red neon. A grey, tall building lurked in the shadows, its windows all shuttered, its entrance more like a private house than a hotel.

'You'll find all you need here,' my taxi-driver promised. The word 'need' had nothing romantic about it. The girls, he also promised, made regular visits to the doctor.

I felt I was visiting the doctor myself. I rang the bell. A large soberly-dressed redhead of uncertain age showed me into a waiting-room, where I was the only patient. The redhead left me, saying it was very late; she would have to see what she could do. What did this mean? I waited. There were no magazines. Suddenly, all I needed was to relieve my bladder. Very badly. But I could see no likely door, and had no wish to invade privacy by choosing a wrong one. Here, of all places.

After a few minutes, a tousled, frowsty harridan in a kimono and heavy-rimmed glasses came yawning into the room. Having given me a mildly hard time for waking her up after midnight, her official closing time, she agreed to let me stay. Very kind, I said, wondering if there was an antisocial-hour premium.

'One hundred francs to view the girls, M'sieur. Then one hundred and fifty per *passe*.'

I did a quick calculation. I had just enough. But I would have to walk home to my hotel on the Left Bank. They say sex is as good as a five-mile walk. I did not feel like eight miles, not that late. Nevertheless, I had to get my facts right. This was research.

'Bring on the girls,' I said, regally as Edward VII getting into his love-seat at Le Grand Chabanais.

I thought of Laurence Sterne's *A Sentimental Journey*, and his adventures with the Grissets (a *grisette* was a seamstress who made money on the side). 'In a few minutes the Grisset came in with her box of lace – I'll buy nothing however, said I.' The flesh proved weaker than such resolve, and the good prelate usually succumbed to the Grisset's charms. Whereas I, confronted by three sulky girls, sleep in their eyes, naked, merely felt sorry for having woken them up.

'Which girl, M'sieur?' Madame asked impatiently. I hesitated further. 'Make up your mind, please. They will catch cold.' She patted my head. 'Say what you wish, chéri!'

I summoned up courage.

'*Où sont les toilettes, s'il vous plaît, Madame?*'

Never has a Madame shown a prospective client off the premises faster. I was not sorry. But my need became even more urgent as the cold night air hit me in Rue de Douai.

I headed for the nearest late-night café, ordered a coffee, and dived gratefully into the basement *toilettes*. I had money for the taxi to my hotel and, what's more, I would not ask the driver for any good addresses.

There were other nights, however. And other girls. I even found the model for the Rapid Hotel in *Irma La Douce*.

I was led to a back-street *maison de passe*, with a red neon light just saying HOTEL. This was more like it: a concierge handing out short-time keys, and making me pay my money in advance; dim lights on all four floors; girls and clients coming and going despite the late hour, furtive passings on the carpetless stairway; the multiple sounds of love beyond cardboard walls, mostly client gruntings and the occasional female cry of simulated joy; the gushing of bidets and the gurgling of drainpipes. We took a room, and ordered drinks to be sent up. And over the drinks, we talked.

I started with the usual question: what's a nice girl like you etcetera? To which, sending me up rotten, she gave me her PR handout to authors: 'So I don't have to work at a dull job and can have nice clothes it's interesting work you meet different people but I never do it on a Sunday I'm a religious girl I go to church I love my old mother who's bedridden I send money back to her in Villerey-sur-Loire . . .' After a second drink, this literary *poule* said: 'You're no Baudelaire, I can see that.' Crafty: a challenge to prove her wrong albeit without the poems. I couldn't resist it.

In my wanderings through Montmartre, I did not find the incarnation of Irma La Douce. But the ambience seemed as enticing as it had to Henry Miller. I knew nothing of its vicious scoresettlings; the underworld of Montmartre still had a welcoming front. It was the sweet and sour, secret Paris of a Brassäi photograph.

I returned recently to Montmartre to see what vestiges remained of Henry Miller's 'pungent and nostalgic' world. How would an ageing Irma La Douce fare, now permanently bathed in 'the glare of the neon light'? I was in for a shock; a whole era of France's history seemed to have ended.

For nearly two centuries France the Libertine had reigned supreme with Paris the sex capital of the civilised world. Two eighteenth-century phenomena coincided to bring this about: free thought to subvert accepted codes of behaviour, and the Revolution to undermine the moral leadership of the Catholic Church.

While Queen Victoria's England and grass-roots America preached pure thoughts, Paris became brothel elect to foreign princes and millionaires. And, more importantly, a place of new sexual freedom (and scandals) for its literary and art world. From Balzac to Baudelaire, Zola to George Sand, there was a celebration of the libido and sexual proclivities. Gide and de Maupassant wrote freely of homosexuality; while Oscar Wilde, imprisoned for it, fled to France to die. Colette's novels have the juicier bits expunged in English translation. Miller and Joyce would have been arrested at home for what they wrote in Paris.

Painters enjoyed the same liberation. From Courbet's explicit nude in *Origins of the World* (1866), to Picasso's *La Pisseuse* (1965), via Lautrec's brothel girls making love, many masters treated the same subject as today's porn' trade – though there the comparison ends.

During the swinging Sixties, the permissive society of New York, London, and other cities took over from Paris and debased the erotic currency. And Paris, no longer supreme, was quick to follow suit.

On a cold winter's day, hands grabbed me from squalid, empty entrances along the Boulevard de Clichy. The live show gorillas were trying to hustle me in from the cold. Rough trade was looking for business.

'*On s'explique, M'sieur!*' breathed a bearded, pasty-faced tout, clutching my sleeve. What was there to explain? In the foyer, vast explicit photos of the show were on view; any child could walk in off the street and get a full sex education on the spot, though the show itself was forbidden to anyone under eighteen.

From Place Pigalle to Place Blanche, on the boulevard's north side, I side-stepped more neanderthal advances; finally, a cool, crisp girl, wearing a uniform not unlike that of an air stewardess, invited me into Le Plaisir. Maybe I would be asked to observe the safety instructions and prepare for take-off?

'*Vous désirez, M'sieur?*'

Monsieur didn't.

Not Le Plaisir. Nor the Sexy Cabaret. Nor Le Jeu. What could Le Sexy Bonsai mean? Japanese dwarfs at it?

The absurd hypocrisy! All those lurid pictures outside the live shows; yet on the opposite side of the boulevard, the endless line of sex shops (including the appropriately named Le Self Sex) must, by law, have curtains over their entrances lest a minor catch a corrupting glimpse of his Oncle Maurice buying an inflatable doll.

From side-streets, fierce old *poules* in fur coats were nodding-and-becking, pathetically desperate for a client.

There was nothing sweet or secret about Montmartre that winter's afternoon. It was tough, aggressive and brassy – far from Henry Miller's flourishing 'in a dim, murky light'.

Determined not to be put off by the squalor of the boulevard, I

turned down Rue Pigalle. The Lolita Club was altogether more
inviting. No gorilla on the door. Credit cards accepted. Even press
clippings in a glass display case, in German and English, saying this
was the sauciest spot in town: middle-aged couples, at the late, late
show, got so excited the actors encouraged them to join in. Brave
of the actors, I thought, and plunged in.

Audience participation also happened by day.

An attractive young couple, more Neuilly *jeunesse dorée* than
Montmartre sex show, were just finishing a bout of simulated cop-
ulation. They sprang energetically to their feet and, holding hands
like a good duo should, took a bow. The only members of the
audience – four young Nordic businessmen strategically placed in
the front row – applauded, and one of them leaned forward to pat
the girl's bare feet like patting a good dog after a trick.

I'd hardly even settled in the last of the comfortable, tiny
theatre's three rows before I was the fall guy. 'Anyone want a
taste?' said the lithe, balletic young man, waggling his cock at the
businessmen. They recoiled. Then, spotting the new arrival, he
sprang across the empty seat between the stage and me, and before
I knew it there was his member not two inches from my face. I
ducked.

The girl shouted: 'If you do not taste, you will be up here with
us for the next show!'

Neither threat, I'm thankful to say, was carried out. But after the
grim gorillas it seemed playfully inoffensive.

The next act was a solo turn. A pretty young brunette danced
about a bit, flashing stocking tops. No wonder the boys had chosen
the front row. Shapely legs entwined their heads. They were sat on,
fondled, straddled, and invited to take her clothes off. Meanwhile,
she talked mildly dirty which the boys didn't understand being foreign. They sat like inanimate sacks, while she occasionally flicked a
toe or finger at their bulging pants.

'How are you called?' she asked one of them in English, letting
her toe rest on his crotch.

'Sven,' said the lump.

The Lolita Club at least presented a certain innocent erotic
humour. It also had a male performer, so couldn't be accused of
just exploiting the female form. He came out of the dressing-

room, clad in a stylish ulster and snap-brim fedora. By this time the
girl on the tiny stage, whose sole decor was a pouf and a rattan
chair, was wearing nothing but Sven's steamed-up eye-glasses.

The actors began a conversation.

'I forgot to feed the parking-meter,' called out the girl, mastur-
bating a little for the boys.

'OK, I'll do it,' the boy replied. 'And when you're through with
this lot, join me at the bar. Don't work too hard.'

The boy left. And so did I. Thanks to the uninhibited attractive-
ness of the performers, it had been an oasis of erotica in a desert of
squalor.

In better mood, I headed for Place de Clichy. The Café Wepler
had a smart scarlet-and-gold awning now, and even in the depths
of winter, tourist coaches were crossing the Pont Caulaincourt on
their way to La Butte Montmartre. No Irmas now roamed the old
bridge's traffic-fumed pavements. They would die of asphyxia.

I was struck by the contrast: as Boulevard de Clichy had become
seedier, so the hill of Montmartre seemed to have gained in charm.
There was even talk of a revival of the Brassäi look, the retro nostalgia that Miller loved, a return to the sights and sounds of a popular Paris that once thrived here.

It had never really left one bistrot in Rue Caulaincourt, Au
Rêve. Behind the bar, a black-and-white photograph showed a
handsome woman leaning against the marble-topped bar.

'Who is that, Madame?' I asked la patronne, imagining it to be
some long-ago star of Parisian music hall.

'It's me, M'sieur,' she laughed.

'How long have you had this place?' Six tables; wash-basin in
telephone box, the kind of old-fashioned phone to dial exchanges
like DANTON and SOLFERINO; newspapers on batons; a
backroom with wooden swing doors topped with engraved lalique
glass.

'Twenty years, M'sieur.'

Just the kind of place Irma La Douce might have bought with
her savings. Her working sisters would be welcomed here. There
is an odd paradox: in Irma's day, a prostitute was known as a *poule*
(hen); now she's known by the tougher word *pute*, a contraction of
putain (a swear-word) with its resonance of malodour. Yet a Paris

prostitute today is no pariah in her community – always addressed as Madame by her baker – and writes 'Hôtesse' on her tax declaration under the category *profession libérale* (freelance).

In a Paris traumatised, like every other city, by AIDS, a return to legalised brothels, mooted by the health authorities and police, was vociferously condemned by the 12,000 members of the Prostitutes' Union. They are professionals. Health precautions, they reckon, are their responsibility; condomless sex is only risked with clients they know well, and 'With or without?' has become a new preliminary.

Some girls believe the oldest profession may have run its course. Wives – *les pots-au-feu*, as the girls call them – are getting more adventurous in the bedroom. An entire network, putting couples and singles in touch with likeminded kinksters, thrives from Carcassonne to Calais, Colmar to Quimper; unvigilant parents find their phone bills soar with kids having a lark on Wednesday's school half-day on the Minitel's *téléphone rose*, a computerised hook-up for people to tap out their fantasies to each other or make dates.

The lower depths of the sex trade are less comic – unless de Sade is your mentor. In the Bois de Boulogne, tough, big-breasted South American transsexuals who live together in cheap dosshouses, as many as ten to a room, earn money to pay for their sex changes; sometimes, at a higher price and health risk to their clients, they are buggered in the bushes by family men who, when caught, bribe the police in order not to have to face a tribunal. Whereas wealthy clients pay a high premium for condomless sex with Thai masseuses or Avenue Foch call-girls or choosy Escort Girls who, if the price is right, will even accompany them on business trips.

There is not much that is 'glamorous and seductive' about the contemporary sex scene, especially in those lower depths where Irma worked. Even Rue St-Denis has lost the tawdry panache it once had. Both sides of the narrow street, just south of Poissonière, the pavements are thick with girls.

Clustered in doorways, they are permitted by the police as any housewife would be – just as long as they do not solicit. No mistaking them for housewives, though: whatever the weather, pink tights, sky-blue tights, purple tights emerge from silver shorts or cheap fur coats; skintight leather pants swelling upwards to matching jackets unzipped to the navel. Some carry switches and vibrators. I once saw a girl costumed in a bear's head, basque, and suspendered fishnet stockings, carrying a ringmaster's whip. Did she take the bear's head off for business, I wondered?

One day, I asked a tall Martiniquaise in thigh boots and blonde wig to show me her place of work. She led the way through a cordon of girls lining an alley that smelt of rotting garbage, and up creaking, carpetless stairs. Along a dingy corridor, she unlocked a door into the cubicle she shared with others – ten minutes a *passe*, so you'd better be quick. There was a wash-basin, and a strong odour of the disinfectant she washed her clients' genitals with. The bed was covered with nothing but a filthy counterpane. And the only human touch were the postcards from clients, a mass of them, pinned to the hardboard wall above the telephone.

'Very important, that telephone,' Shirley Maclaine agreed, when I visited her backstage at the Palais des Congrès where she had just sung the Irma La Douce waltz. Shirley had done much research of her own in Rue St-Denis for the Billy Wilder movie in which she played Irma, and Jack Lemmon her jealous lover. 'If a client gets rough, there's an early-warning system by phone. I accompanied a girl on her beat, and her biggest fear was violence. Getting roughed up by her pimp, or killed by a client. I've played a number of hookers with hearts of gold, and I guess in real life there's very little romance in it, if any.'

I found I was typecast, too. Producers seemed to think I had Paris low-life in my blood, and only a few years ago I found myself working on *Roza*, once again a musical with a *poule* heroine. This time I needed police protection.

Quite how much police protection I never would have guessed: one police commissioner; one plain-clothes lady sergeant in a Hermès scarf; one inspector; and two heavies in brown leather jackets bulging with firearms.

I was visiting eastern Montmartre, a quarter known as La Goutte d'Or – the drop of gold, after the colour of the wine from its once famous vineyard. Nowadays it was the kasbah, mainly a maghrébin ghetto, off-limits after sunset for casual visitors.

A pity, because it is one of Montmartre's most romantic areas.
Fine, dilapidated old houses and gardens straggle higgledy-
piggledy up the hill, on either side of a steeply climbing pathway.
Maghrébin music floats from the dimly lit windows of a mansion.

'That's where one of the biggest Tunisian pimps lives,' says the
commissioner. 'He used to control quite a number of houses.'
Adding with a note of regret, 'Before they made us close down the
clandestine brothels, that is. Ah, M'sieur More, you should have
seen this street before.' We were casing the main street now.
'Every other house a knocking-shop with lines of Arabs for one
whore. She hardly had time to reach up for the sponge on a string
to wipe herself.' In these lowest depths, what shocked was the total
lack of concern for the girl. 'Sordid, you may say, but at least we
could control it. Now vice has gone underground.'

We pass the notorious police station which once had a clandestine brothel over it. 'The girls were very patriotic,' the sergeant
informs me. 'They hung out the Tricolour over the police station
every morning.'

From a Tunisian pastry shop, a boy who's had one drink or puff
of kif too many, weaves across the street towards us. He greets the
Commissioner's posse with a friendly wave. The Commissioner
curtly gives him a nod. Clearly no close friend. Piqued, the Arab
kid says quietly to one of the brown-leather heavies: 'What's the
matter with him? Did he turn gay or something?' The kid is
invited to say that again. He says it again. Perfunctorily, one heavy
turns the boy to face the opposite pavement, then the other boots
him across the street.

'Don't worry, M'sieur More,' says the Commissioner, to dispel
any nausea I may now be feeling. 'Where I am taking you is no
knocking-shop. The girls are part of the family.'

We turn into a bar, and immediately it's time for toasts to be
drunk. We are plied with Chivas Regal from the biggest bottle it
comes in, poured neat into gold curlicued mint-tea glasses. This is
an occasion: M'sieur Le Commissaire is visiting, only the best will
do. And if the Koran forbids alcohol, tonight Allah will pardon a
sin in the cause of fraternity – even if liberty and egality are in
short supply: 'Here's to happy relations between France and
Algeria . . .'

The musicians, all Algerian, begin their music. The Commissioner has serious business with la patronne. She is a hard-nosed peroxide blonde with teeth like gold bricks, clearly a police informer. They confer in a corner.

The girls are much more attractive than those on Rue St-Denis. They wear feminine clothes not fetishist; in their svelte cocktail dresses, they appear more like members of the family on party night than girls on the game. A Berber beauty invites me to dance. The inspector dances, too. My Berber and I are swaying belly to belly to the sinuous, exotic music. She is a very physical presence, very warm. Her scent has all the perfumes of Arabia, her skin a glossy softness upon the bare shoulders moving beneath my hand. I hear her whispering that her name is Aisha and she likes me, she has a proposition, a most attractive suggestion.

And then I see the sergeant looking very beadily in our direction, giving a tug on her scarf. Now the inspector, too, has stopped dancing with his girl and frowns fiercely. The Commissioner breaks away from his conference. And the two brown-leather heavies stub out their cigarettes. Quite clearly Aisha and I have broken some unwritten law. The music continues, but Aisha who has read the signals quicker than I stops dancing. The toasts have been drunk, the goodwill dances danced. And it's time for bed – without Aisha.

I took a taxi home. The driver was a woman of about fifty. She had once been handsome. Her bulldog sat in the front seat, protective as a good *mec*. I watched her impassive, puffy face lit by passing neon lights, a hand occasionally patting her bulldog. A strong lady, clearly used to night work, and not afraid of it.

I began to dream up a sequel: Irma La Douce has retired and she buys this Renault 19 with her savings and, like many former Parisian *poules*, becomes a taxi-driver and . . . that's as far as I got.

5

Valence, 1958

French gastronomy and love have many things in common: a perfect initiation, for instance, leads to a growing appetite. And old habitués, still rising to an occasion, rejoice in the memory of that first great feast.

In 1958, with some money coming in, S and I bought our first posh car. It was the height (or depths) of showbiz flash – a pale blue Ford Zephyr convertible with an automatically controlled roof like most of us had only ever seen in American movies. Blue and white regency striped seats. Just the car for a trip to St-Tropez.

We did it in style. In those days, you could fly your car across the Channel, put it on a train at Le Touquet, get off at Lyons, and drive to St-Trop' for dinner. With only a week's holiday, we said to hell with the expense. Silver City Airways, the cross-channel carlift which once transported camels across the Sahara, is long since defunct, and the up-market way now is to fly as near as possible to one's destination and rent a car. Not nearly so much fun.

Speeding out of Lyons, on the old Route Nationale 7, in our flash car – what a life! Morning mist swirling off the Rhône, the sun burning through it, the precipitous vineyards of the Côte Rotie, our first sign of wine, emerging high above us in a fringe of bright light. We stopped soon after Vienne. Pressed the canvas roof's control button. With a smooth whirring, the roof rose, folded itself and fell away from us like a butterfly's cocoon. Nothing could beat an open car, in the light traffic of June, on the old N7. We flew south, the radio blaring Johnny Hallyday *yé yé* and crackling with static as we passed under electricity cables.

Then I heard S say, quite casually:

'What's that smell?'

'What smell?'

'Can't you smell it?'

'No.'

'Burning.'

'A bonfire, maybe.'

'In June?!'

'I can't smell anything.'

'A sort of hot, oily smell . . .'

S has a very sensitive nose. She could smell hyacinths in a tannery. I had just slowed down for Tain l'Hermitage, and ominous smells have a habit of catching up when one slows down. I had to admit: a slight smell of burning mingled with the newly baked bread wafting from the *boulangeries* of Tain.

'The garage probably overfilled the oil when they serviced it.'

'It didn't smell like that in England.'

'I was going a lot slower.'

'Maybe there's an oil leak.' We stopped. She got out and looked under the car. Nothing. Meanwhile, I had caught sight of more steep vineyards rising above Tain and the vast billboards of their owners: PAUL JABOULET AINE and CHAPOUTIER. I wanted to sniff something a little more elegant than hot, oily smells: the bouquet of a strong heady Hermitage. But St-Tropez called. The sun, by now, had a good warmth in it. We pressed on.

The Rhône curved away from the roadside in a great bend beneath the steep, wooded slopes of the right bank. The valley opened out, and along came our first really good straight stretch of N7 since Lyons. To test the smell, I put my foot down. At eighty, the car smelt. I slowed down. At seventy, it smelt worse. At sixty, it smelt worse still. And then, the smoke appeared. Quite suddenly, the Zephyr's wind went out of it. We limped, shuddering, sizzling, and swearing into a garage just north of Pont de L'Isère.

It was the sort of garage only seen in old black-and-white French movies; but we were in bad trouble, and had no choice. A jumble of junky farm machinery surrounded a dilapidated shed. A beefy man in oil-stained *bleus de travail* emerged from dissecting a tractor; it lay about him in bits which would never reassemble into a tractor. The nearest thing to a car was a Citroën *camionette*, which had clearly seen war service with the Resistance.

'You are in luck!' pronounced Monsieur le Garagiste. He could have fooled me. He walked admiringly round the Zephyr and let out a long, slow whistle of approbation. '*Quelle belle Américaine!* I was brought up on American cars in Chicago!' Who was I to disbelieve him? He spun a brief, plausible tale of emigration to America and return to France, a sadder but wiser mechanic.

'If you're too busy', S proposed obligingly, 'just tell us where the nearest Ford dealer is.'

'Right here,' joked our friend, who had gingerly opened up the bonnet to inspect the damage. Wagging his head and sighing: 'Did you have your car serviced recently? Yes? And did you have antifreeze in it for the winter? Yes? Well, your fool of a *garagiste* should have taken it out – for summer. In this heat, it makes the water evaporate. You've blown a gasket – and the piston block's bent with the overheating. I can fix it for you, but it will take two or three days.'

Two or three days? Out of our precious week? Where would we stay? Pont de L'Isère was a one-tractor town – and that was in pieces. It did not augur well. What would we do here for two or three days? Swim in the Isère? Monsieur le Garagiste wiped his hands with an oily rag, wound up his telephone into a frenzy and spoke very old-boy-net to his correspondent. Then, 'I have booked you into the Restaurant Pic, Valence,' he announced.

'Thank you, but we need more than a restaurant,' S said.

Monsieur le Garagiste winked. 'You will have more than a restaurant, Madame, I assure you.'

Pique? I had only heard our friend speak the name, and tell the taxi-driver where to take us. Pique was what we felt, pique was appropriate. In our ignorance, we had never heard of the Pics, the great restaurant family of Valence. Already, they were well known to travellers of the N7, who built itineraries around Pic lunch stops, siestas in the Pic garden, or overnight stops in one of the Pic guest rooms.

With the popularity of road travel in the Thirties, André Pic, second generation and one of the great chefs of France, had the sense to move his 3-star Michelin family restaurant from the hills of the Ardèche to the outskirts of Valence, a block or two from the N7. Valence, then a Rhône-side town of some 30,000 inhabitants, was a transitional place between northern and southern France, with the red-tiled roofs of Provence and the solidly bourgeois Haussman-style architecture of nineteenth-century Paris. Neither one thing nor the other, it was a town the traveller only stopped in for a meal, a night's rest, or if a car broke down. Or, in our case, all three.

Our taxi dropped us in the rue Colbert, a side-street off the long Avenue Victor-Hugo. Only later did we find out that through this modest entrance had swept the Aga Khan, Rita Hayworth, the King of Morocco, and Fernandel – to the restaurant of the stars, tucked away in a quite ordinary house in the suburb of a provincial town.

Quite out of the ordinary, however, was the Pics' welcome. André, rotund and beaming as a medieval friar was then sixty-five, already an invalid who moved as little as possible; his wife, Sophie, and son, Jacques, twenty-six, recently married to Suzanne, were clearly a solid back-up team. And all four, with the modesty of excellence, did us proud during our short stay.

The scent of lime blossom from the fine trees and flowers of the Pics' garden drifted around our room, a light room in which we could rest our increasingly heavy bodies. In 1958, Londoners were unaccustomed to *la grande bouffe*; restaurant eating was not the cultural event it now is. We pigged it occasionally in King's Road bistrots and Soho, and tried out Elizabeth David recipes at home. That, except for the very rich, was the extent of it.

Pic problem: how to occupy our time healthily between the baby chicken in saffron and cream sauce, crayfish tails, sausage of pike in *sauce nantua*, and the next gourmet treat. Three great meals a day, including a sumptuous breakfast of home-made brioches, croissants, jam and café-au-lait, wrought havoc with our constitutions. Alka-Seltzers sizzled permanently in glasses; supplies got dangerously low. A trip to the chemist was yet another excuse for yet another brisk stroll – either to work up an appetite or to walk off a sauce.

'We haven't seen the sanguines,' S announced.

'The what?' I thought she was referring to some arcane local mushrooms about to appear at dinner that night. But no, she meant the red-chalk drawings of landscape artist, Hubert Robert, the prized collection at the Valence Municipal Museum.

'I think', I said, 'we should stay out of doors.'

'We've done Valence out of doors.'

It was true.

Indoors, outdoors, Valence in those days could be done in half a day flat. And at that, slowly, spinning out the sanguines for a couple of hours. We had two or three days.

We covered the waterfront – on both banks of the Rhône. We strolled the main drag, remembering on the Boulevard Général de Gaulle what André Pic told us: 'When the General ate with us, he couldn't get through the courses fast enough. However, he did say thank you nicely.'

Round and round the Parc Jouvet we walked, up and down Les Côtes – steep narrow streets with long, cobbled steps. We penetrated the dilapidated Old Town, the dark, cool wastes of the heavily restored Romanesque Église St-Jean and cathedral. The smell of incense made us queasy.

We paid homage to the town's historical celebrities. Napoléon, as a sixteen-year-old army cadet at Artillery School, became an avid reader here, thanks to a local bookshop owner. Peynet, the cartoonist, was inspired by the bandstand in the Champs de Mars to draw his famous lovers by it. Renaissance writer François Rabelais was a student at the University, and had his roistering young hero, Pantagruel, pass briefly through the city, in *Faits et Dits Héroïques du Grand Pantagruel*:

> . . . but he saw there was not much to learn there, and that the rogues of the town set about the scholars; in spite of which, one fine Sunday when all were dancing publicly, a scholar wished to join in the dance, which the aforesaid rogues did not countenance. Seeing which, Pantagruel sent them packing to the banks of the Rhône, and would have drowned them all, had they not burrowed into the earth like moles, a good half league under the Rhône. The holes are there still.

These we gave a miss but, by the time our Ford Zephyr was repaired, we had become quite fond of Valence. And devotees of

the Restaurant Pic. In St-Tropez, having spent half our money on
the car repair and Pic, we would willingly starve.

A Pizzeria Rabelais now adorns the Place de L'Université and
Benetton has a shop under Napoléon's digs. Valence Old Town,
transformed by restoration, is alive with design-conscious enterprises. We hardly recognised it: a warren of neatly paved streets for
pedestrians only; boutiques, boutiques all the way with the latest
prêt-à-porter fashions; the beautifully preserved Maison des Têtes, its
façade of elaborate stone-carved heads and interior courtyard, a
Renaissance masterpiece; a sunken alleyway with a chic, brightly
painted iron stairway to the Karate Club, conveniently close to the
Club Gambetta, which offers *musculation*.

So Valence in the Nineties is as obsessed with self-defence as the
rest of France. It has much to defend. Now the most important
agricultural and industrial town of the Drôme, with a population
that has more than doubled since the opening of the Restaurant
Pic, Valence is a city on the move. Served by TGV from Paris, the
old N7 much improved – our blessed tractor garage metamorpho-
sised into a smart Talbot-Peugeot *concessionnaire*, the Autoroute du
Soleil streaking along the quayside, where once we walked in
bloated tranquillity, and an airport with businessmen opening the
gatefolds of their *Lui* magazines, as the 6.15 a.m. flight takes off for
Paris.

Business booms: industrial zones surround the city on all sides
like twentieth-century ramparts; near Valence Sud autoroute exit,
roads curl and squiggle and switchback over each other in an orgy
of interchange, serving an area of giant supermarkets and business
hotels. Casino Géant, Novotel, Mammouth, Bricorama, Leclerc,
Maxi-Cuisines – so near and yet so far from the Restaurant Pic.
But where there is business, there are business lunches. And the
Pic is booming, too.

In a desert of soulless urban expansion, today's Pic is an oasis of
conviviality, with its white, southern walls and red-tiled roof.

We entered through a gate on the Avenue Victor-Hugo.
Crossed a patio for summer dining beneath the stars, passing

flowers in pots, winter pansies, and globe lamps. And were welcomed by a new Pic daughter-in-law, Marie-Hélène, wife of Alain
Pic, bearded heir to the ovens he shares with his famous father,
Jacques. Jacques Pic we remembered, but on our first visit Alain
was not even born.

Ubiquitous Japanese gastronomes graced the dining-room, six at
a table big enough for video cameras and notebooks as well.

'My husband makes trips to Japan,' Marie-Hélène told us. 'To
give demonstrations of *haute cuisine*. But Osaka is not Valence, and
he likes to get back here.'

The Pics do not constantly jet between the kitchens of the
world, like the culinary stars, Paul Bocuse and Co. Their secret is
to be on the spot, a presence felt, if not visible until after the meal.
A name chef actually manifesting himself to reassure his guests is an
endangered species. The younger Pics are traditionalists – like the
André Pic we knew.

But André Pic had died, quite simply, from overdoing it. He
loved to eat, he loved to drink. He made himself ill. He lost two of
his Michelin stars. And it became the mission of Jacques, sworn to
a more balanced life than his father's, to put his house in order and
regain those two stars. He has more than succeeded.

'When you were here', Jacques told us, 'I was beginning to
experiment with lighter sauces, taking over from my father. He
had taught me a lot about sauces. But tastes were changing and
people were happy to find they could have a gastronomic meal
with no ill effects. A *crise de foie* is a bad French joke.'

We remembered Valence through a liverish haze: how would
we shape up to Jacques Pic's Menu Rabelais?

The menu card's cover, designed by Peynet, was light enough.
'I'll love you more', says the girl to her lover on an outing in a vintage barouche, 'when you take me to dine chez Pic.'

And the ambience is light, too. We are there on the first
Saturday of 1990. The elegant, enlarged dining-room is filled, not
with tourists or businessmen on expense accounts but prosperous
Valentinois, the weekend regulars, extending the *fêtes* of the
Christmas holidays to one final binge. It's a family ambience –
grannies and babies, a small boy in a white bow tie and American
T-shirt, a little girl in a black velvet dress with white lace collar.

'We have a special dessert trolley for the children,' Marie-Hélène, herself a mother of two, tells us. '*Bon appetit.*'

First comes *Galette d'Artichauts Homardine*: slices of lobster with heart-shaped beetroot on top, a slice of artichoke heart between. Drunk with this was a white Hermitage '87 from Grippat – earthy with a taste of mushrooms. Next, *Pétales de St-Jacques et Feuille de Saumon sauce Verdure*: slices of scallops with caviar for the petals, a green bean for the stalk, and two slices of salmon for the leaves, served in a green, creamy sauce. Then, *Minute de Turbot*: turbot slices stuffed with truffle, and lobster claw flesh, served with another white Hermitage '87 from Chapoutier this time, well made in an unspecial year.

Pause for a *Sorbet au Marc*: water-ice made with more *marc* than water.

Our gargantuan Menu Rabelais continues with *Suprême de Col-Vert en Choucroute* (wild duck and sauerkraut), followed by *Millefeuille de Cerf aux Morilles* (wafers of venison and morel mushrooms, with a relish of veal-and-truffle). With this, a red Hermitage '87 from Paul Jaboulet. King of the red Côte-du-Rhônes, Hermitage – Hugh Johnson calls it 'the manliest wine of France'.

Fromages include almost any French cheese we could wish for, with a wide choice of local Drôme goat's cheeses. And the *Dessert Friandises* . . . chocolate mousse with wild strawberries, ice-cream and orange slices, cakes and tarts in profusion, all confected by the pastrycook-in-residence, one of the thirty staff behind the scenes.

After lunch Jacques and Suzanne Pic kindly put up with our reminiscences.

'This time, you came not by accident,' Jacques said, looking calm and cool after a four-hour stint in his kitchen. 'I hope it was as good.'

'Better.'

Suzanne added: 'I'm sorry we can't offer you your old room for a siesta. We only have two rooms and two suites now, and they're always full.'

But we didn't need a siesta. Nor a walk round the town. As we left, we felt as light as a Jacques Pic sauce. We even felt like driving.

And this time, we had a car.

It was a chance, finally, to explore the Rhône Valley surrounding Valence. To take a trip to Tain l'Hermitage where, previously, we'd been too preoccupied with getting to the South to taste the wines. After the robust Grippat and lusty Chapoutier chez Pic it was time to put that right.

During other trips on the Autoroute du Soleil, I had always wanted to explore the hilly, farming country behind Tain. But that contagious disease, autoroutism – catching the speed bug and an uncontrollable urge to 'get there' – had prevented it.

Now I fulfilled an old dream, winding up through the vineyards of the Hermitage and Crozes-Hermitage *appellations*, on single-track roads without a sign of another car. Through villages like Chantemerle-les-blés with open-sided barns and bales of hay tightly bound against the wind.

Our tranquil D-road took a bridge across the autoroute. And we rejoiced to be where we were, headed not for some anonymous Service Area but the romantic-sounding Belvédères des Coteaux du Rhône.

These view-points are the highest spots on the steep escarpments above the Rhône Valley. They are spectacular. Most dramatic was the Belvédère de Pierre Aiguille, up behind the Jaboulet and Chapoutier vineyards. The D-road becomes a twisty C-road then, suddenly, a dirt track leading to the vantage point. The wind whistles. It's vertiginous, as you look down on a toy river, toy villages, toy TGV speeding north to Lyons, and toy cars on the N7 hugging the bends of the river. I waver a bit with cliff angst, and to steady myself, my eye levels to the panorama: westward to the high forests of the Ardèche; eastward to the faraway snow-capped peaks of the Vercors.

Down, down our road zig-zags, past precipitous vineyards to the valley. Through Crozes, the central village of the *appellation* with a moat-like stream running down its middle. No signposts to Tain and no one to ask. We guess. Soon we can actually see the town way below us. How to get there via the maze of unsign-posted vineyard roads is another matter, and six wrong turns and near-divorces later, we arrive for our appointment with Max Chapoutier.

'Lucky you were late,' said our bespectacled young host, short, portly and dapper in a discreet English check suit with clubman's tie. 'I've had Swiss clients all morning. They only just left. And . . .' The phone rang: a very important Italian client. 'Excuse me . . .'

Chapoutier is to Rhône wine what Pic is to food.

I was happy to watch a girl sticking labels on miniature wine bottles, a publicity handout. Short of office space for our meeting, Max had installed us among the wine – magnums of Chante-Alouettes, bottles of Les Meysonniers.

'So you enjoyed our '87 white chez Pic?' Max beamed – and had us taste it again, chewing and swilling. 'We're known for our white. The terrain is rather special, you see. Steep, south-facing slopes. Plenty of sunshine. A perfect mixture of chalk, granite, and peb-' The phone rang: an important client from Belgium. 'Excuse me . . .'

I contemplated the straw-coloured liquid in my glass. And tasted again. It didn't taste like the wine I'd drunk chez Pic. Why? It was all that it should be: full-bodied, dry without being acid, velvety without being sweet. And yet?

Max Chapoutier explained: 'This wine should be drunk with food – like you had it chez Pic. Try it with a curry sometime.' And he turned to eulogies of his friends, the Pics. As a special favour for us, they did my brother's wedding. And mine.'

'What was the menu for yours?'

Max's glasses steamed up with the memory. 'Pigeon stuffed with truffles, lobster salad, *loup de mer* with caviar. But what I love about the Pics is their kindness to friends. We Chapoutiers get behind, returning their fav-' The phone rang. Max Chapoutier excused himself yet again. Clearly it was time to leave – but not before buying two dozen bottles of the wine we'd liked so much chez Pic but which hadn't tasted the same chez Chapoutier. We trusted Max's explanation. But sad to tell, it didn't taste the same chez More, either – with or without food.

By now we were like members of a fan-club, in pursuit of all things Pic.

'The former Pic restaurant?' said Madame Darona, a small wine-maker hidden away in the hills of St-Peray, on her own admission so bad at maths that she charged a flat rate of twenty-eight francs a bottle, good year or bad. 'Yes, it's still there. But don't expect it to be like the Restaurant Pic in Valence!'

We made a pilgrimage, way up into the Ardèche hills, twenty minutes of serpenting on the Le Puy road. By the time we reached the Auberge du Pin, it had begun to rain. Lowering clouds hung over the pine woods, and a door creaked and slammed in the wind.

Now it was a ghost-inn. No one about. Tables and chairs stacked for the winter. And that mysterious front door left open was not welcoming at all, even a little threatening. Had the present owner gone away for the annual closing and forgotten to lock up?

The desolate Auberge du Pin seemed to symbolise the whole flight from the land in France; how astute of the Pics to relocate themselves in the up-and-coming valley town of Valence, with its all-year-round clientèle.

I tried to imagine Sophie Pic, grandmother of Jacques, way back in the last century, serving her chicken fricassé and sautéed rabbit to hungry hunters and travellers. Now this solid old coaching inn was entirely bereft of its household gods. I could smell a faint, lingering odour of *frites*; in a few months, the summer tourists would return, enjoy the view, and gulp a formula menu without even knowing what illustrious futures were formed here.

6

Nice, 1960

'It's nicer in Nice', went the old song from *The Boy Friend*. And I really didn't imagine it to be a violent place. Not a place for a quiet Englishman to be threatened by a gangster. Not in the off season.

Rain dripped from melancholy palm trees. The Promenade des Anglais had never looked more *anglais*, and the Municipal Casino seemed like the best place to pass a wet November afternoon. Ostensibly, I had come to Nice in search of a house to rent for the family next summer; I was a sober family man having a flutter of a few francs on Premier, Dernier, Milieu, the safe roulette bet of the unadventurous. Well, I won a couple of hundred francs, quite a haul in 1960, and decided to bust it on a little seedy, lonesome night life.

Nice was then and still is the Côte d'Azur's most surprising town. Anything can happen. Far from the blandness of that song, its beauty conceals the kind of loucheness I love in a city. Its closeness to Italy, its past link with the House of Savoy, its population descended from Sardinians whose King once ruled it, and the Piedmont architecture make it a typical Mediterranean hybrid. Whereas Marseilles is North African, Nice is Italian. Yet both are unmistakably, bloody-mindedly French.

Nice only became attached to France in 1860, a reward to Napoléon III for helping King Victor-Emmanuel of Sardinia boot the Austrians out of northern Italy. But the emotional attachment went back much further – to Masséna, a Niçois soldier who became Napoléon I's Marshall of France; and it continued with

Garibaldi, also Niçois, who helped mastermind the unification of Italy and later served with the French against the Germans in 1870.

Both Garibaldi and Masséna have noble squares named after them. In either you could be in Italy. The Place Garibaldi is yellowy ochre, leafy tranquillity in midtown with fountains, a statue of the hero, and a baroque Chapel of the Holy Sepulchre. The Place Masséna is pinky ochre, an echo of Turin, all arcades and hanging lanterns. Garibaldi and Masséna are not names one associates with the Mob, but it was just off Place Masséna that my adventure occurred.

Wallet pleasingly full from my casino gains, I turned blithely from that stunning square into Rue Masséna where, I was told at my hotel, some action could be found. At that time most large French provincial towns had their version of The Crazy Horse Saloon. I scanned the wan displays of attractions outside various nightclubs, and settled for the one where among the faded photos of stripteuses, novelty dancers, and magicians there was a large blonde with a slanty smirk and a cobra between her legs.

The show was due to start around midnight, the barman told me. It was just after eleven. I decided to sit it out at the bar, and watch the action. There wasn't much to watch. I was the only person in the club, and the band played the barman's requests.

A customer arrived.

He was clearly well known. The barman shook his hand, and the customer flashed massive cuff-links studded with jewels.

'You drinking alone?' he smiled. I mistrusted the glittering affability.

'Before you, there was no one else to drink with,' I replied.

'Have a drink then!'

The customer bought me many drinks. Each time I said 'My turn!', he held up a lordly hand and shook his head. He was very tanned, his shoulders very broad, and I was feeling very pale and weedy, hoping other customers, less menacingly hospitable, would appear. For what seemed an eternity we discussed, unbelievably, the British Trade Union movement. The customer, who wore rings of lethal sharpness, did not approve of striking workers, he said. France had too many Communists, too many foreign trouble makers.

'You agree with me?'

'No, actually not.'

'Oh? You are British, aren't you?'

'Yes, but . . .'

'Most of the British residents in Nice would agree. If they were here now, they would contradict you.'

'They wouldn't understand the conversation, Raoul. Most British residents of Nice never have and never will speak French. It's a principle they have – like not speaking in the club.'

'Which club?'

'Any club. The British, you see like silence . . .'

Tactless, that. Raoul's eyes gave a warning flash. I did not want the argument to get out of hand, by either defending the British working man or the rights of foreigners in France too vociferously. After so much liquid hospitality, I was bending his ear too boldly and my host was getting fidgety. We were mercifully interrupted by the cabaret.

By this time, thank God, the joint had a few more customers, and the girl with the cobra was received with a polite patter of applause. She was followed by a stripteaseuse called Mylène.

I rather fancied Mylène. She was short, sturdily built, and did her stripping with a certain gaiety at odds with the surroundings. She was dressed as a French maid, making the most of her feather duster on the bald heads. She looked a little like Monica Vitti, one of my favourite Italian actresses at the time.

After the show, Raoul had business with a couple of gorillas waiting for him at the other end of the bar. Mylène, dressed again, wore spangly glasses, a crucifix on a silver chain round her neck, and butch leather blouson over a little black dress. She peered myopically at me over the top of her glasses, and smiled. I bought her a drink.

I told her I liked her act. Nobody, she said, had told her that in two months. In two months there had been virtually no one in the club – except Raoul and his cronies.

'Lucky you had him then,' I said. Mylène gave a doubtful grunt. 'He couldn't stop buying me drinks.'

'And you accepted them? From that scum?'

'Scum?'

'One of the scummiest gangsters in Nice. He lost his mother last summer, so he's got nowhere to go nights. That's why he's always in here, buying suckers like you drinks and making trouble.'

Let's get out of here, I thought. Too late. Raoul was with us. He offered to buy Mylène a drink. She said she already had one. He offered to buy me a drink.

'Thanks, Raoul. I've really had enough.'

'So now you are refusing my drinks.'

'Raoul,' Mylène snapped at him, 'Julian does not need any more of your drinks.'

'Julian?!' He turned on me with a mean grin. 'How does she know your name?'

'I told her. Like I told you . . .'

'Be careful, Juliano *mon ami, Mylène est une entraineuse!*' A polite way of saying Mylène was a hooker. Which Mylène, a respectable stripteuse with parents in Monte Carlo, did not like at all.

Mylène gave Raoul a hard time in Nice patois, and Raoul gave it right back. The gist of it, I gathered, was 'Piss off, Raoul, and take your gorillas with you', which seemed foolhardy of a girl accompanied by one slewed Englishman of meagre fortitude.

Surprisingly Raoul and the gorillas pissed off.

Mylène looked pleased with herself, and bought me a nightcap to prove she wasn't on the make. Then I said good night.

'I'll come with you,' she said. I did not object. We made our way to the front entrance. The doorman looked grim. Raoul and the gorillas, he warned us, were waiting in a car. As they left, the doorman had heard him threatening to kill us. Kill us? For what? Well, he wouldn't go that far when it came to it. Just chase us down the street in his car, confuse us like scared rabbits with his headlights until we fell and he could run over our legs. Good, clean fun.

So we took the doorman's advice and left the back way. Mylène, concerned for my safety, suggested I skip the six or seven block walk back to my hotel and stay the night at her place, conveniently round the corner. Again, I did not object. Mylène was a good sport.

Raoul had not exactly lied when he made out Mylène was a hooker. Oddly and chastely, I found myself sleeping on her couch. She had a bad leg which needed plenty of space and could not sleep with a man in her bed, she said. She got cramps and had nightmares.

Over breakfast next morning, she apologised for my uncomfortable night. 'I still haven't recovered from the accident, you see.'

'What accident?'

'A car accident. I had both my legs broken.' She laughed when she saw my expression. 'Oh, nothing to do with Raoul.'

And what of Nice low-life in the Nineties? Rue Masséna had become a street for pedestrians only; no cars waited and no one looked like a leg-smasher.

Smitten with Niçois nostalgia I just had to find that joint – if not Mylène who would no doubt be a granny by now. I would like to have seen her again. You don't meet her sort every wet November night in a Nice nightclub. Even if I wouldn't have recognised her, nor she me, we shared that one small adventure and could at least have had a couple of laughs about Raoul.

I walked the length of Rue Masséna on a cold night. It had become antiseptically touristic. Le Fast Food everywhere: the Hamburger Quick tried to rival the Elysées Masséna boasting its Pizza-Paella-TexMex-Pâtés-Salades-Poissons. There were Sexa-shop, Cartier, Manfield, and stylish young Niçois hanging out at the Brasserie Le Mirador. There was even one nightclub of suitable sleaze called Cha Cha Cha. An old crock in a thick fisherman's jersey, smoking an evil-smelling pipe told me: 'The show's around midnight.' Familiar words, unfamiliar place. I passed.

A group of German convention delegates with badges strolled purposefully by. They had one woman with them, so I guessed they must be on the look out for more. I followed them.

To the hideously dull new Ruhl building which houses the Meridien Hotel they led me, pausing only to check out Promotion Mozart. 'Make your dream come true,' suggested an ad in the window, 'own an apartment in the Belle Époque Villa Prat.' Indignant rumblings came from the Germans about the name Mozart being used by French property developers. But not nearly as indignant as I was to find McDonald's typically installed on the city's best corner between Avenue de Verdun and the Promenade des Anglais.

I followed the Germans, like a sleuth, into the Casino Ruhl. A tombola lottery ticket with a prize of a Golf GTi, displayed glossily in the entrance, went with the price of admission. The gaming room was pure Las Vegas. Girl croupiers worked a crowded black-jack table. A few Italians, sharp, tough, and wiry, had crossed the border for an evening's fun. An old-time mamma, in red pageboy hat and grey fur coat, gave some much needed style to the Punto Banco table. But nobody could compete with my memory of Mylène and Raoul.

I slumped disconsolately into a deep red leather armchair and thought: I know what's the matter, today's Nice gangsters are just too damn respectable. They look like bankers or surgeons, living in smart villas up in Cimiez with twice-a-week-hairdo wives, and children growing up to be creative accountants. Picking up strip-pers was passé, too. Some of those wives, bored with the hairdos and shopping, played *Belle de Jour* now and again. Maybe I should check out tomorrow's *thé dansant* at the Negresco; or Ladies' Night at Centre Ville, the disco that claimed to be the in-spot of the showbiz and sporting crowd.

For this, of course, was the Nice of Jacques Médecin. Even without him. Only a few months back, he had fled the country in disgrace.

The Médecins, Jean and Jacques, *père et fils*, had ruled the city as mayors from 1928 to 1990. Quite a run. They were Nice's royals, and evoked the same kind of populist affection and jokes as Britain's. Up till 1982, mayoral power was, however, limited by Paris. Then new decentralising legislation gave provincial mayors and presidents of regional councils more power. Jacques Médecin was both Mayor of Nice and President of the General Council of Alpes-Maritimes.

During 1990, French mayors of all political persuasions wal-lowed in scandal: Marseilles – corruption and murder in dubious clinics; Bordeaux – mysterious disappearance of millions of francs of football club funds; and Nice – gigantic misappropriation of municipal subsidies in kickbacks, ostensibly in the pursuit of the city's considerable culture and leisure developments.

Jacques Médecin, never mind the culture, now had plenty of leisure. In September, the sixty-two-year-old mayor with playboy looks belying his workaholism decided to resign and do a bunk, rather than answer a court summons for non-payment of personal income tax of fourteen million francs, and questions like how did five million francs of Nice-Opéra's subsidy get loaned to a friend of the girlfriend (and colleague) of the opera's director. Better to slope off sharpish to Punta del Este, Uruguay, before the shit hit the fiscal fan. No one was surprised when French Customs, rustling about in Monsieur Médecin's follow-on luggage, found enough crisp banknotes to finance a string of polo ponies. Which led supporters to believe he had been framed by political opponents; Jacquot would never take that kind of risk, they said, not in his dodgy position.

Fuel was added to this theory when the Socialist government compulsorily purchased the missing Médecin's private house at the price of his tax debt – a figure well below the market price. 'Later', said a Government spokesman, 'when the property market takes off again, we will sell it at a handsome profit.'

But I was not in Nice for a newspaper or to espouse any cause célèbre. Graham Greene, a much braver warrior than I, had already risked much by taking the Médecin regime to task in his pamphlet J'Accuse, challenging its alleged underworld connections.

The Médecin heritage fascinated me. How much had Jacques really done for Nice culture and leisure? The name Médecin is close orthographically to Medici, from whom he claimed descent. If you looked into the Medicis' Florentine government, the unacceptable face of capitalism might be equally evident. But it doesn't stop you enjoying the pictures in the Uffizi. Admittedly, Médecin's projects used public funds, whereas the Medicis' were generally private patronage. At least you could say for Médecin: he had been the people's elected mayor.

So just what had he done for the people of Nice?

'Oh, you should have seen the ballet of cars!' said Madame X, an employee of the Acropolis, Nice's Arts, Tourism and Convention Centre shaped like a super-modern cruise ship, she was showing me its 2,500-seat Apollon Theatre. 'Car manufacturers love to have their conventions here to launch new models. Renault, Rover, BMW. What a show SAAB gave us! The cars danced!'

Which reminded me: I had not filled in my Ruhl Casino tombola form for that Golf GTi. Damn, Nice was a city of cars – dancing at the Apollon, lotteried at the Ruhl, double-parked on main streets, plunging eternally into multi-level, subterranean car parks designed for shoot-outs. Not for nothing were Médecin and his American wife frequent visitors to Los Angeles. That city's influences were much in evidence. The Bay of Angels twinned with The City of Angels. Without the smog.

Madame X was a Médecin loyalist; many people she said, had betrayed him. She wore a snug tweed jacket and beautifully cut cor-duroy trousers, relit cigarillos with quick nervous movements. 'Of course it was a witch-hunt! The Mitterrand government was jealous of what Monsieur Médecin did for Nice. Ten years ago, Nice was just a French tourist town. He put it on the map internationally!'

I would see the change, Madame X assured me. The Acropolis was the only convention centre in the world – flash went her lighter – with a permanent art exhibition. 'That picture of Louis Armstrong is by Moretti, the sculpture down there by César.' There were works by local artists Arman, Venet and Tobiasse.

Under Médecin's regime, an organisation called Nice Com-munication had grouped together Nice's cultural activities: art, music, opera, ballet, theatre, cinema, museums, tourism, theme parks and leisure. Nice Communication had a 14 per cent share of the city's budget. And quite a bit of that share went missing. That's where the trouble began.

'Have you got an appointment with Jean Oltra yet?' Madame X was keen to know. Oltra, Médecin's right hand man, had been General Director of Nice Communication, which was cursorily disbanded by the new regime at the Hôtel de Ville, and some forty Nice citizens implicated in the accusations.

'No,' I said. 'Monsieur Oltra's phone was off the hook on Saturday.'

'Yes. He gets all kinds of calls. He is the only man still loyal to Monsieur Médecin.'

'But I spoke to him Sunday evening.' Monsieur Oltra had been most affable. 'He wasn't quite certain of his movements this week, but would definitely see me. He promised to call last night before I left home.' He had not called.

So Madame X in her brisk, efficient manner, picked up the phone to call Jean Oltra. He was not at home. She spoke with Madame Oltra. Of course, just as soon as he returned Madame Oltra was sure her husband would call me at my hotel.

So while waiting for Monsieur Oltra, I decided to see how the Niçois-in-the-street had taken the Abdication. As one of King Jacquot's hobbies had been local gastronomy, I started with the chefs and restaurateurs. Médecin, among his other talents, was author of *La Cuisine du Comté de Nice*.

'A keen amateur,' was the verdict of Claude Duret, son-in-law chef of Catherine-Hélène Barale, whose traditional family restaurant livens up the nondescript Rue Beaumont. 'Jacquot will have plenty of time to cook now.'

'But will he get the ingredients in Uruguay?' I wondered.

'Oh, we can always send him proper Nice olive oil, basil, and anchovies – between the five-hundred-franc notes!'

There was affection in the joke. If Jacquot got away with it, good luck. It didn't seem to occur to Monsieur Duret that Jacquot had not got away with it. In his kitchen, business as usual: chopping *blette* (Swiss chard, a spinach-like vegetable) for two Niçois recipes – stuffing for raviolis and filling for a tart. I had a brief lesson.

For the raviolis, the *blettes* were mixed with onions, cheese, eggs, and three meats (two kilos of beef to half a kilo of veal and pork, cooked in a daube before chopping). For the tart, the chopped vegetable combined with raisins, pinenuts, apricot jam, rum, rhubarb and figs.

'Simple, family cooking,' said Claude. 'Before the Médecins, Nice was a poor town!'

Like a queen of the neighbourhood, Catherine-Hélène Barale holds court from nine-fifteen every morning. Neighbours drop in to buy *tourte aux blettes* or *pissaladière*, and for a gossip. I was given a slice of flaky light flan of onion, anchovy and olive, and a tumbler of rough red wine. It was a sublime breakfast.

'I was just saying,' Madame Barale brought me into the conversation like a good hostess, 'how we are all obsessed with ill health.

My sister keeps count of the times a day she does *pipi*. She's up to seven — and the whole neighbourhood knows.'

Madame Barale, spry and spare, in her mid-seventies, was born in the house where she has her restaurant. It was a relic of the old Nice I had been hoping to find again. Here was a private museum of local memorabilia: player-piano with cylinders, a copper bath, two vintage cars, cartwheels, old telephones, horn gramophones, even a silk pennant embroidered *Bataille de Fleurs 1910 Antibes*.

When I left, Madame Barale was in fierce argument with a young, plump bearded Niçois who accused the Russians of not working. 'Of course, they work!' she said. 'There were women in the trenches!' The precipitate Médecin departure was not a subject for argument, however. He'd gone, and that was that. Nice and Madame Barale had been there longer. I left her folding her freshly laundered red and white napkins for tonight's dinner, just as she did every day.

It was reassuring. The Old Town, too, had business very much as usual. Six-storey, seventeenth-century houses in a labyrinth of alleys and steps, nestled beneath the Château's bosky hill. Incense wafted from the baroque cathedral, and the fish market smelt properly fishy. Petrol fumes did not reach these quiet precincts of the poorer Niçois, and even garbage was being collected by a little electric train. Only marginally gentrified was Médecin's Old Town: despite some newly-painted terracotta façades and green-grey shutters, the Genoa-style washing hanging from the windows revealed only one trendy beach towel marked BEACH in English.

In the Rue Droite, so narrow you can reach across the street and join hands with your neighbour opposite, I found la patronne of Aux Palmyres more indignant than Madame Barale. Emerging from a bower of tulips and carnations fresh from the nearby Flower Market, she brought the stockfish stew to follow my stuffed cabbage leaves.

'We certainly miss Monsieur Médecin,' she said. 'But what a funny way to leave us!'

A note of sadness, too, greeted me in the Cours Saleya. The Cours, favourite tourist street in Nice, not only hosts the markets but is hard by the corridors of power: Hôtel de Ville, Palais de Justice, and Préfecture. Among its people, there was a feeling of being let down – almost like when Edward VIII had abdicated and left hastily for France. 'We are more royalist than the King,' someone put it. Nice was in shock.

But some things are immutable.

Next day, the fruit and vegetable market was just packing up for lunch. Pigeons were already lunching luxuriously on rich peckings of *socca*, the little chickpea pancakes, scattered around one girl's pitch. '*En la miéu ritornella, viva, viva Nissa la Bella,*' she sang, as she put on her coat to go home. And the refrain kept returning, with its royalist overtones: Long live beautiful Nice!

'I saw Jacquot often,' she told me. 'He used to come walking here. A real lady's man. I fancied him, I must say. There should be more mayors like him, whatever he did.'

I had been recommended to La Cambuse for lunch. I dug into a feast of a Niçois dish: *Filet de loup avec ses 5 légumes*. The five veg' with the sea-perch were: beignets of onion; stuffed baby courgettes; stuffed tomatoes; aubergine moussaka; and the best French fries in town. After that, I did not honestly give a damn what the gargantuan Madame Rioch, La Cambuse's owner, thought of Médecin, but she told me: 'Oh, he's done some bad things, but a lot of good for the town. I can't judge him. It's not for me to say. We Niçois care a lot about Nice, and anyone who lets us down . . . well, it's sad.'

I walked lunch off on the Quai des Etats-Unis. The sea was blue, the sky was blue. And the Bay of Angels, with water gently lapping the pebbles, showed not a hint of menace. Then I saw a poster on the boardwalk. It showed Honoré Bailet, the new Mayor, a smiling, honest-looking chap if ever I saw one, giving his message: 'In 1991, together, let's continue to work for the future of Nice. Best wishes.'

Continue? Continue what exactly?

I returned to my hotel. Still no message from Jean Oltra. I had been told there was no point in contacting the Mairie; the present Municipality were a bunch of interim temporaries, supported by the Socialist government to get Nice out of a jam until municipal elections could be held. In the mean time, investigations into corruption were being pursued by the Préfet and the Cour des Comptes, which sniffs out and tears apart creative accountancy in the public sector.

But why not contact the Mairie? If I couldn't talk to the old regime (Oltra), the new regime (Bailet) might illuminate rumours about slashing economies in Nice's cultural budget. Whose cut would be the unkindest, I wondered? Art, opera, carnival – or personal bank accounts in Switzerland?

Finally, after a verbal tour of the Hôtel de Ville's telephone exchange, I made an appointment with Madame Y in the Cultural Affairs Department.

Curiouser and curiouser. The address she gave me didn't seem right. It was not in the Hôtel de Ville, but round the corner in an even more inauspicious street. Flash though the private life style of Jacques Médecin may have been, his place of work was modest; back-street Mairie with simple café opposite where people waited to see him for breakfast meetings at seven-thirty. No designer offices for his publicity team. More like Naples than Nice. Through a dingy archway, into a rickety elevator, two dilapidated floors up, and no sign on the door. Inside, a different scene. The low-key approaches led to the well-appointed but unflashy offices of . . . Nice Communication. Hang about, hadn't that been disbanded?

Yes, it had, explained Madame Y, but they hadn't had time to get the logo off the reception wall yet. It was understandable; everything in Nice was moving too fast. The new administration was a bit *bouleversé*, to put it mildly.

'But you must see someone in the Mayor's office,' Madame Y said. 'Someone more in the know than me.'

While making several calls on my behalf, she discreetly let it be known that she, like Madame X was a Médecin loyalist. In the culture-and-leisure domain, 'continue' meant continuing the good work of Jacques Médecin.

'I have an English author here . . .' On the other end of the line, whoever it was in the Mayor's office spoke for some time checking out my credentials. The British press, I knew, had given Nice a rough handling over the Médecin affair, and I wanted it known I was just a poor, honest writer of travel books not an Insight team. 'Well, we must receive people,' Madame Y told the Mayor's office, ironically insistent on my behalf. 'After all, Nice is not closed.'

Monsieur Untel, high up in the mayoral hierarchy, assured her a Monsieur Chose would contact me at my hotel. In the mean time, why didn't I check out what was being continued?

For France's fifth-most important city, it was impressive. Nice had always been a major art town. But Jacques Médecin established a veritable chain of modern art habitats. And unlike Paris, the municipal museums were free (except the Marc Chagall). From the new Matisse in its noble Italianate villa, to the waterfront Dufy, Médecin had housed his artists as well as the Medici family housed theirs in the Uffizi.

Among the steep, winding streets of Nice's modern town is the Musée des Beaux-Arts.

In a nostalgic nineteenth-century Genoese villa and park, up cool marble stairs the walls are adorned with fey, floating *chérettes*, the name Niçois poster artist Jules Chéret gave to his highly romanticised girls depicted amid turtledoves, bluebirds and children. But there are, alas, no posters like his marvellous one for the Palais de Glaces. Rather too chocolate-box for my taste, the Chéret paintings lose out to the one superb room of Van Dongens, which include my favourite *Tango of the Archangel* with the Archangel Gabriel in a tux dancing with a nude in flowery garters and pink stockings. Jules Chéret would not have approved.

And of his fellow Niçois artists, Chéret would surely have preferred Alexis Mossa to his son, Gustav-Adolf. To me, both were a revelation. And in 1990, a new small gallery of their work opened on the Quai des Etats-Unis. Alexis did heavy official art portraits, but also – and miraculously – time spent with Courbet at Barbizon inspired light, touching watercolours of the Nice countryside.

Gustav-Adolf was altogether stronger meat. In the first decade of the century, he predated the surrealists with weird, symbolist visions. A voluptuous femme fatale just called *Elle* with tiny skulls and two crows in her elaborate hairdo sits on a pile of tiny corpses; there are equally minute bloody handmarks on her thighs. *Lui* is a pallid young hermaphrodite in a flimsy dress, looking at 'himself' in a mirror; beyond the arches, a phalanx of top-hatted, evening-suited gay-bashers approach with menace. *Le Système de Doctor Forceps* shows a couple in bed being approached by a doctor with spidery, red fingers.

Jacques Médecin, whatever else may be his mayoral legacy also left behind him the Promenade des Arts. In 1990, this flamboyant cultural complex opened its doors to the Theatre of Nice and the Museum of Modern and Contemporary Art. The insistence on the word 'contemporary' was a just tribute to the many young artists experimenting in Nice at this time (some thirty privately owned galleries are also listed).

All French political leaders like to be remembered by a monument. Paris is already bristling with President Mitterrand's – from the arch at La Défense (known as the Wind Tunnel) via the Louvre Pyramid, to Opéra-Bastille, and more, like the new high-tech National Library, on the way. So who can blame Mayor Médecin for having his little flutter with the Promenade des Arts? A fine monument and a credit to its brilliant architect, Yves Bayard. Médecin obviously picked up a thing or two from the LA City Center Arts complexes. It is appropriate: the collection includes works by Warhol, Dine, Rivers and Stella. Between theatre and art gallery, built of luminescent grey Carrara marble, is a fountained, festive promenade where children whirl about on skateboards, narrowly missing senior citizens being herded to culture shock within.

Four towers are linked by transparent walkways of glass and elliptical steel – like some New-Age fortress. The senior citizens, wondering quite why Christo wanted to package a girl in plastic or César thought a crushed car worthy of his time and theirs, were happier up top of the battlements. Here, Japanese hump-back bridges join the turrets, and the old folks clutched on to one another with much giggling on the steep slopes. Yves Klein's environmental *Wall of Fire* (300 burners alight at night) and *Garden of Eden*, a water garden, add to the excitement. The views of Nice are exhilarating: south, over the rooftops to the wooded castle hill and Old Town, the sea beyond the waterfront skyline and the Negresco's landmark cupola; east to port and mountain corniches; west to the long, curving beach city stretching as far as the airport; north to the surprisingly unbuilt-on hill of the observatory.

The feeling of space is reflected within the museum. It is built for large works like Olivier Debré's monumental *Ocre Rose aux*

Taches Bleues; and smaller constructions like Martial Raysse's tree of plastic *trouvailles*, bottles of all shapes and sizes probably found on the littered beach at Golfe Juan where he lives.

But Yves Klein, for me, was the surprise of the show. Born Nice 1928, died Paris 1962, he produced wonderfully tactile works like *Blue Venus*, a sumptuous nude in synthetic resin on plaster; or a startling violet nude man, cut off at the knees, against an even more startling gold background. A collaboration of Klein and Christo gives us a witty kitsch wedding of a bemedalled Ruritanian wimp with a soppy Princess Bride.

Eyes bleary and feet sore, I returned to my hotel. I asked for my messages. Monsieur Oltra I had given up, but Monsieur Chose from the Mairie hadn't called either. Silence prevailed.

Next day, I pursued the Médecin heritage, taking in two theme parks.

The Parc Phoenix, dedicated to the world's wonders of nature, is itself something of a wonder. I was welcomed by Monsieur Machin who asked me when I was last in Nice.

'Thirty years ago,' I answered, wondering if he was born then.

'Well, you remember the *bidonville* out here by the airport?' Meaning a shanty-town of old tin cans and boxes, where the poorest of the poor lived. 'Full of maghrébins. They were . . .' Monsieur Machin made an eloquent gesture of expulsion.

'To Marseilles?'

He grinned. 'Ssssh!'

'That *bidonville* was here?' I could hardly believe the change. High-rise buildings, all coloured glass, towered beyond the park.

Monsieur Machin nodded. 'A company called Semaren developed the land. Fifty-one per cent Nice Municipality, six per cent Alpes-Maritimes Department, the rest private finance.'

'Mixed economy was popular.'

'Monsieur Médecin, who was naturally the company's president, liked to do things that way. You see, by law, wherever property was developed within the city, seven hectares in twenty-five had to remain green.'

So rather than make a municipal park which had to be free, Médecin had made a theme park which could run at a profit to private investors and the city and help pay for the museums.

That was the theory. At Médecin's departure, Nice was substantially in the red.

I paid my entrance fee and set off around the world in what seemed like eighty environments. One minute I was in the Mediterranean – surrounded by olive and citrus trees, a heady odour of herbs engulfing me in a rock garden; the next, lost in a labyrinth of bamboo, where enchanted children played hide and seek; then, crossing a desert dune; delving into an Aztec pyramid where underground plantlife thrived; inspecting the bonsais (another of the former Mayor's hobbies); taking in an island of primal forest, surrounded by a lake of lotus blossom and lilies; and the world's biggest hothouse (25 metres high and 7,000 square metres), where I sweltered in the Louisiana Bayou and marvelled at Thailand's orchids and had a Planter's Punch in the Gingkobilobar.

Nature's 'music' accompanied my every move: 'Squawk! Grunt! Caw! Gurgle!' went the atmospheric soundtrack piped to all corners and climates.

From jungle and savannah, I became more locally orientated – in the Parc des Miniatures, which showed the history of Nice in model buildings.

In a lush Belle Époque garden of cedars, cypresses, and pines, I walked along a network of paths. The walk alone, with glimpses of the Mediterranean through aromatic trees, would have been pleasant enough; an added attraction were the scale models of everything from the Romans' Forum at Cemenelum to Jacques Médecin's Promenade des Arts.

Miniatures of famous Belle Époque villas reminded me that I must be getting back to mine. In Le Petit Palais I had chosen one of the best small hotels in Nice with its fin-de-siècle charm, standing on the wooded hillside of a residential neighbourhood above the city. Good air to breathe, quiet at night. And impeccable message-taking. Even if one never received any.

My God, I had! A certain Edith Knight of Côte d'Azur Développement had called. Who was she? Some English or American lady trying to flog me a villa?

'The Mayor's office suggested I call,' Madame Knight said in faultless English. 'What is it you would like to know?'

I was cautious. First I wanted to know what Côte d'Azur

Développement might be.

Well, it was an organisation to co-ordinate development in the Alpes-Maritimes Department, outside Nice, to find foreign finance for new enterprises, that sort of thing. It sounded kosher. So I opened up.

'Are you British, by the way?'

'Oh, no,' said Madame Knight. 'I'm a Bounin.'

Bounin? National of some young African country? Silence, while my mind raced. I should have known. One of the oldest Nice families, the Bounins.

Madame Knight put me wise.

'And your perfect English?'

'I was educated in America and England.'

'Where does the Knight come in?'

'My husband.'

'British?'

'Neapolitan.'

'I see.'

'The Knights came over with Nelson from Stratford-upon-Avon.' Curiouser and curiouser.

I liked Madame Knight with her international background and openness. I wanted to know more. Apparently, she'd only been back in Nice a year. Her husband, a banker, had wanted a change of scene. His parents had Jamaican, Swedish, Dutch and Italian blood – and only the common language English between them. Educated at Eton and Cambridge, he was finding Nice a good spot for new enterprise, in spite of the city's temporary fall from grace.

'And what does the new Mayor mean by "continue"?' I asked.

A pause. 'Well, the future will be more conservative. We must wait and see. Things were going too fast, too flamboyantly.'

'Budget cutbacks, do you think?'

'Maybe the Carnival will be less elaborate this year.'

The 1991 theme was the King of Fools. It was cancelled.

'All this Médecin business . . .' Madame Knight made dismissive noises. Here, at last, was the authentic voice of the Nice establishment. 'All terribly Mediterranean, you know. Nobody from the north understands it.'

'What about Graham Greene?'

'I'm just rereading "J'Accuse". Personally, I would have done exactly the same in his shoes. He was being very Mediterranean, in fact. Championing a close personal friend, because he was in a position to do so. "I have friends, I can help you" – that's a good thing, isn't it?'

'Very Mediterranean, yes.'

'I was brought up on it. My Uncle was the youngest Nice Deputé. And there's even a Cult of the Dead, very strong among us. My first cousin Paul, when I returned, gave me the key of the family tomb. "Take it," he said. "You're head of the family now." We like to pay respect to our ancestors. Don't forget, we're descended from Sardinians.'

'And did people of the old families like yours pay respect to Médecin?'

'They're very snobbish, you know. They loved all his black-tie events, the galas, though they pretended not to. In fact, they say in Nice there are not enough nights in the week for dinner parties. The town is full of cliques. There's a network . . .'

As Madame Knight talked, I watched the twilight beyond my balcony. The sky turned to violet over the sea, and the lights began coming on, till the whole town lay twinkling, and it was like Christmas in the tall Aleppo pine outside my window. The Promenade des Arts, illuminated, was a rival to the Promenade des Anglais. And that's how Jacques Médecin would have wanted it.

When I got home, three hours drive from Nice to the other side of Provence, tired after my voyage of nostalgia I turned on the TV news. Lucien Salles, director of Nice-Opéra had just been arrested and was in jail. Also with warrants out for their arrest – but missing from Nice – were Elisabeth Arnulf, the girl alleged to have fiddled the 5 million francs, and . . . my elusive old pal, Jean Oltra.

No wonder he hadn't called me last Tuesday. That very day, rather sensibly in my view, he was already winging his way across the Atlantic to join Jacques Médecin in Uruguay. But there was a sequel: being a man of honour, Monsieur Oltra later returned to Nice – to face trial and a year in prison.

As for Médecin himself, he did not return to be tried for non-payment of taxes in January 1992. In contempt of court, he was sentenced to one year in prison, fined 300,000 francs, and forbidden to hold any public office in France. His lawyers are appealing under the Rights of Man.

When last heard of, Nice's ex-mayor had already built a sumptuous mansion in Punta del Este and was selling T-shirts to the South American jet set.

Viva, viva, Nissa la Bella!

7

Grimaud, 1961

'Could we have more blankets, please?' S asked, shivering in a glacial *salon*. For the umpteenth time a force eight mistral had blown the French windows open. On the terrace palm trees flapped like angry birds. 'For the beds . . .'

Our landlady looked surprised.

'The central heating's on the blink,' I said.

She looked even more surprised. She was the young, efficient wife of a wealthy carpet manufacturer. Nothing in her life was ever on the blink – not even her aged husband.

'I will send a plumber.'

'And a little more coal and wood, please,' suggested S.

'And how does the hot water get from the boiler to the bath?' I asked.

'Nobody has ever asked that before,' our landlady said, in amazement. 'You must ask the plumber.'

For the villa, with its comfortable bourgeois furnishings, Louis-Philippe fruitwood and tapestry-covered chairs, was no drab holiday let; it had been the dower house of the carpet manufacturer's mother. She had died in it, and I did not wish the same fate on my family.

April can be a bitterly cold month in the Midi. Poor British fools, we were counting on cloudless blue, arriving all eager from London to Grimaud in search of *le bien-être*. Impossible to translate. Something much more subtle than well-being and indefinably French, *le bien être* is a happy, hedonistic state induced by sun and wine, often preceded, so that the contrast should be properly felt, by stress. Although no one used the word much then, twitchy Parisians fled south so that *le bien-être* could massage their driven, competitive egos.

So far we'd only encountered the stress.

In 1961, the St-Tropez area acted like a magnet to the upwardly mobiles as well as the made-its. Brigitte Bardot lived there, and was occasionally sighted – to the orgasmal thrill of the sighter. Three years before, our rented flat in the town had overlooked the patio of her parents' house. As the entire Bardot family sat at Sunday lunch, we had our first BB sighting. She was dishier than a flying saucer, and her sister Mijanou wasn't bad either. Plenty of *bien-être* about that family, and us too, basking on our terrace with olives and pastis. But that was June, and now it was April, and where had all the *bien-être* gone?

In theory Grimaud was just the village to celebrate a Broadway hit for a few months, making the most of good times while they lasted. I would begin new work. S and I would lead a glorious double life: by day, lavishing new experiences of nature on our London-born, three-year-old twins, Camilla and Carey; by night, whooping it up in St-Tropez. Not forgetting holidays for our parents.

S's father was a Roman archaeologist, and could make trips from us to Arles, Nîmes, and Vaison-la-Romaine; her mother was a keen botanist and could revel in Mediterranean exotica unavailable in Essex.

My own mother and father had not been to the Riviera since before World War II and then only rarely. They would visit my Great-Aunt Bessie, a professional gambler in Menton; she and her meek husband traipsed daily from the Pension where they lived to the casino, both dressed from head to toe in white, he a few steps behind her, like the old couple in Tati's *Monsieur Hulot's Holiday*.

Another trip, my parents had been guests at a grand villa on Cap d'Antibes, owned by a multi-millionaire called Davidson. My paternal grandfather and Davidson were once Civil Service clerks together. 'Willie,' said Davidson one day, 'get out all your savings. There's a chap called Eastman who's looking for partners, and he's on to something that can make us a fortune. It's called Kodak Film.' Well, Davidson invested his savings; my grandfather remained a civil servant. And the rest isn't history.

I always comforted myself that, as a Kodak heir, I could have been rich, miserable and uncreative. Instead of cold, miserable and uncreative as I now was in the Grimaud house. I spent many April hours, puffing Gauloises into a red glow to thaw out my fingers sufficiently to tap a typewriter.

Worse was to come.

'Oh, it's nothing,' said my mother, giving one of her ricochets of eight sneezes as she came out from a swim.

We were on the beach at Beauvallon, huddled together like eskimos. The sky was blue as our noses. A mistral made the water popply, like moving ridges of snow-capped mountains. My mother was used to the icy waters of Wales, and thought she could easily take the Gulf of St-Tropez. Well, I couldn't; the twins couldn't; and evidently, aged seventy, neither could she.

Next day she was in bed, still saying 'Oh, it's nothing!' and the thermometer saying 103.

Our house was just the place for parental sickness. One-storey, easy to deliver meals. Fine view of palm trees from the sickbed, a vineyard shimmering beyond the terrace, and old Marius tending his vines or delivering wine, therapeutic sunsets and, at night, the soothing song of nightingales. In summer, that is. It was not yet summer, and my mother gazed rheumily upon the lowering landscape.

Above us, on its hill, medieval Grimaud rose to the clouds via winding, narrow streets to its landmark ruined castle. Having outlived the Ligurian tribes of the Gallic Celts, Phoenicians, Romans, Saracen pirates, the warring Counts of Provence, and a spiteful Louis XIV who knocked it down, the castle was symbolic of Grimaud's survival. Somewhere in the village there must be a good doctor, I thought. And there was.

Docteur Garouste diagnosed pleurisy. My mother was much sicker than any of us imagined – most of all, herself. Docteur Garouste was the embodiment of attention. He prescribed a whole medicine chest, as is the custom of French doctors who, cynics believe, get kickbacks from the pharmacy or have shares in the pharmaceutical company. I could never believe such things of Docteur Garouste; he had saved my mother's life.

'If one's got to be ill,' said my mother philosophically, 'this is quite a good place to be it.'

She was nursed to recovery, aided by the potent infusions of Madame Campdorase, a sturdy, determined lady of Majorcan origin who came in twice a week to cook for us. Her patent remedies with herb, blossom and berry killed or cured. She could be seen burrowing about in the copse on the edge of the vineyard, searching for camomile and fenugreek.

'Very good for the palpitations, fenugreek,' Madame Campdorase pronounced.

'But I don't have palpitations!' my mother protested, bravely downing the disgusting infusion. One could not gainsay Madame Campdorase; she knew best.

'Never eat mayonnaise after the setting of the sun!' was another of her many maxims. As a result of her cooking, my father ate unusually heartily and never complained of his usual indigestion.

Things were beginning to look up. My mother recovered. We even planned an outing to St-Trop', just S and I discoing. Then it was S's turn.

'You look awful,' I said, after she'd done yet another there-and-back to Nice airport with yet another batch of houseguests or parents. 'You need a holiday.'

'I've got toothache,' she groaned.

So we got to St-Tropez finally. To the dentist. He was young, keen, and at that time the only one in town. He decided S's offending tooth would have to come out. S was in too much agony to protest. At the end of the session, the delectable young dentist, who resembled Gérard Philippe playing the part, proudly held up the tooth and exclaimed triumphantly: 'My first extraction!'

A couple of days later, it was Carey's turn. She fell and gashed her knee on some jagged concrete. Blood streamed. We rang Docteur Garouste; he was out on call. So there was nothing for it but to head back to St-Tropez, this time to a decrepit old beast of a doctor.

With trembling hands, he got at the stitching like a short-sighted tailor, saying there was no time to give Carey an anaesthetic. We protested. He took no notice. The heart-rending yells stayed with us for days, and the French medical profession took a temporary dive in our estimation. But Carey's wound healed perfectly, and she showed it off on the beach with great pride.

Then Camilla and I were for it.

If there had to be a faulty fairground aeroplane at the Ste-Maxime fair, it would inevitably be mine and Camilla's. I pulled the joystick and got no joy; our plane resolutely refused to take wing. Camilla and I hurtled round and round at ground level, as though in a plane which has reached its cruising speed while still on the runway. Anyone with even the skimpiest knowledge of aerodynamics knows how that would feel. Especially when the runway is circular, and you're trying not to crush your three-year-old daughter as the centrifugal force pushes you outwards, entangled in her candyfloss.

'I don't like it, Daddy!' yelled Camilla.

'Hang on, darling – it'll soon be over.' It seemed to go on for ever. With fairground music drowning our cries for help, the operator was deep in the racing page of *Nice-Matin*, and didn't see what was up: two non-flyers buried in candyfloss.

After this fiasco, we had paid our stress dues, and finally, God took pity on us. The South of France began to resemble what authors like Colette said it should.

Madame Campdorase had much to do with it.

'*Quel bordel!*' was Madame's low opinion of the kitchen. Our landlady had been as stingy with the crocks as the blankets. Under Madame Campdorase's supervision, S bought pots, pans and utensils that we have to this day. The eccentric kitchen range was fired by coal and wood. It inspired not tantrums but cackles of wild laughter, and Madame Campdorase became a merry witch at her brew. Somehow, she juggled heat levels by adding a lump of coal here, and a stick there, so dishes requiring different heats could be cooked in the same oven.

She prepared dishes in advance, and gave S precise instructions about how they were to be reheated: '*Vous le sortez demain à onze heures pile, et vous le réchauffez comme ça dans le four – tout doucement. Et à midi, c'est prêt.*' Midday – the sacred hour for lunch when only the odd cat could be seen in the Grimaud streets.

From Madame Campdorase we learned the basics of French

cooking and marketing. She taught S how to pick the best vegetables in Ste-Maxime market; what pot to use for which fish:
bouillabaisse in this casserole, *loup de mer* with fennel in that fish kettle, *daurade* on the charcoal grill; the difference between a fennel
bulb and wild fennel; how to make pastry short, flaky or *tourte* for
pizza (the twins' favourite); where to find dandelions, lamb's-
lettuce, and wild chicory for *mesclun*, the salad of Provence; and
her own recipes for veal with sage and green olives, a pungent
daube and succulent *courgette gratin*.

Camilla and Carey loved her. They went on their own to visit
Madame in her dark, rudimentary village house where she lived
with her son, a frequently unemployed mason. Masons in
Grimaud had not yet become millionaires. It was still a village
where the sound of a concrete-mixer was rare.

When the summer finally appeared, so did the smell of drains
from the street. Not enough to spoil the twins' teas with Madame
Campdorase. Two hours stuffing themselves on tiny paté sandwiches, *îles flottantes* and layered chocolate cake especially made for
the occasion.

Her teas kept our daughters happy, while S and I had no qualms
about inviting gastronomes to her lunches or dinners. Inhibitions
of every kind were disappearing as the summer hotted up.

During one of Madame Campdorase's feasts, a desultory discussion of modern art, ranging from the Cocteau sailor's chapel at
Villefranche to Picasso's Valauris pottery, was suddenly enlivened
by a Belgian art historian.

'Let's go to the nude beach,' he proposed. This legendary naturist's paradise was tucked away somewhere towards the less popular
end of Pampelonne Plage because nudism was illegal.

'Have you been?' his wife asked S.

'We've had too many sick people,' S replied.

'There', the Belgian reassured her, 'you will see many healthy
Germans.'

'I can't wait,' I said.

Just with the Belgian couple, comparative strangers, we would
probably have balked at the idea. However, Edward and
Christiane Behr were also at lunch. They were old friends, had a
house in Ramatuelle and were very much more *au fait* with the

local mores than we were. The nude beach was second nature to them. And they reckoned we should give it a whirl.

So, fortified by the rough Varois red of Marius the farmer and a particularly succulent guineafowl from Madame Campdorase, we set forth.

The twins had always had the run of our bathroom and were used to us naked. Like the Behrs, they took nudity in their stride. They joined the naturist kindergarten, little blonde cherubs of both sexes gambolling about the sand with unselfconscious abandon. Whereas their parents did not instantly feel at home among stout Herrenvolk playing energetic volley-ball, on a beach a-wobble with an excess of bronzed flesh.

It was not a pretty sight. But we duly stripped, and we and the Behrs and the Belgians (who were evidently practised at it, too) streaked for the sea.

Almost at once a low-flying helicopter buzzed us.

'Stay in the water!' advised our friends. 'They're taking pictures.'

'Who are they?' I asked.

'Police.'

So we stayed in the sea till the chopper passed, then returned to our mattresses for a siesta. Later, I was awoken by the passing of the chopper on its second sortie of the afternoon. Too late to put my swimming-trunks on.

Later that day, we sat enjoying an *apéro* at L'Escale. Our pleasure was only slightly marred by sunburn in unfamiliar places; then, considerably more so by the arrival of a police car. Two *flics* began circulating, trying to match faces to photographs.

It was a choice of two evils; run for it and be arrested for not paying our drinks bill; or face the photograph bravely. I signalled desperately to the waiter, who resolutely refused to have his eye caught. He arrived – coincidentally with the *flics*. I paid. Then . . .

'Is this you, M'sieur? Madame?' one of the *flics* challenged us. An aerial shot showed S and me full frontal, not smiling for the camera.

'We were asleep, Officer,' I protested. 'Otherwise we'd have covered ourselves with towels.'

'What my husband means is . . .' S had no idea. 'We normally sleep naked in the hot weather.'

'Not on my beaches, Madame!'

A second, more important *flic* came in gravely, passing sentence: 'You have committed an offence against public morality, M'sieur, 'dame. I'm letting you off with a warning.' He indicated Choses, the nearby boutique, with its array of swimsuits. '*Allez acheter des maillots de bain.*'

We were now thoroughly initiated. More and more part of the scene, an impermanent scene of friends and acquaintances coming and going. Someone brought Allen Ginsberg to lunch. Film people appeared after the Cannes Film Festival. Edward Behr, then working on *Newsweek*, was called to the telephone of the Pampelonne beach club where we were lunching, returned, kissed his wife Christiane and all of us goodbye. 'Just off to Vietnam,' he said. He stayed there reporting the war for six months.

Eleanor Fazan, a choreographer friend, taught us the Madison, the latest dance craze from America, and we were all childishly excited when we introduced it to L'Esquinade, St-Trop's perennially 'in' disco, that very night.

I found myself sitting in a corner of the disco, Scotch-Perrier in hand, discussing an idea for a musical with Françoise Sagan. *Bonjour Tristesse*? Surely not. Anything was possible. We all had plans for all kinds of crazy ventures, plans buoyant on a wavecrest of *bien-être*, then sinking into oblivion where they probably best belonged.

Another favourite friend was Claire, married to a Spanish count. Claire and Carlos were most sociable but hated snobs and the more pretentious aspects of the area. She ran a decor shop, and introduced us to a couple dealing in antiques, Anne-Marie and Pierre, who invited us all to dinner one night. We were to sit on what they had us believe were genuine Louis XV cane-bottomed chairs. The chairs turned out to be beautifully baked fakes – unfortunately just a little overbaked. We sat. One after the other, the cane seats collapsed, leaving us helplessly laughing, bottoms stuck firmly in the chair frames.

The next year, with characteristic kindness, Claire and Carlos offered us their handsomely converted *bergerie* for a nominal rent. Hidden away in the pine-forested hills of Les Maures, this house confirmed S and me in our determination one day to have a place of our own in France. On rare wet days, its vast, beamed drawing-room resounded with the laughter of children; on the terrace, the click of *boules* and the croaking of frogs engraved the Midi twilight upon my subconscious, and on particularly fraught winter days in London, the scent of pines in the midday heat would come back to me.

Under one particularly fine parasol pine, I sat at my typewriter every morning, going through the motions of work, a Gauloise stuck in my mouth, and several rolls of fat too many over the top of my Choses pants. Now, recalling the welcome sight of Madame Campdorase coming to tell me lunch was ready, I wouldn't have missed it – not for all the money in Kodak.

It would need all the money in Kodak, or a large chunk of it, to settle in the St-Tropez area nowadays. Or so our disenchanted friends told us. It had become, they said, a haven of rich arms deal-ers, the lunatic fringe of the peerage, terminal yachties and geriatric golf bores, and every bimbo-and-brat pack under the sun. We would hate it. We decided to see how true this dismal picture really was.

On the road where we once saw two snakes, their heads inter-twined lovingly as they slithered along in the morning sunshine, a grim sight greeted us.

To the left and right, the hills of Les Maures were covered with charred tree-stumps, a black skeletal landscape stretching as far as the eye could see. Giant parasol pines, like the one I loved to work under, had gone with a mistral-fanned inferno.

Later we heard an ugly rumour that property developers had started that particular conflagration. Burn-and-build is the system: after ten years, deforested land has no building restrictions. Greens in local government are lobbying to make it twenty years to dis-courage executive arsonists. It will be a tough battle.

The gangster brutality behind respectable Riviera businesses is nothing new. It is becoming more evident as the whole coast sprouts concrete where once there were trees.

From that familiar Le Muy to Ste-Maxime road between ravaged hills, we caught our first, breathtaking glimpse of the Gulf of St-Tropez. We were in for a demographic shock. A roadside poster increased the bad vibrations: ON THIS ROAD ONE DEATH A MONTH.

Ste-Maxime was unrecognisable, a riot of over-development, and it was not till we reached Claire and Carlos's old house that anything like home appeared.

I was pleased to see that neither my favourite parasol pine nor any of the cicada-haunted wood around the house had been burned. Claire and Carlos had long since sold the property; that much we knew, but not who the new owners were.

We were greeted by familiar faces. The caretaker and his wife had stayed on and, astonishingly, remembered us after nearly thirty years.

When we asked about the house now, they seemed only to want to talk of our stay there. Good caretakers, we thought, on their guard against nosy questions. But they did show us round. The house was closed up and needed a coat of paint. A huge swimming pool had been built; at the bottom, two black flippers lay in the water. The vast, airy drawing-room had been converted into suites of luxurious bedrooms giving on to the terrace.

In one bedroom, family photographs reminded us of our happy times there: smiling father and mother with children, on beach, by pool, barbecuing, sailing. No wonder the caretakers had been silent: only afterwards did we learn that the smiling father was serving a six-year prison sentence for shooting and killing his wife in a *crime passionnelle*.

No part of France evokes in me feelings of melancholy affection like St-Tropez and its surrounding countryside. As one of the world's most beautiful places, it deserved protecting better; too bad that Brigitte Bardot, that great campaigner for the safety of seals, whales, and other animals, should have deserted it in its hour of need.

St-Trop' had become a tourists' toilet, Bardot said. Fifty million Frenchmen (and others) were peeing in her Baie des Canoubiers. And she was tired of all that naked flesh. 'Who started it?' asked an indignant Mayor of St-Tropez with some justification.

And God Created Woman, Bardot's French debut (she began her career with Dirk Bogarde in the British *Doctor at Sea*), gave the town its sexy image and enticed mass tourism in the Fifties.

The trouble is, God also created promoters. And promoters, in league with their deeply unoriginal architects, have now created shopping malls and marinas and golf courses with dinky villas ruining one of the world's most perfect landscapes.

'I've nothing against promoters,' claimed Alain Spada, Mayor of St-Tropez. 'They've got their work to do, here or elsewhere. Personally, I'd prefer it was elsewhere, for my job is to protect the natural patrimony of the Commune. The bamboo, the sand, the tamarisk, the parasol pines are just some of the elements which attracted painters to St-Tropez at the beginning of the century. Let's preserve this nature, it's the guarantee of permanent success for the peninsula.'

Fighting words. But the St-Tropez peninsula is only part of the area. There's the whole Gulf of St-Tropez – from St-Tropez to Ste-Maxime with the communes of Cogolin and Grimaud between. Other mayors tolerate the promoters doing their worst elsewhere, where land is cheaper and workers, in a limited summer economy, find all-the-year-round construction work.

The western end of the gulf, where once nothing blocked our view from Beauvallon beach to Grimaud castle and the Massif des Maures, was a beach city in the making. Giant cranes possessively brooded over their building sites.

Port Grimaud has a lot to answer for. Which is not really fair, because it was the first and best of the marina towns, designed by a visionary town-planner, François Spoerry. Reclaiming a mosquito-infested swamp, where the hunters of Grimaud once shot wild duck, Spoerry's builders constructed a Provençal village of 2,000 fishermen's houses (though not for fishermen!) not one like another, each with its own mooring and connected by a labyrinth of canals and quays and bridges.

Now that the new paint has weathered with the years and bougainvillaea, lemon and orange trees have taken root in the gardens, I could even grow to like it. Especially if Port Grimaud had not been ripped off by other promoters.

Like a canker, the marinopolis around the gulf has spread in hideous growth. The words 'port', 'marina', and 'park', once romantic, have become synonymous with Florida-style resorts.

Roars of anger came easily that day; roars of laughter, too. The roundabout at La Foux, where four important main roads meet, had become a comic circus, featuring the motorist as clown. Even in the Sixties, it was notorious for back-ups; now greatly enlarged, it is a cat's cradle of feed lanes, easy to negotiate if you know where you're headed, hopeless if, like most of its tourist users, you don't.

We imagined we did. Even so, round and round it we went, as though magnetised by the Géant Casino hypermarket which has been astonishingly built in its midst. Surely La Foux must be the world's only roundabout whose central island contains a shopping centre with '38 boutiques at your service'. Eventually, I orientated myself by Luna Park's familiar ferris wheel on the right, and knew I was on the road to St-Tropez.

These approach roads are laughingly called an infrastructure. But the main arteries are in such bad shape, it's a case of arteriosclerosis. Strictly to be avoided from 15 June to 15 September.

In high summer, residents of the country villages of Grimaud, Gassin, and Ramatuelle used to regard St-Tropez as a place for early morning marketing or late night discoing only. Between those hours daytrippers were welcome to its endless backups. Now, sadly, those villages seem perilously close to the sprawling gulfside conurbation, and in danger of being sucked into it; while St-Tropez itself, by comparison, seems to have retained the charm of a Riviera fishing-village – with the likes of Kenzo, Hermès, and Cartier discreetly tucked away into its narrow streets.

It felt good to be back. Aloof from the mishmash development of the hinterland, the town struck us as more modestly welcoming, less intimidatingly flashy than we'd remembered. And the broad perspective of the port, I was astonished to find, was still not much different from Albert Marquet's 1905 painting. Even Paul Signac's sunset of 1896 shows recognisable rooftops and church tower, whereas little was recognisable on the shoreline of the Gulf since 1961.

Admittedly, we were out of season. Talk in the bars was of winter tasks – refurbishing, repairing, and reviving spirits after the summer madness. All but a handful of the peninsula's fifty hotels were closed. We settled for Les Palmiers in the Place des Lices, where I had previously stayed in November; the splash of rain on the palm trees had kept me awake all night. Tonight, behind its garden full of ripening lemons and grapefruit, the hotel seemed much improved.

The hotel manager advised: 'Chez Angèle for dinner, and the Annonciade Art Museum is open at nine tomorrow.' Information is erratic off-season: the owners of the restaurant had decided to leave for their annual holiday in Senegal that very day; and the museum was closed for the winter.

Pity. We'd passed this waterfront home of Braques, Rouaults, Dufys, Matisses, and Bonnards many times – with children, parents, or friends eager for drinks or ice-creams or a ringside seat at Senequier for the action of the port. The coming-and-going of yachts and the street acts were the nearest we got to culture. Somehow culture was not what you came to St-Tropez for in the early Sixties. I had managed to catch up with the Annonciade on a later trip, and I wanted to share it with S.

The old town was a rich substitute. I had never really explored its back-streets at night. Lamplit and trafficless (after five, no motor vehicles by law), a warren of paved alleys led us from one little square to another, and down to the beach of La Ponche where gentle water lapped the sand. And up, up, to the top of the town where a restaurant appeared to be open.

'I'm afraid we only do fish,' said the starlet waitress with short, dark hair. 'Personally, I hate fish.' Anyone who liked fish was clearly an imbecile.

A St-Tropézienne, if ever I saw one, taking the contrary line whatever.

The restaurant was near La Citadelle, the eighteenth-century fortress dominating the town. The street was undergoing open drain surgery. Drains were one of the Mayor's preoccupations, and no wonder with a population of 6,000 inhabitants swelling to 80,000 in summer. Too much sewage was seeping into too many wrong places; the sea, for one. I remember a potentially idyllic boat trip, spoilt by our not being able to find a creek where the water was not a garbage dump. Not nice at all: what were the fish feeding on? The fish-hating waitress could have a point.

'Sorry, the chef's not here yet,' she continued. 'Come back at eight.'

'Is there a bar near by?' She looked blank. 'Or perhaps we could have some wine here?'

'Of course, if you don't mind waiting.'

'For the wine? Surely . . .'

'No, I mean – for dinner.'

She brought the wine list. We ordered a Cassis, the dry, flinty *p'tit blanc* served by Marcel Pagnol's César in his Marseilles bar.

'Personally I hate white wine,' the waitress declared, as she poured. 'But if you like fish, then I suppose you have to like white wine.'

The chef arrived. The waitress returned.

'We have fish.'

'Good,' said S. 'Could we see a menu?'

'We don't have a menu.'

'Oh.'

'We have fish soup, and then squid with prawns, followed by red mullet.'

'How much?'

'Just a minute.'

She consulted with the owner, one of those who makes a point of never speaking to his customers unless they are regulars. The chef, his hair in a pig-tail, addressed his Teflon frying pan with great ferocity, hurling into it pieces of squid which spat back at him indignantly. The waitress was assisted by the chef's beguilingly helpful nine-year-old daughter. It was all studiedly amateur.

The waitress returned.

'Five hundred francs.'

'For two?'

'Just a minute.'

She consulted again.

'For two.'

'Wine included?'

'Just a minute.'

Another consultation.

'Wine included.'

What had seemed a classic St-Trop' rip-off now began to be a deal: the wine being 155f. on the wine list, the balance was 345f., making our three fish courses 172.50f. a head. For St-Tropez, one of France's most expensive towns, neither a steal nor a stinger.

'Done,' I said.

And the meal, astonishingly, was very good.

Encouraged, we continued our search for good old-fashioned French quality. We found it at the carpet factory, now our only connection with the house we had rented at Grimaud.

Our landlord, the carpet manufacturer, had long since died, leaving the business in the capable hands of his widow. By the time she had retired there were international showrooms in London, Munich, and Milan.

The small, Victorian factory stood in the midst of sprawling, traffic-clogged Cogolin, and was established in 1928 to absorb the local Armenian immigrants who had special carpet-making skills. In spite of world fame – carpets for the White House and Versailles – it retains an artisanal, almost folksy front. The telephone plays 'Greensleeves' while you wait.

The factory manager Monsieur Michel, resembling an amiable university professor, welcomed us like old alumni. Each carpet, he explained, was specially designed and never duplicated – with prices to match; a Louis XVI design of exquisite intricacy for an English country house cost £70,000. Clearly this was not a factory tour where one emerged with a souvenir; our interest remained purely academic, as we followed our prof. towards a huge wooden frame on which a canvas was stretched. It looked like an outsize artist's easel. Two girls worked on it from a lift like a window-cleaner's, winching themselves up or down each time they'd finished a section, shooting wool into the design with a thread pistol. Other techniques involved hand-knotting the pile, or cutting it with huge scissors for relief designs.

Clients are encouraged to design their own carpet. A Cocteau-influenced motif in green was signed by actor Jean Marais, star of Jean Cocteau's *Orphée* and *La Belle et La Bête*. American abstract artist, Otto Fried, had one made with twenty-seven different blues in it.

'When money's no object, no problem is insurmountable,' smiled Monsieur Michel. Everyone seemed to know more about art nowadays. Clients were clearer about what they wanted. 'We are the Yves Saint Laurent of carpets.'

He showed us one carpet especially designed to go under a Paris dining-table weighing – literally – a ton. It was tailored with holes in it for the feet. Another, at drawing-board stage, required precision dimensions to fit a mansion's complex curving staircase in Toulon.

'Still a lot of rich people about . . .' I observed, watching some of the forty employees, mostly girls, at their clickety-clacking looms, soothed by piped Mireille Mathieu.

'And luckily they don't all just want Ferraris and off-shore racers.' Monsieur Michel spoke with increasing passion for his trade. 'If handicrafts like ours were taken more seriously, and the time needed to perfect an object respected and paid for, I guarantee there'd be fewer young people on the streets. Not so many computers, more hands working. One can't blossom in the mind without working with the hands.'

We left the Cogolin carpet factory suitably uplifted. Here was French excellence at its best. In our search for *le bien être* we had once known, we found it either very expensive or costing nothing. And a walk still cost nothing.

S and I climbed to the Castle of Grimaud. Good to find it superbly restored, thanks to the high standards of the Commune's award-winning municipality. But the surrounding hills now bristled with the inevitable mock Provençal houses, each different but managing to look exactly alike. Colette, who bought a house near St-Tropez, La Treille Muscate, in 1928 prophesied the rot from what she saw around her even then. In *Belles Saisons I* she says, 'If I dared, I would write: "The real Provençal house can be recognized by its lack of conformity." But I would see rise up against me the army of Midi-lovers who have built, in the south-east of France, a meridional house, covered in curly tiles and pink stucco.'

Like the streets of Grimaud, still in the paroxysms of new building, uniformly *bon chic, bon genre*, French good taste can be as exasperating as French bad taste. Here and there I longed for a rickety gate to a derelict garden, an original worn façade. Just something to make Grimaud less perfect. In the narrow street where Madame Campdorase once lived, now spotless with paved steps and tubs of geraniums, her house had been sandblasted and painted out of recognition. It was the bijou holiday home of a Parisian, occupied for maybe two months of the year.

It is not every day one has nostalgia for a whiff of drains. And how we longed for that once wonderful, clear view across the plain to the Gulf and St-Tropez!

Not all was lost, however. Vines still grew, and where there are vines, land is protected by strict laws. Pockets of resistance to the invading constructors remained. Despite the thirty-six beach clubs and detritus of used syringes, condoms, and discarded beach-shoes along Pampelonne Beach, the Commune of Ramatuelle has at least prevented the shoreline becoming a beach city. And Sylvabelle, our favourite small beach on the south coast of the peninsula towards Cavalaire, still had not a high-rise in sight; the winter *gardiens* of villas were jogging up and down, exercising themselves and their killer guard dogs.

'Oh, everyone complains,' said our old friend Claire. She and Carlos had remained faithful to the area. 'We've moved house four times, each time nearer to St-Tropez. It's nice to be able to stroll down to the village and shop.'

The village. That's what Claire called it now. Somehow I'd never thought of St-Trop' being a village. Suddenly I saw what she meant. Sophie Rallo was now queen of the discos where, in our day, Regine had reigned; next year, it would be someone else. But the village would still be a village.

And Claire, a witty raconteur of its fortunes, would still have a tale to tell.

When she and Carlos arrived in 1957, she told us, they met an old antique dealer who lived in the château. She was known for her stutter. And when Claire asked her how she liked living at St-Tropez, she replied, all those years ago: 'St-Tr-tr-op-opez is fin-fin-fin-' But she never finished her sentence.

8

Médoc, 1965

'Is over there another country?' asked Camilla, as the car ferry crossed the mouth of the wide Gironde from Royan to Le Verdon. She was used to Channel crossings – with another country at the end.

'No,' I started. Then it occurred to me it really was like another country in some ways. 'Well, sort of . . .'

'Sort of?' Carey pinned me down. 'What d'you mean, Daddy?'

I hesitated. Would I be confusing them?

'It's the Médoc,' I continued, 'a part of France visited and lived in by quite a lot of English and Irish. Who make or sell or buy wine.'

'Oh.'

We had picked the twins up at Saintes, where they'd been staying with Chantal, a favourite au-pair girl. Her father was a funeral director. And it was a short distance from gravestones to *graves*, the stones deposited by the Gironde River millenniums ago; stones which make the vineyards of the Médoc specially propitious for the production of fine wine. Drinking it was almost a sacrament to Englishmen like my Great-Uncle Horace who had baptised me, aged twelve, with Château Larose.

But how did one tell the story of the claret connection palatably to seven-year-olds in 1965?

As a legend, perhaps? Once upon a time there was a widowed French queen called Eleanor. In 1152, she married an English king, Henry II. And for a dowry, he received a big chunk of south-west

France called Aquitaine. The English, being sensible, hung on to it for 300 years. Partly because English wine was grotty, and Aquitaine's wine was super. It was called *clairet*: in French, because it was a lovely pink colour – much lighter than today's claret which is dark, a little dry on the palate with a taste of fresh fruit and smelling of old cigar-boxes.

'Will they have Orangina?' the twins asked, even before I could begin. So that was that. It was clear as *clairet*: baptism with Château anything would wait a few years.

'They' were Jasper and Jane Grinling, friends from London, who, with their three children, spent summer holidays at Château Loudenne. Jasper was a great-grandson of one of the original W. & A. Gilbey partners, and Château Loudenne had belonged to the firm since 1875.

Wine merchants to the people, Walter and Alfred Gilbey became rich from selling claret to the Victorian middle class. Château Loudenne was Cru Bourgeois in the classification of Bordeaux fine wines by *cru* (growth or quality of vineyard). In other words, not as grand as Cru Classé – and certainly not Premier Cru Classé like Châteaux Margaux, Lafite, and Latour. The Bordeaux region was quite classé-conscious enough for the British; and the Gilbeys, sons of a stage-coach owner ruined by the coming of the railways, had, by the purchase of Loudenne from Vicomtesse de Marcellus, become landed gentry in France.

The tall, thin spire of a grey church was our landmark. Very flat, Médoc: you could see the spire for miles. Just beyond the village of St-Yzans, we took a turn to the left, leading from marshland through vineyards towards the Gironde. At the end of a tree-lined drive stood the riverside château.

Camilla and Carey showed real interest suddenly. To a seven-year-old, it had the makings of a fairytale castle. But an Englishman's château is not necessarily his castle – at least, not in the Bordeaux region where the word signifies a wine property (sometimes with no house at all) rather than a noble pile. There are more than two thousand such châteaux, their houses varying from the eccentric chinoiserie of Cos d'Estournel to the understated charm of Château Loudenne. Definitely more manorial farm than stately home.

Standing on a low hill, its brick arch with the Gilbey wyvern crest welcomed us into the courtyard. Two wings housed offices and stables, attached to a one-storey château with two witch's-hat turrets.

It was English country house life combined with *la vie du château*.

Grinlings and Mores played hide-and-seek in forgotten cupboards, under a Victorian billiard table, up to dusty attics, behind countless curtains, such a vast assemblage of hiding places, some of the darker, dingier ones quite scary if you weren't found quickly. Then there were games of Murder where hands would squeeze your neck as you crept up the spiral stone stairway of a turret. Aaaaagh!

Beach trips were frequent. The Médoc was imbued with the luminosity and lethargic piny smells of the Atlantic seaboard. Within half an hour, miles and miles of sand-dunes were shared only with plovers and seagulls. Surfboards rode the breakers, and the breakers, on a speeding tide, knocked down our sandcastles.

On rainy days, the children did paintings of the house.

Château Loudenne was a gift of a subject: a rose-pink, grey-turreted eighteenth-century Carthusian monastery which had avoided the crenellated additions so beloved of Victorian Médoc château-owners. Its gardens, beyond a paved terrace, sloped romantically from croquet lawn to vineyard to river bank. The twins' paintings depicted a castle more in keeping with the Brothers Grimm than the Brothers Gilbey. Carey even had the Gironde come swirling up around the rose-pink building, as the poet Gérard de Nerval describes a similarly romantic château – 'with a river bathing its feet and running between the flowers'.

No wonder Walter and Alfred fell in love with it.

I found reminders of them everywhere. Especially in the library. Along with *The Economics of Brewing*, *Sermons Preached in Manchester*, and the AA handbook of 1925, Alfred Gilbey's meticulously Victorian record of visits from England was a social document of the period. The brothers came twice a year: in spring for the flowering of the vines and 105 days later for the autumn vintage – a journey of some twenty-six hours from London.

Their obsession with weather seems comically British. But they

had become wine-makers as well as merchants, and knew the haz-
ards of late frost, freak hail, or summer rainstorms. Thus I read:
'The winds had shifted during the night from NW to NE, the
morning was cold, the river rough, which prevented the young
people, in the charge of Sir Spencer Wells, from going for a sail.'

S and I would wake in our ground-floor bedroom to see a merchant ship, silhouetted against the sunrise, surrealistically gliding
past the window like some behemoth loose in the garden. And I
thought of all the boats that had taken barrel upon barrel, bottle
upon bottle of claret past Château Loudenne on their way to
England from the city of Bordeaux 40 miles up river. The Gilbeys
had their own port for transport of wine and guests; our children
played on an old overgrown tramway that once linked the smart
new Victorian *chai*, where wine was made and stored, with the
port.

Other games included vicious croquet on the lawn, whacking
opponents' balls into the vineyard. Recovering with tea on the
terrace, I thought of Sir Walter (as he had become in Edwardian
times), entertaining the locals from grander, Cru Classé châteaux.
In 1907, 'Mr Barton motored from Château Langoa and remained
to tea. A heavy storm delayed his departure and he could not
inspect the vintage or the *chai*.'

Storms of a different kind often delayed our lunch: from the
kitchen, rumblings and crashes as the Austrian couple had one of
their ding-dongs. At the table, ravenous from the outdoor life, we
waited and waited. Jasper poured out glass after glass of Château
Loudenne, the children consumed bottle after bottle of Orangina.
Eventually Johann, knuckles raw from punching a chopping
board held in defence, or cheek scalded by a glob of well aimed
sauce Bordelaise, would slam in and hurl lunch at us. Did Sir Walter
have this aggro when 'the curé and mayor of St-Yzans came to
déjeuner'?

I imagined not. The Edwardian era of Château Loudenne was,
after all, its heyday, calm and prosperous. During world wars and
Depression, claret was drunk only by the seriously rich or those
with inherited cellars. It did not become popular again till the late
Fifties, when a new, never-had-it-so-good middle class rediscov-
ered its pleasures.

The Gilbey family responded by once again selling good, popular claret as W. & A. had done; and Jasper Grinling, as marketing director, led a move to renovate the château as a PR base for entertaining clients. French elegance combined with English comfort (the touch of Jane Grinling) made Château Loudenne quite a place to stay. In 1965 it was still very much a family home.

During our visit, the Union Jack was billowing from the terrace flagpole – as it had done for ninety years.

Since moving to France in 1976, our daily wine has become as natural as bread.

Thanks to my wine guru Steven Spurrier, the Englishman whose Paris wine school and shop became a magnet to budding winos-about-town, I was initiated into the joys of lesser-known French wines like St-Pourçain and Madiran. And in 1978, I willingly graduated to an investment in that year's superb claret.

Having now enjoyed our Léoville-Barton for several years, it seemed high time to revisit the Médoc to see for myself how its special character was faring in these days of wine trade speculation and hype.

Naturally, I began at Château Loudenne. First impression: they had put out more flags. It looked like an Olympic event.

This time, I drove up the avenue as guest of International Distillers and Vintners. A series of Byzantine takeovers had long since eliminated all members of the Gilbey clan from the board. The new company, a French subsidiary of IDV, was called Gilbey de Loudenne. By using the name, the vast conglomerate wished to preserve the 'family' ambience.

Now it was a corporate château – a new genus in claret country – with summer concerts, art exhibitions, a restaurant, a wine school (with a five-day course for more than £1,000), and capable of large-scale entertaining.

'We always hoist the flags of visitors,' explained Pamela Prior, the company's châtelaine, as she welcomed me. The Irish flag for Morgan & Furze had become entangled with the stars and stripes for Chemical Bank, so they couldn't get them down in order to hoist the Dutch flag for a very sniffy Amsterdam wine club. And the Greek flag for ten Metaxa brandy directors.

'One of your companies?' I asked.

'IDV's, yes.' Though as welcoming as a château owner, Pamela was careful not to sound proprietorial. She had just taken the Greek directors' wives shopping in Bordeaux and to lunch at La Tupina where the chef is called Xiradakis.

Pamela insisted on helping me with my sparse, overnight luggage. I was embarrassed to see her carrying my disgusting old Reeboks, flung hastily into the car.

'Just the shoes for tramping about vineyards,' she said, cheerfully showing me to my room.

I went out and tramped.

The cannon was still there on the terrace. And the dilapidated gardener's cottage. And there was still no swimming pool. So far so good. Edward Heath had planted a centenary tree, and Hugh Johnson designed an arboretum, but the garden still looked a bit disorganised with dahlias, chrysanthemums and apple-trees batting for England, clipped box hedges for France.

In my room, a picture over the mirror showed a little girl with a net chasing a butterfly and I thought of that happy summer holiday. It was the Pink Room; now all the rooms were named by colours or grape varieties. I could have been in Merlot or Petit Verdot. All had appropriate decor and furnishings, baths with brass taps or old-tiled showers. Like a family home turned into a private hotel. And a very good one at that.

In the Adam green drawing-room, a fine Paul Klee carpet, abstract and pastel, seemed much too adventurous for a wine trade CEO. 'The powers-that-be hate it,' sighed Pamela. 'It'll probably have to go.'

The visitors' book had become business-orientated. Gilbey relatives and their English guests had long since given way to clients from Fortnum & Mason, Mecca Ltd, Madrid, Canada, Japan. And Ernest Gallo, the Californian wine mogul of the mass market.

'How many is a full house of guests?' I asked.

'We once had thirty-two from a supermarket chain,' Pamela sounded faint just telling me. 'Complete with their Indian accountant and his two kids.'

'Do you do dietary food, then?'

She looked at me as if I was mad. 'Well, vegetarian, if necessary.'

The cook, Josette, was one of the best in the Médoc. She and her husband, Silvain, striped-waistcoated and black-tied, were about to celebrate twenty-five years of corporate service. 'Pity we just missed you,' I said, remembering the stormy Austrians, as Silvain offered me a pre-dinner drink from the entire IDV range: Bailey's Irish Cream? Malibu? Bombay Gin? Jack Daniels? Ouzo? I stuck to Château Loudenne white.

'I'm afraid there's just me for dinner,' said Pamela. What happened? Did Chilean vintners or Korean distillers cancel out? I felt quite guilty. So much trouble for just me – candlesticks, best crystal and silver, Pamela's hand-written menu, wines thoughtfully chosen by Charles Eve, the present Loudenne director: '74 white with the solettes, '70 red with the quail . . .

In the absence of Charles Eve, Silvain guided me through the wines, proving to be a fine sommelier as well as butler.

'As you were last here in 1965, M'sieur,' Silvain said. 'M'sieur Eve thought you would appreciate a La Gaffelière of that year.'

How could I not? It had a mellowness to match my mood.

'I don't know where I'd be without Silvain,' Pamela said. 'He waits, cleans, hoists the flags.'

Next day, the flags had been disentangled and the Norwegian flag was already flying at breakfast time. A special tasting had been arranged for me, before the Norwegian group's tasting at midday. Although the *chai* with its Victorian clock was outwardly the same, inside was a world of high-tech vinification, supervised by a crack Burgundian wine-maker, Jean-Louis Camp.

'First a taste of this . . .' Jean-Louis siphoned me a glass fresh from the vat – 1990 Merlot, harvested just two weeks before. A tannic zonk in the palate. '*Costeau, hein?*' I reeled.

In the tasting room, Jean-Louis told me about their white Château Loudenne, one of the very few whites made in the Médoc; how they were tailoring it to the tastes of new buyers from the States, Canada and Japan, making an easy, crisp, perfumed wine that retained the character of the grapes.

I tasted two methods: the traditional method and the new method, provocatively called Skin Contact. That meant tasting two lots of each grape variety: Sauvignon (acidic, gorse-flower flavour) and Sémillon (supple, plenty of body for ageing). And two final blendings of '89. The Skin Contact method won, naturally.

And, thanks to the oenology of Jean-Louis, Château Loudenne white now also had longer shelf life. Shelf life means a wine can be displayed on supermarket shelves in appalling conditions (upright, neon-lit, wrong temperature) with minimum ill effects; the balance must be just right, or the drinker wakes next day with a gimlet between the eyes.

We proceeded to the three elements of Château Loudenne red, still made by the traditional claret method: 40 per cent Merlot (fruity), 5 per cent Cabernet Franc (spicy), 55 per cent Cabernet Sauvignon (dry). And the final blending of 1988.

Very few châteaux let you taste the three elements of claret separately. Anyone can try Château Loudenne. Holiday-makers could drop in from the Atlantic beaches, taste one white and one red without charge, and go away having bought nothing. It would be bold but not impossible.

Whereas you can never just drop in on a Cru Classé château whether you intend to buy anything or not. Appointments are *de rigueur*, and then only if you're in the trade or on the network. Buy nothing at your peril: no sale means no fun. A big buyer might get invited to play polo at Château Giscours where the owner, Pierre Tari, has his own team.

Cru Classé claret is reputedly the best, and certainly the most expensive. And, however archaic the virtually unrevised 1855 classification, most Cru Classé claret is pre-sold during its year of making, before it has matured in barrels for two years or been bottled. Much speculation and hype goes on. If a good year is prophesied, the wine trade, journalists and experts start sniffing around during the depths of the winter following the vintage. But proprietors will hold off till the last possible minute to sell, as the price rises – or, if they leave it too late, falls. In spring, sales start in earnest; by summer it's all gone to the wine trade who can never be absolutely certain how it'll be at first drinking-time maybe five years later. A dedicated claret drinker, along with its maker, takes a gamble all the time.

From a British corporate Cru Bourgeois château, I moved on to a privately owned Irish Cru Classé château. Like an entry in the Gilbey record of visits from England, I was off 'to Château Langoa for déjeuner at Mr Barton's'.

The Bartons had been in the Bordeaux region for eight generations.

I parked the car by the gates of Château Langoa and pulled an ancient bell, which clanged out over the gravelled courtyard. Nobody seemed to be about. The great house stood there in all its glory – classic eighteenth-century Bordelais mansion with ground-level cellar; directly above, a drawing-room full of Irish ancestral portraits and glittering French antiques. Somewhere a dog barked.

The dog, I discovered, was Anthony Barton's Irish setter which eventually led me to his master in the courtyard of the *chai*, where he was in mid-vintage.

I felt uncertain. I had not seen Anthony, present owner and Cambridge contemporary, for many years. Having failed his exams, he'd gone straight to Bordeaux to learn the family wine business in 1951. Was this an invasion of privacy on my part? He and his Danish wife, Eva, had recently experienced a great personal tragedy: the death of their only son, Thomas, in a car accident.

My reception was courageously light. I was treated by the resilient Bartons like an old family friend, and we talked immediately of the vintage.

Among the hundred grape-pickers, some were Czech on a first trip to Western Europe since the collapse of Communism. I can think of worse introductions to private enterprise.

Lunch break. The grape-pickers trooped hungrily into the vintagers' kitchen across the courtyard. We would be having the same lunch: five courses with wine. 'But not with them,' Anthony said. 'It inhibits them, if I'm there.' A semi-circular window separated le patron's canteen from the vintagers below; a couple waved and raised glasses, matey as in a Dublin pub. 'And you'll get better wine,' he added.

The Bartons are the oldest Cru Classé family in the Médoc, predating the Rothschilds (1869) by nearly fifty years. Along with the Boyds, the Kirwans, the Phelans, the Clarkes and the Lynches, they were the Wild Geese – eighteenth-century Catholics escaping Protestant persecution by fleeing to France to become mercenaries.

'French Tom' Barton, founder of the Bordeaux dynasty, was neither political nor religious but a sharp trading Anglo-Irish Protestant. And his grandson Hugh bought Château Langoa in 1821.

'1822,' Eva corrected Anthony.

'No, you're confusing it with 1722, when French Tom came to France.'

'Want a bet?'

Anthony laid fifty francs on the table. 'Sorry about this, Julian . . .'

A delicious rosé, which must have resembled the original *clairet*, accompanied the soup and charcuterie. With the roast chicken and green haricot beans, a Léoville-Barton '62. I hesitated, worried about missing out on the right taste and smell. It was a long time since I'd sniffed an old cigar box.

'Wine's become too cerebral,' Anthony reassured me. 'We spend our meals with noses in our glasses. Eating should be convivial.'

With the cheese, Léoville-Barton '55. An amazing wine. I had been honoured.

'A nose of wet dog, don't you think?' I thought he was being serious for a moment. The Bartons, after all, are very serious winemakers. But no. Anthony, I found, was a merciless mocker of wine pretensions. 'Wet dog has joined pencils, beech twigs and sweaty sandals in the ridiculous jargon of wine columnists.' He patted his Irish setter. 'And there's a world of difference between a nose of wet setter and wet chihuahua.'

After lunch we strolled through a garden which might have surrounded some great house in County Cork.

'We never became French, you know.'

Anthony and I compared our Cartes de Séjour: both our photographs made us appear instantly deportable. Anthony looks a little more villainous than I; normally handsome and clean-shaven, his face in the photo has somehow grown the stubbly beard of a terrorist on a long sentence.

'Do you feel foreign?' I asked.

'Oh, yes. The Bordelais French are very closed. Most of our

French friends are from other parts of France. They find it easier to integrate with us foreigners than with the Bordeaux people.'

'I get the impression that the Médoc is full of foreigners. Am I right?'

'Depends what you mean by a foreigner. Many of them, like the Rothschilds from Germany and the Mentzelopolous from Greece, took French nationality.' There were about 400 good châteaux – many, many more if you include the so-so domains. 'Most, good and bad, are French-owned, of course.'

Top drawer French families have always had a Cousin Didier or Tante Florence or Tonton Guillaume making a *bon p'tit bordeaux* for their own cellars and friends and family.

Anyone can play – at a price. A mega-yen Japanese architect, Keichi Fujimoto, fell in love with Château Citran and completely restored it, vineyards and all. And a British company once sold Château Latour to another British company for £4.5 million an acre, making it at the time the highest-priced agricultural land in the world.

But when the French government comes out of its corner for the nation's heritage, it comes out fighting. Robin Gold, another old friend from the Gilbey clan, later negotiated the purchase of Château Margaux from the Ginestet family for his American employers, National Distillers. 'We'd signed a contract in seventy-seven which included the crops of seventy-five and seventy-six. It had been OKd by the French ministries of agriculture and finance. Then Valéry Giscard d'Estaing stepped in and stymied it.'

The President insisted it be sold to a French supermarket owner called Mentzelopolous. Franco-American relations were understandably strained as a result. Mentzelopolous paid £7 million, and Château Margaux is now masterminded by his daughter, Corinne, with a 1990 market value of £350 million.

A run of good claret years in the Eighties coincided with new wealth in the West and Far East. Masters of the Universe wanted Vintages of the Century to humiliate their friends at dinner parties. Demand soared. So did prices.

'Threatens to be yet another Vintage of the Century,' was Anthony's wry comment on 1990. 'We get them regularly every five years.'

He was off to Los Angeles soon; selling the Vintage of the Century to Century Fox execs when the dollar was weak could be tough. There were other problems. He rustled through the mass of papers on his desk to show me a copy of complex US Government health warnings, compulsory label wordage far more lengthy than 'contains sulphites'. Even the Gilbeys, fighting Victorian temperance in the Liberal party, didn't have to put warnings on their labels.

But the Gilbey tradition was continuing at Château Loudenne, the Barton tradition at Château Langoa. The British-Irish connection with the Médoc seemed as strong as ever. With the Americans and Japanese in hot pursuit.

I left Anthony to his harvest, and continued along the narrow D2 which winds past châteaux signposts romantically familiar to wine-lovers. I passed the hundred Barton grape-pickers, surprisingly energetic after their lunch, and crossed the Gironde from Lamarque to Blaye. Bright sun shone on the high-priced west bank. Somewhere in its rays, inland and hidden by the trees of the riverbank were the farmhouses or mansions with wall-to-wall vineyards between them: Latour, Langoa, Lafite, Mouton Rothschild, Beychevelle, Cos d'Estournel . . .

On my return home to the Midi, S and I treated friends to a bottle of Léoville-Barton, '78. Just the wine to accompany tender young Drômois lamb. What's this, they asked. I told them. A Vauclusian wine-lover, whose favourite tipple with lamb was naturally Châteauneuf-du-Pape, sniffed and sipped suspiciously, then beamed broadly.

'I haven't much experience of Bordeaux, but this wine,' tapping his nose with approval. 'Superbly made.' Later in the meal he joked: 'These days, the Americans and British know our wines better than we do!'

Even the wildest exaggerations have a grain of truth. And I refilled his glass gratefully.

9

Bargemon, 1966

Two years before 1968, when the tanks and flying paving stones of the second French revolution brought down President Charles de Gaulle, S and I were already confronting student protest in the village of Bargemon – from our nine-year-old twins.

'I am not going to a silly French school!' Camilla announced.

'A village school,' Carey added scathingly. They were London girls.

'But Colette's gone to school. What'll you do without her?'

Colette was the daughter of the Santini family from across the street, same age, same interests; they communicated more by giggles and hopscotch than the language of Voltaire or Shakespeare. Term had begun three days before. Colette had indeed gone to school – or her Corsican father would have dragged her there by her hair. Not the twins. If I dragged, they'd kick.

'Colette's French!' they chorused. 'It's all right for her.'

In London it had seemed such a good idea. We would all work in France for a bit: S at French gastronomy, me at my typewriter, and the twins at French irregular verbs. It was clear who got the worst of the deal. S and I felt pangs of guilt. How could we have been so irresponsible? Taking our daughters out of school in London, expecting them to knuckle down at a village school, high in the Var hills, at nine years old hurled into the humanities, maths, science, rhetoric, philosophy, and all in French, too. We must be mad. I'd even been to see the headmaster, Monsieur Delpui, prepared to plead for their inclusion. I needn't have worried. 'But, of course, Monsieur More!' he assured me. 'Primary school is open to everyone, whatever nationality, race, or creed.'

The pride of laic State education, free and for all. Only in 1968 to become a free-for-all.

For the twins, the days continued schoolless and happy in the little village house belonging to a writer friend, Venetia Murray. It was a corner house in the ramparts, the best place to be in a medieval fortified village. Friendly narrow streets. A vast view from the terrace towards the Mediterranean and the distant craggy hills of the Esterel.

Even so the house felt claustrophobic. On rainy winter days, 'Where's my . . . ?' became a constant cry as a treasured book or toy from the limited selection we'd brought from England went missing, to turn up in someone else's unmade bed or under the kitchen table. There weren't family rows, just rumblings; we were having too much fun to fight. But the house just couldn't contain all that pent-up, well-fed energy.

On fine days, to keep the twins happy, we hairpin-bended higher into the hills – to the Table d'Orientation of the Col du Bel-Homme. On a clear day, you could see Corsica. It was a clear day.

S said, 'That's where Colette's father comes from.'

'Are you missing her?' I added.

The twins exchanged a look.

Another day, we took them tobogganing, even higher. The sky was once more limpid.

'Is that Corsica again?' Camilla asked, pointing over misty blue hills to a distant mass in glistening water.

'Right!' said S hopefully.

'That's where –'

'We see Colette after school, you know,' Carey cut me short.

'Not for long, you don't. She has about four hours of home-work. And if she didn't do it, you know her father would certainly kill her!'

Colette was indeed in awe of Papa Santini, however amiable he and wife Monique may have been to us. And I thought of taking a lesson or two in parental discipline from him. His daughter would drop in for tea after school, and was quick to depart.

Days without their chief chum were long. And any friends of Colette's were friends of the twins. The *copains* were sorely missed, too – especially a handsome boy, Jean-Louis Lagadou, son of the local estage agent who had sold Venetia the house. It was all, as it were, in the family. Too bad the twins didn't see it that way.

At lunch on the third day, S could contain herself no longer. 'You know at least five children by now. Why don't you go to school and see more of them?'

'Shy.'

'It's in French.'

'We'll look silly.'

'Not all French children are necessarily brilliant at French,' I argued, hoping to give them confidence. 'Like some English children have trouble with . . .' My mind went blank. '. . . their spelling.'

'Where are we going this afternoon?' Carey asked, changing the subject.

'Why don't we go to the beach?' Camilla suggested brightly.

'It's trying to rain. Why don't you – ?'

S and I gave up. The best education, we believed, was between consenting human beings. We talked of other things: home, mostly – as one does when abroad is not shaping up. School was taboo.

Suddenly Carey got up, put on her anorak, and opened the kitchen door which led on to the street.

'Where are you going?'

'School.'

We were dumbstruck. And off she went – just like that.

'What was it like?' Camilla asked later.

'Super.'

'What did you do?'

'Dissected a cockroach.'

'In FRENCH?'

Next morning, Camilla couldn't wait to accompany her sister. By eight twenty-five, they had joined a broadly grinning Colette and heavily satchelled gang, to find out whatever mysterious joys, besides the dissecting of cockroaches, the school might hold for them. If this was the common foundation of French civic liberties, I was all for it.

That afternoon they returned, exhausted, but in a great state of excitement. They had had an English class.

'And we did all the work!' Carey said.

'Wasn't there a teacher?'

'Yes, but she said it was better if we spoke the English,' said Camilla. 'So we read out a story. And then we had to tell everybody about the things in it – like Big Ben, the Houses of Parliament, and the Tower of London.'

'We really didn't know, as you've never taken us there,' Carey added.

'But we had to work terribly hard!'

'Only in English?' S asked, disconsolately.

'Yes – but we never stopped!'

That was the first time they had really shone at any school subject. Their confidence fairly glowed. And, from then on, you couldn't have kept them away from that school. Plans of feudal castles, long division, how sheep's wool became a sweater, more dissection (the great favourite) – the facts came pouring in. And the French language with them.

They even offered to go shopping.

Sometimes a Sunday joint of meat would not fit into our small oven. So, when the twins went for the bread, I would accompany them to the bakery with a heavy baking tin – a shoulder of lamb spiked with garlic, on a bed of sliced potatoes sprinkled with thyme and olive oil. 'Un baguette . . . un baguette . . .' Camilla repeated, rehearsing her bread order for Madame Clavier, the baker's wife.

'Une baguette,' Carey corrected. 'S'il te plait.'

I began: 'You don't tutoyer –'

'Tais-toi, Daddy!' Camilla interrupted. 'Carey, Madame Clavier's not Colette, so you vous her.'

'Une baguette, s'il vous plait,' they said more or less in unison, as I handed the lamb to Madame Clavier who took it to her husband. This would wait until the last baking of bread was finished, and be cooked, together with other villagers' lunch dishes, in the great bread oven which held its heat for hours. We would then return for our joint with its succulent aromas, and be tucking into it soon after.

Such practical, every day usage really made the twins' French come on apace.

One day, S went to pick up a pair of shoes which were being mended by the cobbler.

'I've a surprise for you, Madame More,' he said. 'Come!'

The smell of leather gave way to sizzling sugar, as the cobbler opened the door between his shop and home. There, in the kitchen with his three children round the open fire were Camilla and Carey, feet up, toasting marshmallows, going through the motions of homework.

As the log fires of winter became unnecessary and a carpet of spring flowers unfolded on the meadow below the ramparts, homework was transferred to an olive grove.

We were trespassing, but nobody seemed to mind. These flower-strewn, grassy slopes in the shade of ancient olive-trees were for all to enjoy, and here Camilla and Carey would draw and read and translate parts of the body with Colette. Like the French lesson in *Henry V*: '*La main, les doigts, les ongles . . .*' went the twins; Colette, at a disadvantage on her home ground, had as much trouble as Katherine, daughter of French King Charles VI, did with 'De hand, de fingres, de arma, de bilbow . . .'

When Colette left for her summer *colonie de vacances*, the twins were inconsolable. Other children faded away, amid tearful farewells. The Bargemon school had closed for the summer, and we returned to England.

Nineteen sixty-eight came and went, and the twins' basic French served them well over the years. And what years they proved to be for French students, not to mention their parents!

The trouble began much earlier – with the best of intentions. By the laws of the great Third-Republic educationalist Jules Ferry, between 1881 and 1886, primary education became free, compulsory and laic. Religion was not taught but the Wednesday half-day remains traditionally time off for parents to arrange whatever religious instruction they, not the State, think fit.

Private education does exist, but it is mainly professional or

Catholic. Fee-paying schools are known as Free Schools which leads to the same confusion as US public schools where you don't pay and British public schools where you sure as hell do.

The freedom from compulsory religious instruction has always given the French school system the edge on civic liberty. The lycée is a melting-pot of class and race. A banker's child works side-by-side with a plumber's, a Muslim next to a Jew. It is a fine democratic principle, but like many fine democratic principles is fraught with problems.

Little did Jules Ferry know what he'd started: the snowballing of an educational system, imitated and envied worldwide, till it is now near choking on its own success. Standing room only is the order of the day in many lycée classrooms. All pupils' parents want qualifications that will take their children to higher education, that minimum diploma without which you can't even get a job in a laundry.

A foreigner may wax enthusiastic about the French school system from the safe distance of a South Kensington or Los Angeles lycée. Or even a village school in deepest France. This was where every peasant child learned to spout Racine, right? Where budding Louis Pasteurs were born. Where my own children would learn the French of Voltaire and a little more about the world.

Hang on.

Today they'd also learn a little more about the media, the police and the President of the Republic. 'I have understood you,' said Uncle Mitterrand, quoting de Gaulle, after 100,000 students had vigorously protested in Paris – against lack of money for their schools and the prospect of hard work now for no work at all later. Articulate young Toulousian pressure groups and others TGV-ing in from the provinces confronted the head-nodding Minister of Education and benchloads of advisers. A peaceable, serious debate; a field day for six TV channels. There was violence, too, not just from the bitter, marginal gangs living in soulless suburbs for whom the future is likely to be the dole queue or jail. Middle-class students, spoiling for a fight, also joined *les casseurs* leaving a trail of smashed shop windows and overturned cars.

Turning a blind eye to pillaged supermarkets, teachers and parents were mostly supportive. As was the CRS, the traditionally hated and feared arm of riot control. A certain solidarity, for once, prevailed: the *flics* had children – equally fed up with classes of forty, classrooms collapsing around them, inadequate teaching and no security staff for schools where drug pushers and child molesters could walk in off the streets.

And what of the future? Was there life after lycée? Or was the exam factory a dead end? That was the most nagging question of all.

All of this seemed somewhat academic when S and I returned to visit the Bargemon school. The problem of the day was practical and familiar: how to get the basics of English into the heads of nine-year-olds without putting them off foreign languages for life. 'It will be the common language of the European Community,' said Monsieur Nicollet, now headmaster. 'We must all speak and write it well.' Here was a village teacher with a more realistic attitude than many a talking head or politician.

The school looked much the same. A big, nineteenth-century four-storeyed building like an exam factory. The kind of place where Marcel Pagnol's father might have taught; appropriately, *La Gloire de Mon Père* was playing at the local cinema that very week. On the school façade, stone-carved, was *Écoles des filles* at one end, *Écoles des garçons* the other. Girls and boys had long since joined forces.

Monsieur Nicollet welcomed our visit to the weekly English class. He was interested to know if we saw a change. We had to admit we had never attended when the twins 'took' it; we'd never have dared.

It was a manageable class, twenty-five boys and girls of nine and ten years old. Experimental, Monsieur Nicollet warned us: not a conventional language class at all; more of a self-expression group. Television stifled imagination, he said, and this class aimed to stimulate it. 'Once they get confidence in English,' Nicollet continued, 'they'll have it in any language.'

S and I sat at the back. Monsieur Nicollet kept order, while his energetic young teacher, François David, educated in Brooklyn (among other places), animated the fun. And fun it was. 'OK? Now the days of the week.'

'Monday, Tuesday, Onesday,' started a child.

'Wednesday!' corrected the star pupil, a fat boy looming all the larger for his vivid lime green tracksuit.

Before fifteen minutes had passed, François had whipped them through the days, months, and the translation of the tonic sol-fa into English notation. Somehow the few slips François made – 'Look to your book,' – mattered little. What mattered was the spontaneity of response, the throwing about of words like balls in a playground.

'What is this?'

'It is a cassette of Madonna,' piped a black girl in the front row.

'Yes, and we'll hear some of it at the end of the class.'

Monsieur Nicollet explained to us: 'Start them young – with their own interests – and by the time they reach secondary school at eleven years old, they'll be bilingual. That's our idea, only the authorities haven't quite accepted it yet. We hope they will when they see the results.'

'I am under the table.' A tall blonde Finnish girl had difficulty acting this, and banged her head. 'Shit!' Her English was already fluent.

'*En anglais, comment allez-vous?*' François never picked on one particular member of the class; he let the answers come freely.

'Who are you?' 'Who do you do?' came the cascading answers.

'How are you?' corrected the star pupil condescendingly.

'I am well.'

'You can say "fine", too,' said François and referred to us: 'Is "fine" OK?'

'Just fine,' we assured him.

Then it was time for the Monster Game, a variation on Snakes and Ladders. Each member of the class in turn threw a dice which led them to various instructions on the board about constructing their monster. Thus they practised English numerals, addition, parts of the body, as well as drawing and colouring monsters, some of which were state-of-the-art self-expression.

They had reached sixteen: 'GIVE YOUR MONSTER SIX RED EYES.' The next player threw five.

'Sixteen and five is?'

'Twenty-and-one.'

'No, we say "twenty-one". Read out what you must do.'

'Draw . . .' the girl was a Tunisian called Auaffi. '. . . four lit-tle
. . . ears . . . on your monster.'

With his final lightning change of interest, François brought the
class to fever pitch with Madonna song titles. He wrote 'Material
Girl' on the blackboard and I was afraid he would ask me to translate it into French. *Fille matérielle?* Didn't sound right somehow.
Fille de tissu, perhaps? Wrong material. On to the next . . .

A girl had already written 'Love Don't Live Here Any More' on
the blackboard. I could see what was coming.

'"Don't" is not good English, right?'

'Colloquial,' I said. 'Not BBC or Daughters of the American
Revolution.'

'So, OK, you rub out "don't" and write "does not".'

The girl did so and tried to fit 'Love does not live here any
more,' to the music. The extra beat foxed her and made the song
sound absurdly stilted. So the class ended with everyone happily
singing 'Love don't live here any more,' which would come in
handy if any of them grew up to become delegates at a European
Community agricultural conference.

In the street afterwards, we congratulated François who, it
turned out, was a diplomat's son. He seemed to love his class, and
they clearly loved him. 'Well, I learned about children the hard
way,' he laughed. 'I have one in America with my first wife. Now
I am married to an Australian and we have three together and
another on the way.'

'With Finns, and Arabs and all the English around,' I said,
'Bargemon has become very cosmopolitan.'

'That's village life today!' he shrugged.

Villages of the Riviera hinterland, earlier in the century, had
emptied with a flight from the land; now they are being repopu-
lated with a flight from the sea – second-home owners fed up with
the crowds, noise, dirt and burglaries of the coast. At the other end
of the social scale, immigrant workers find work there.

The cosmopolitanism of Bargemon had affected its Frenchness
little. Walking in the Place Moreri, we could have been nowhere
but France. *L'art embellit la vie* was carved on a stonemason's house;
the art that embellished his life, quite simply, was two stone carvings on either side of the door, one showing himself with hammer

and chisel, the other his wife at work in the kitchen. In the shade of a huge *micocoulier*, the nettle-tree without which no Midi square is complete, stood a noble nineteenth-century statue to Louis Moreri, author of the Historic Dictionary, priest, doctor of theology, born Bargemon 1643 . . .

'How do you do?'

Auaffi, the Tunisian girl, had recognised us from the English class. With three languages – Arabic, French, and a little English, she seemed as confident of expressing herself as Monsieur Nicollet would have liked. In ten years, she'd be more than holding her own in one of those student protest debates on French TV.

'Would you record a little English for me?' I asked.

'If . . . you wish . . .'

Without any shyness, Auaffi spoke into my tape-recorder: 'I do not . . . like Madonna . . . I like Cheb Khaled.'

Let's hear it for the independently minded nine-year-olds of Bargemon school. Some day they grow up to be Colette Santini, now a single parent with a daughter, Sophie, and running a crèche in Nice; or Jean-Louis Lagadou, determined that Bargemon village shall be preserved, however many new villas and swimming pools sprout in the surrounding countryside; or our own daughters, reluctantly starting French there, eventually speaking it well enough to play leading roles in a French movie, *Le Jumeau*.

IO

Côte d'Or, 1970

Most francophiles have their idea of the perfect French village. Some have been there, others only imagine it. For me, the perfect French village is like a lost chord. Once I struck upon it, quite by chance, then with the dying fall of that exquisite, never-to-be-remembered harmony, my village disappeared. Stupidly I had forgotten to circle its name on the map.

In 1970, I was motoring through Burgundy. Or was it '69? Anyway, I know I was alone. S certainly wasn't with me, or with her Proboscidean memory she'd have remembered the village's name. Who else could I have been with? Was I on my way to Switzerland to see Peter Ustinov to work on a musical of *Romanoff and Juliet*? In a blizzard that all but ditched the car? Buried in snow all Burgundian villages look much of a muchness, so it can't have been in winter. No, it was Spring '70. I'm sure of it. And I was alone.

On the slow route south, eschewing the autoroute for D-roads, I did not just dream it. My village was flesh and stone. My village had everything a village in Burgundy is supposed to have. Church with polychrome tiled roof; a romantic, dilapidated château of some suitable century; an auberge buoyant on butter, cream and velvety wines; woodsmoke and manure wafting from a farmyard in mid-village; a herd of friendly white Charolais cows nuzzling your car in the main street; geraniums bursting their windowboxes and a canal. A canal? But of course a canal. What is a Burgundian village without a canal?

'Could it have been Pernand Vergelesses?' S suggested.

'No canal.'

'You can't have everything.'

'This village did.'

Burgundy is a large province. And I deduced that my village must have been in its most ravishing département, the Côte d'Or, one of the few in France not to be named after rivers. Its romantically inclined gastronomes insisted that 'Côte d'Or' – those golden slopes of the Burgundian plateau which spawn some of the world's most famous wines – had more relevance to their fortunes than 'Saône-et-Seine'. And with characteristic Burgundian determination, they got their own way.

Some years later, S and I had set out on a voyage of rediscovery. Our *recherche du village perdu* began just beyond the vineyards of Aloxe-Corton. The glinting church spire ahead looked familiar; so did the woods beyond, and the cluster of houses on a slope of intense verdure. But what were those grape-pickers doing? Very picturesque in their brightly coloured shirts. Very energetic in close formation between vines clipped neat as topiary. But . . . 'I don't remember vineyards near it,' I said.

That ruled out Marey-les-Fussey, too. Pity. Vineyards of the Hautes Côtes shared gently undulating hills above Nuits St-Georges with the forest of Chaux. Already the leaves of walnut, oak, hazel and beech were turning. Our car delved into a narrow, winding corridor of early autumnal tints. Round a corner, a tall grape-picking machine was upon us, its orange warning-light flashing, and we nearly disappeared under it to be plucked like a row of vines.

Also maddeningly off the list were other secret wine villages a few kilometres away from the great names: Monthélie behind Volnay (for reds); St-Romain behind Meursault (for whites).

St-Romain Le Haut was high above its vineyards, so it could be the one. We headed for the hills. By the roadside, an Air Escargot balloon hovered over the vineyard of Auxey-Duresses. Grape-pickers on a break watched with sardonic amusement a wine buff balloonist lecturing his rich tourists on the finer points of Pinot Noir and Chardonnay. Bursts of hot air from the burner kept the balloon manoeuvring a few feet above the vines. Any moment, it seemed, its brightly coloured Vasarely patterns might suddenly flare up and the whole poetic absurdity vanish in flame like Christmas cracker magnesium.

If only St-Romain Le Haut could have been my village!

An eighteenth-century cul-de-sac perched on a wooded hill. No commerce, cars, hotels, or done-up cottages. Not even a café. Pigeons cooed in Burgundian towers covered with virginia creeper and topped with flag-like weathervanes. An imposing gateway invited entry into a romantic manor's courtyard. And Alain Gras, a small but highly recommended maker of Bourgogne Aligoté, Meursault, and St-Romain welcomed us to a nine-thirty tasting – unlike the grander producers down in Meursault who require three weeks' notice. A good St-Romain is better than a so-so Meursault any day, and the white wine we bought from Alain Gras was well worth the detour.

But St-Romain Le Haut was not my village. You could pass through my village; if you passed through St-Romain Le Haut, you would pitch some hundreds of feet from the ruined castle into the vineyards below. Another thing: my village had a substantial auberge.

'The Auberge du Vieux Moulin?' S suggested. We were driving through Bouilland, a strong contender. Its auberge seemed too up-market; if I had been there, I remembered it simpler – no Michelin-starred food or designer decor. 'Were there dahlias as big as dinner plates?' Perhaps, perhaps, but there was no farmyard, not in the middle of the village of Bouilland, and I could hear them still, those melodiously lowing cows outside my simple auberge window.

Ternant did have a farmyard – animals and open barns in mid-village, just as I'd remembered. Its church had a plain grey slate spire and was rather ugly. My church's tiles sparkled.

Descending through woods, we caught a glimpse of Quemigny-Poisot. Ah. Could be. From above, definitely. Then red roofs clustered enchantingly around a church spire revealed themselves as modern villas with alpine eaves transplanted from the suburbs of Grenoble. Anyway, I was forgetting the château. Quemigny-Poisot had no château.

A shame, then, that the Château de Montculot was a kilometre or so outside the village of Urcy. Its crumbling eighteenth-century façade, shuttered to the world, overlooked the Mont de Siège. Beyond the table mountain was Dijon, city with the lowest crime rate in France, and no one locked doors or cars at Montculot either. Entering the gateless farmyard, we could have knocked off the pick-up trucks, station wagons, and agricultural machinery, walked through the open back doors of the château, now clearly converted into separate dwellings, and stolen pots from the pottery. Where were the potters and farmers and their families? The whole place seemed deserted.

'It's Saturday,' I rationalised. 'They've all gone shopping.'

'It's Friday,' S said. 'You lost a day as well as your village.'

We returned to the front of this Marie Celeste of a château, and discovered from a plaque that it had once belonged to the Burgundian poet, Alphonse de Lamartine. It was as romantic as his poetry. He had inherited it from Abbé J-B François de Lamartine, an uncle, and grew up there in a state of bliss. Its peace inspired several of his 'Meditations'. And after the wayward fortunes of a poet had forced him to sell it, he wrote, 'I sold the château but not its memories, the woods but not their shade, the streams but not their murmurings. All these things are within my heart, and will only die when I die.'

In a state of divinest melancholy, we drove on. Other châteaux beckoned, châteaux actually in their villages. At Commarin, I felt I was getting somewhere: Louis de Vogüé's stately home, a moated Renaissance pile, was just off the main street. Lush parkland surrounded it. From stables in the twin-towered front courtyard, generations of nubile countesses had no doubt galloped out into the morning mists swirling through tall lime-tree avenues, hellbent on some dangerous liaison.

Imagination was stirred. Until we checked out that main street. Despite a passable Burgundian church, the village itself let us down yet again. Perfection is a cruel yardstick.

I had staked a lot on Châteauneuf-en-Auxois. Even as we climbed to this fortified medieval burgh perched on a landmark hill, my spirits rose. Fine architecture came at us in a pot-pourri of centuries, as we parked by an eighteenth-century manor in the encouragingly named Place aux Boeufs. The heady odour of fresh manure rose off the street, leading past rose-and-vine-covered fifteenth-century cottages to a genuine mid-village cowshed. There was a nip in the October air. Already the scent of woodsmoke was intoxicating guests of the local Logis de France, a modest Renaissance auberge.

The fortress, too, blended architecture of several periods. Across a drawbridge, six round towers, from which enemy forces might be spotted for miles across the Morvan (now a nature reserve), were built for the Knights of Chaudenay in the thirteenth century. Later, Philippe Pot, Lord of Le Rochepot, sensibly modernised it with a touch of Flamboyant Gothic. And in the eighteenth century, mullion windows were replaced with larger ones to make the most of the view.

'This is it,' I confidently declared.

'So where's the canal?' S said as gently as possible.

'Since when does the Canal de Bourgogne run over hilltops?'

'Exactly. And you said, when we were beginning this crazy quest, it couldn't have been Pernand Vergelesses, because it didn't have a canal.'

Right.

Regaining our car, I trod in a cowpat. It did not bring us much luck.

We looked at the canal. At Pont-de-Pany, I rallied. This could definitely be it. I had a sudden memory of my magic village being on a mainish road, one of the French kind with no traffic.

'And I've seen that lock-keeper's house before, I know it. And the *fin-de-siècle* hotel . . .' We drove slowly past a Burgundian farmhouse.

'And the château?'

'Where?' I looked excitedly round.

'Nowhere.'

No château, true. But we persevered. The Ouche Valley was beautiful enough to explore, lost village or not.

St-Victor had horses rolling in meadows, lambs in an orchard, but the old folks' home I did not remember.

La Bussière had a different retreat: Cistercian abbey with watergarden, weeping willows and ducks on the lawn. I suppose I could have remembered it as a château. Sure enough, the old village backing on to Notre Dame had a greensward surrounded by medieval houses. We left town by an archway where an old man leaning on a fork gossiped with neighbours. Perfect – if there had been a farmyard. And the mooing of a white cow or two.

Pont d'Ouche boasted a canal port, which in no way resembled anywhere in my village. A barge lay in a filling lock. On the deck, six American tourists had paid twelve thousand dollars for a five-day cruise. They sunned themselves luxuriantly on deck, glasses in hands, faces glued to paperbacks, while a Cambridge undergraduate on a vacation job did his stuff with the lock-gates, opening and closing them for the barge to pass through.

'I do thirteen of 'em between here and Dijon,' he said uncomplainingly. 'Plus washing the dishes. But the perks are good. Yesterday I had a balloon trip with the clients. They get that thrown in, by the way.' For twelve grand, I should hope so.

It was a British charter firm. A villager watched from the bridge with caustic amusement: 'They pay the price of American palaces for an old barge. The British – pardon me, M'sieur – *ils les plument à nu*.' But the Americans seemed more than happy to be 'plucked naked'.

S and I, however, were beginning to lose heart. In the serenity of Fontenay Abbey, where St-Bernard had taught his monks to forget their pasts, I came to a momentous decision. I would give up my quest. It was time for Cistercian practicality. A certainty of belief. And I could at least be sure of having previously been to Saulieu. Most people driving to southern France on the old N6, before the advent of the Autoroute du Soleil, stopped there, either for a meal or a night's rest.

Though not a perfect village nor even a specially interesting town, Saulieu had received in its time Walt Disney, Edith Piaf, Archduke Otto of Hapsburg, Orson Welles, and the Marquis de Cuevas among many other celebrities – for one very good reason.

On the pre-autoroute road to the Côte d'Azur, the Côte d'Or, Saulieu's three-star Michelin hotel-restaurant was a must, presided over by the late, great Alexander Dumaine between 1932 and his retirement in 1964. The Burgundian prince of chefs was the chef of princes – and God help any who pulled rank. His braised beef has gone into the annals of classic recipes. And the big bear's growling is legendary.

When Alphonse Daudet's journalist son, Léon, smothered his beef with half a pot of Dijon mustard, Dumaine snatched his plate from under his nose, with the devastating comment: 'I imagined Monsieur Daudet to be a *gastronome*. He is merely a heavy eater.'

Little did I know, as a mere anonymous traveller stopping over at the Côte d'Or, how Alexander Dumaine would once again enter my life, twenty-five years after his death.

It was Brazilian Year at the 1989 *Foire Internationale et Gastronomique de Dijon*. The pulsating of live lambadas and sambas shook the vast halls of the *Parc des Expositions*. Girls from Ipanema wriggled and rubbed crotches with their chaps in carnival mood. Black beans went with the bongos, barbecue smoke with the jazz guitars; *churrascos* and *cozidos* were a far cry from Alexander Dumaine's braised beef. At chic little boutiques, swimming costumes sexily cut for Copacabana Beach caused ripples of excitement among the young girls of Dijon.

Meanwhile, rather more soberly, a prize was being presented for the year's best book on gastronomy. It was the *Prix Littéraire Alexandre Dumaine*, founded that year in memory of Burgundy's greatest chef and funded by the local tourist board and the town of Saulieu.

A jury of food journalists, top chefs, and regional dignitaries had awarded the 15,000 francs to *Provence Gourmande*. And it must have come as a considerable surprise to some of them that the perpetrators of this *œuvre*, originally entitled *A Taste of Provence*, were British: I was the author, my daughter Carey the photographer, and S was in charge of recipes.

I tried to imagine Frenchmen awarded a prize for a book about cricket. Would the reception be as warm and uncompromisingly friendly as ours at Dijon? Even the long official speeches had a light touch. There is a certain effortless formality about the French language that makes speech-making if not easy, at least bearable. And in my short (but not too short) speech of thanks, I dared the odd joke, promising Monsieur Dumaine I would never again put mustard on my beef – even Dijon mustard. The generous laughter was out of proportion to the wit.

At the six-course luncheon that followed, I was the only man at my table without the Legion of Honour. The Mayors of Beaune, Nuits St-Georges and Saulieu gave the wines a hard time. The Batard Montrachet '83 was shrugged off mercilessly, but the Chambolle-Musigny 'Les Amoureuses' '80 passed. Quietly, I enjoyed them all. I was in uncritical mood. And desperately trying to pace myself for the night to come: a six-course banquet at Clos-de-Vougeot. All in a day's work for a Burgundian mayor.

'Once I was on the jury of a dessert competition,' Philippe Lavault, Mayor of Saulieu, told me. 'Twenty desserts to taste in a morning, with the right sweet wines to accompany each. Followed by an official lunch.'

Luckily, the Mayor of Saulieu was also a doctor.

That evening, fanfares and pennants and colourfully medieval public relations greeted us at the 708th Chapter of Gastronomy, held by the Confrérie des Chevaliers du Tastevin. In the massive stone Cistercian cellars of the heavily restored Renaissance château known as Clos-de-Vougeot, six hundred guests were being entertained by the Chevaliers to a Rabelaisian, black-tie *disnée* at which new Chevaliers – showbiz, diplomatic corps, wine trade, local dignitaries – would be enthroned.

Despite the medieval *mise en scène*, the Brotherhood is not that ancient. In 1934, to combat a slump in sales of their world famous wines, a group of energetic Burgundians founded the bacchiac society to publicise the wines of France in general and those of Burgundy in particular. Ten years later they bought the former monastery of Clos-de-Vougeot and began their series of world-famous PR binges. And highly entertaining they are.

After the Grand Master's 'harangue of welcome', we sat ourselves at long refectory tables. I was delighted to find Docteur and Madame Lavault near by; a medical mayor at hand could be useful. The rites of Chevalier enthronement are taken from Molière's play *Le Malade Imaginaire*, and this was no place for illness, imagined or otherwise. I was an official guest, and official guests should get a menu like this down without gasp or burp.

PREMIERE ASSIETTE
Le Fois Gras de Canard en Brioche
escorté d'un Bourgogne Aligoté 1987 frais et gouleyant

DEUXIEME ASSIETTE
Les Filets de Lotte aux Petits Légumes
humidifiés d'un Meursault-Perrières 1984 subtil et parfumé

ENTREMETS
Les Oeufs en Meurette Vigneronne
arrosés d'un Cote de Nuits-Villages 1985 fin et bouqueté

DORURE
Le Civet de Chevreuil de la Forêt de Cîteaux
accompagné d'un Beaune 1er Cru 1985 suave et prenant

ISSUE DE TABLE
Les Bons Fromages de Bourgogne et d'Ailleurs
rehaussés d'un Latricières-Chambertin 1982 de noble lignée

BOUTEHORS
L'Escargot en Glace – Les Poires Glacées en Tastevin
Les Petits Fours

Le Café Noir, le Vieux Marc et la Prunelle de Bourgogne
fort idoines à stimuler vapeurs subtiles du cerveau

En disnée, met et vins se hument, au café tous tabacs se fument.

With the sixteenth-century French of Rabelais went the classic cream-butter-and-wine cooking of Burgundy. But, like the wit of the speeches and songs that interspersed them, each marvel had the lightness of excellence. A lightness echoed in the speeches. When the Chef took his bow, he received a teasing rebuke from the Grand Master.

'To health and good living!' the Chef toasted.

'Thank you,' replied the Grand Master. 'But the venison could have been cooked longer.'

The Chef acknowledged the ribald laughter with a good-humoured but utterly unrepentant bow.

The songs were relentlessly hearty, and one *chansonnier* sang and ate at the same time while guests below him ducked. Hunting horns heralded each course, borne by a regiment of serving ladies at full gallop, so all six hundred of us seemed to receive our dishes piping hot and at the same moment.

A corpulent dignitary timed it badly, returning from a pee just as serving ladies were beetling up the narrow aisle between tables with dessert. Blocked by the fat VIP, a *serveuse* bearing a large snail-shaped ice-cream cake gave him such a look, he seemed to shrink before her very eyes. I never saw a fat VIP make himself thin faster.

A practised ease in the ritual had the banquet running as smoothly as a High Mass. Christian and pagan elements manifested themselves in the speeches, celebrating the bread and wine of life: 'One must look after the body for contentment of the soul.'

There were French schoolboy jokes too. When we were toasted for our prize a speechmaker quipped: 'It is perfectly all right for the English to earn a prize for French gastronomy. Shakespeare was, after all, a Frenchman.' Ooohs-and-boos from the several British present. 'His real name was Jacques-Pierre.'

International *bonhomie* culminated with the enthronement of ten ambassadors to the United Nations as Chevaliers. In a mock-Latin ceremony, each was touched on the shoulder with a vinestock as though receiving some bibulous knighthood. In his speech of thanks Finnish Ambassador to France, Matti Hakkanen, President of the Chapter, observed: 'An ambassador who has a good time is less dangerous than one who works.'

My wine glass, sacrilegiously used for water at one moment, was nonchalantly swilled out by the sommelier with Latricières-Chambertin so that the wine's noble lineage should not be contaminated. But I was past caring and so was he. Having a good time had none of the tensions of correct behaviour. The spirit takes on a whole new dimension of lightness, transcending all such dreary thoughts as 'What glass should I be using?' or 'Who's driving?'

'If you're ever in Saulieu', said Docteur Lavault as we made for our cars, 'be sure to give me a ring.' The Mayor's invitation was genuinely pressing, and the following autumn we took him up on it.

Our pilgrimage to the shrine of Alexandre Dumaine began at the Lavault home, a solid, Flaubertian house in its own *parc*. Its lights blazed welcome and Madame Lavault greeted us like old friends.

'I'm sorry,' said Madame Lavault. 'My husband is not yet back from his meeting in Dijon.'

With Mozart playing and pink champagne well iced, we awaited Docteur Lavault. More dessert-tasting, I wondered? It was eight o'clock, Saturday evening; the Mayor certainly worked hard for Saulieu. Then I saw a BMW turn through the gates. With an air of amusement, Docteur Lavault apologised for his lateness: 'Seven hundred regional mayors descended on Dijon to hear the Minister of Finance explain tax changes. So you can imagine how many questions there were!'

While we strolled up to the Côte d'Or, the Mayor – once Alexandre Dumaine's doctor – filled us in on recent developments.

'What happened to the hotel after he retired?' I asked.

'Well, it ticked over – until the arrival of the Autoroute du Soleil.'

'And it boomed again?'

'My God, no! The autoroute acted as a bypass. It killed us.'

'It really made that difference to Saulieu? With its reputation for good food?'

'At first, catastrophic. With virtually no through-traffic, we became a desert. For centuries, Saulieu had been a gastronomic stopover and staging post. Madame de Sévigné, in one of her letters, recalls having such a good meal she got sozzled for the first time in her life. Suddenly our hotels and restaurants were empty.'

'Tonight I couldn't get a room at the Côte d'Or. What made the change?'

'The vision of locals like Bernard Loiseau.'

A chef with his name in lights. On the recently refurbished front wall of the Côte d'Or, 'Bernard Loiseau' shone like a star in the Burgundian night.

'You'll find Bernard's food very different from a Tastevin banquet,' the Mayor said. 'And from Dumaine's.'

'It's the new Burgundian taste,' Madame Lavault added. 'Very revolutionary.'

'More health conscious.'

Was this a restaurant or clinic I was entering? God help us, was *nouvelle cuisine* not dead and buried in Burgundy? I thought a pigeon's wing with sliced dwarf kiwi on a bed of polenta still only flourished in the Falkland Islands.

I need not have feared.

Much hand-shaking greeted our party in the hotel lobby. I admired the portrait of Alexandre Dumaine. 'Not a good likeness,' said Madame Lavault with feeling.

The Mayor was a little miffed not to be in the small front dining-room, where the in-crowd normally ate. And where was Bernard? 'With the Michelin team in the front room,' apologised Hubert, the restaurant manager. 'There are five inspectors, and it's their third visit.' Bernard was sweating on his third Michelin star – a must for American gourmets, we learned.

The Lavaults accepted the back room with good grace. There we ate what those Michelin men would not get spare tyres from: *cuisine à l'eau*, the culinary invention Loiseau has perfected over the nineteen years since his apprenticeship with the Troisgros brothers.

Bernard, like many of today's top young chefs, believes a gastronomic meal is a spectacle. Going to a restaurant is like going to the theatre, he reckons. Making a hit requires showbiz panache as well as culinary invention. *Cuisine à l'eau* – steaming vegetables using natural meat and fish juices rather than oil and butter – was presented as a star performance.

Next morning, Bernard proudly took us backstage. Last night he had had the critics in but wouldn't be getting the 'notice' till next year's Michelin Guide. No point in worrying. In fact, three months after our visit, Michelin awarded him his coveted third star, and it was treated as a major media event – and not only in France, either.

The third star would carry him through the long Burgundian winter when previously there were sometimes more staff than guests at the Côte d'Or. Three Michelin stars helped fill the house all year round. It's the gastronomic equivalent of a Tony or *Evening Standard* theatre award.

With a nine-million franc bank loan for hotel improvements, Bernard exudes confidence: 'Inventive chef, OK. But you have to be able to sell yourself. Some genius cooks can't string two sentences together. Me, I love going on télé and mixing with le showbiz in Paris. I want to make this just the best place for

Parisians to spend weekends.'

Having recently had President Mitterrand as a guest, Bernard was engagingly cocky, a Jack-the-Lad among hoteliers. Perhaps because he does not come from a catering family, he doesn't take himself too seriously.

His father was a traveller in hosiery from Clermont-Ferrand. It wasn't easy working his way up to the three-star firmament, a celestial position often helped by family connections. The Pics, the Troisgros, the Lameloises all have deeply planted roots. Some of the older chefs look on Loiseau as a flashy upstart with perverse culinary ideas.

'Is it true', S asked, 'that your favourite food is potatoes?'

'Perfectly,' Bernard laughed. 'I like them so much, I want to have a complete potato menu. The potato has infinite possibilities.' I wondered what potato ice-cream would taste like. 'I don't mind causing a scandal with my cuisine.' He looked as though he positively enjoyed it. 'Anyway, I'm retiring at fifty. Who wants to spend their life in a kitchen?'

When we saw the kitchen, we weren't surprised. Bernard was building a new one, but at that time still occupied Alexandre Dumaine's – hardly a kitchen you'd associate with gastronomic miracles, then or now. How he and his act performed on such a tiny, cramped stage with perilous ups-and-downs and dilapidated-looking equipment was in itself something of a miracle.

La Salle Alexandre Dumaine, the famous front dining-room, had the class of the 1850s. Ornate pictures and furniture were perfectly matched, though cutlery and glasses of a simpler kind adorned the tables. Little bouquets of flowers were in Dumaine's old silver ice-cream cups. And I thought: maybe I once ate a sorbet out of one of those cups.

To lose a perfect French village, as Oscar Wilde might have said, is carelessness. But thanks to Alexandre Dumaine and friends, Burgundy had been delectably regained.

11

Le Nid du Duc, 1975

If the equivalent of an Oscar could be awarded for Best Foreign Home in France, nominations would roll in for film and theatre director Tony Richardson's Le Nid du Duc. For originality, art direction, intrigue, action, sharp dialogue and X-rated scenes (not explicit), Le Nid du Duc had the fans coming back time and time again – including S and me.

Tony himself was an unconditional fan of France, and at Le Nid du Duc could behave like an opulent man of the left. His home was there to be shared, his drink drunk, his food eaten, his pool swum in and his cars smashed by an endless flow of jolly comrades.

In France, to be of the left and rich was no sin. In the shadow of Britain's dark, satanic mills, such a contradiction was still deeply suspect. Tony always hated the nay-saying of Nanny England, left or right; between his productions of *Look Back in Anger* and *Tom Jones*, a time of revolution in Britain's theatre and cinema, his life-style, even when relatively poor, firmly eschewed the puritan. When the creators of *Tom Jones*, including Tony as director, worked for no salaries but a share of the profits, its unexpected box office success is said to have made five sterling millionaires. In the Sixties that was money.

People like Tony take their pleasures seriously. And now he could invite friends and family to share those exotic pleasures in France, where he was a most generous and, at times, unnerving host.

Mind you, he himself would never call his home exotic. 'It's terribly simple,' was how he described it to me before my first visit. 'You'll hate it and be bored stiff.'

This terribly simple, boring house was actually a converted hamlet in a clearing in the forest of the Massif des Maures. The *hameau* of Le Nid du Duc owed its aristocratic name not to a duke but a horned owl with tufts of feathers on its head. It was quite a lot of real estate for one owl's nest.

You approached through chestnut and oak woods, much of them belonging to Le Nid du Duc. Tony seemed vague about where his land began and ended, being nonchalant about property and never locking doors or shuttering windows ('Who'd ever want to break in?'). By the standards of most second-home owners, it was vast and its forest a welcome protection against property developers in the highly desirable hinterland of St-Tropez. The long, rough, purposely unmade-up drive was a deterrent. When movie producer Harry Saltzman arrived in a limo, having taken three wrong forest tracks, Tony saw instantly that their movie project together was not to be. Harry was not even amused by the sign *Canard Méchant*.

In fact, there no longer was a dangerous duck, but a flock of vociferous peacocks which flew up to nest in the great lime trees at night. With wild shrieks, they welcomed guests at the car park where stood an old jeep suitable for the forest tracks, a beat-up Citroën for marketing in St-Tropez, and a gleaming Mercedes convertible for the Polish chauffeur, Jan, to pick up guests at Nice airport.

Tony would always greet people as though they'd been invited, which very often they hadn't. At least, not precisely that day. 'You must come and stay,' was his open invitation in wild moments, and strange voices would be on the phone from the call-box in La Garde Freinet, and only vaguely familiar faces would arrive minutes later. It could be a screenwriter from Los Angeles, a couple of back-packers on their way home from Thailand or friends of somebody's secretary. It was, on the face of it, a most democratic household.

'Do you want a drink?' would be Tony's first question, and if they didn't, his face would cloud with incomprehension and suspicion, as though they might be subversives from Nanny England.

The main farmhouse was where older guests like Tony's parents stayed and the rest of us congregated before dinner. Music was opera or rock. The living-room had works by David Hockney, not displayed in any show-off way but because Hockney was a friend and frequent visitor; nothing at Le Nid du Duc seemed to have been done by design which meant Tony had spent hours and a fortune planning its insouciance.

On the terrace, where a long farmhouse table was often set for between fifteen to twenty-five diners, first-time guests would gasp at the view – from the head of a thickly wooded valley down to the plain, where Tony, spindle-thin and demon-legged, would lead walks at a marathon pace.

With all those trees, there was enough shade even in high summer to siesta outdoors. Hammocks bulged with replete bodies. Down steps past lemon and orange trees, the first house was where Tony lived in two rooms. Guests had the rest of the straggling hamlet, converted into cottages with cool tiled floors, reasonably comfortable beds, and a theatrical knight or Broadway playwright to share the shower.

At the bottom was a whole cottage converted into one vast rumpus room, with a stage-set flight of stairs suitable for the plays of Natasha and Joely, Tony's children from his marriage to Vanessa Redgrave. You could also find yourself acting in a charade with the likes of Jack Nicholson. A vast plate glass window gave guests the option of the valley view when their loved ones made fools of themselves. Further down the hill, a swimming pool was far enough away not to spoil the rusticity.

S and I, during our own house-hunt in France, returned there in November, 1975. 'Stay as long as you like,' Tony had told us with characteristic rashness. He would not be in residence, no one else was expected (which meant there could be a hundred for Christmas), and but for the *gardien*, Jean-Pierre, we would have the place to ourselves.

Jean-Pierre was a young and sociable companion resembling the hero of Truffaut's *Quatre Cent Coups*. He darted about the place, fixing this and that, swigging from the ever-open bottle cf Vidauban *rouge* on the kitchen table, and feeding the many animals. He was glad of the company, he said. Being *gardien* of Le Nid du Duc was a lonely life in winter.

'Tony may come for Easter,' Jean-Pierre announced in early

December as though it were tomorrow. 'Maybe I will go to America in the February holidays.'

In fact, he took time off to go to Italy, leaving us in charge of the animals – whippets, chickens, ducks, geese, rabbits, an aviary of exotic birds and the famous peacocks. One day a peacock, bored out of its crest with lack of guests to screech at, came exploring in the house. I startled it and it flew out of a window which was unfortunately closed at the time. It left its shape in the glass like a Tom-and-Jerry cartoon character.

Friends of Tony's dropped by, including the English horticulturalist Hiram Winterbotham who lived in the Lubéron. Hiram was an erudite English country gentleman, and he taught us everything we know about French mushrooms as we searched the Le Nid du Duc woods together. Avoid mushroom books, Hiram said; colour prints can be misleading. Anything white should be mistrusted – could be *vénéneux* or even *mortel*. When in doubt, take your mushrooms to be checked at the local pharmacy.

One of the Le Nid du Duc regulars, and high priest of high camp, was Giancarlo, a flamboyant Italian, pre-Raphaelite in his velvet medieval pageboy's cap. Star of the impromptu summer 'festivals', he dressed in drag as Mimi or Tosca, entertaining us with his opera buffa mimed to playback. Now, in the depths of winter he was forlorn and pale, far from his extrovert self.

'Whatever's the matter, Giancarlo?' we asked.

'I was in prison,' he said. 'I am fix with some stupid charge of stealin I never in a million fuckin years done.'

Jean-Pierre had brought him back from Italy for rehabilitation. Giancarlo's life, like many of Le Nid du Duc's guests', hovered on a razor's edge. But a kind of complicity united us. At this time, S and I were feeling a bit lost too, having left England with no solid plans, and when we went later to Paris, Giancarlo lent us his bachelor pad on Rue du Dragon. Le Nid du Duc was that sort of place: one unlikely thing led to another.

For a more permanent home in France, we were considering the conversion of a ruined aviary at Le Nid du Duc. Another of Tony's friends, engineer and arts patron Jeremy Fry, had done basic plans for it, and David Hockney considered making a pied-à-terre there. Jeremy had converted his own *hameau* at Oppedette on the

Vaucluse plateau, and was generous with much-needed practical advice.

Now S and I spent many happy evenings, working on our own variations for the aviary. But I am superstitious; I wasn't sure I could live with the ominous cry of those peacocks through an entire winter and, much as I loved the place, I wasn't sorry when our plans, like Hockney's, were shelved.

It was, however, a perfect base for a house-hunt. If there had been any houses worth hunting. In the mid-Seventies, South of France options revealed nothing but horrors at our modest price. We came to hate a recurrent speckled mock-marble floor, named presumably after the Marseilles gangster who had first installed it: Sol Granito. A fierce lady house agent, when we told her all we wanted was a wreck of a farmhouse to convert to our own taste, yelled aggressively: 'C'est introuvable!' We have news for Madame Introuvable. Later we found it, way up on the northern borders of the Midi. But that's another story.

At that time, hunting a house was as frustrating as hunting game in the Massif des Maures. Rare was the wild boar that managed to cross the autoroute from the Upper Var. We left Le Nid du Duc at first light on an icy February morning to pursue our hunt in the Loire Valley. And as the headlights pitched and flickered on that familiarly rough ride through the chestnut trees, I rounded a corner to be confronted by a massive shape blocking the road. The wild boar's eyes glinted red and its breath was smokey in the freezing air; it was a mythic beast, guardian of the forest road. I was glad I wasn't on foot. But, after a forbidding glare at us, it lumbered off into the undergrowth and let us pass.

My visits to Tony in France had begun in the Sixties. I was no stranger to his singular life style, and the people who helped make it.

Our theatre and movie generation, some of us from working-class backgrounds but mostly middle-class, ranged politically from blood red to insipid pink. We supported Women's Lib. We sent our children to State schools. Our hi-fis croaked out Brecht and Weill in the original German, our tellys were tuned to the satire shows, and we got drunk at the Establishment Club. We were solidly pro-CND and anti-Vietnam War. One memorable Sunday

I found myself in full-scale conflict with the police in Grosvenor Square, when a demo got irretrievably out of hand while Vanessa Redgrave was delivering a signed petition to the US Embassy.

But I do not remember Tony Richardson's South of France scene as a hotbed of trendy lefties. Far from it. The ambience was refreshingly classless and anarchic. Tony firmly believed that art was not for the soap box, and tubs could be thumped elsewhere. His home was a place for letting go – a far cry from the British middle-class drabness many of us had suffered in our youth. No turning in early with a cup of Horlicks. More likely it was Dom Perignon for elevenses, and there's nothing in any manifesto that says socialists can't enjoy their money. In these surroundings, I saw a very different Vanessa Redgrave from the ardent campaigner and political activist.

I was working on *Red and Blue* with Tony, and Vanessa at the time was playing the lead in *The Prime of Miss Jean Brodie* at the Wyndham's Theatre, London. Tony, in France, suggested we come down for a conference.

After Vanessa's Saturday night performance, we repaired to Sybilla's, the disco of the day, and danced till it was time for our night plane to Nice. We danced a little too long. The flight was at 3 a.m. and at 3.05, we were dashing down a Heathrow corridor yelling, 'Stop the plane!' Well, they did stop the plane which was leaving its bay; they trundled it back and we boarded breathlessly.

An open Mercedes was there to meet us at dawn. On the autoroute Jan hit his usual 120 m.p.h. through the Esterel, and Tony in his bathrobe greeted us with the usual welcome: 'Do you want a drink?' It was six-thirty. If this was work, we were all for it.

We spent Sunday and Monday mornings working on beaches and round the pool, and caught the Monday midday plane back to London. Vanessa was in plenty of time for Miss Jean Brodie. 'Have a nice weekend, dear?' asked her dresser. 'Oh, quiet,' Vanessa replied. She had not turned in early with a cup of Horlicks, that's for sure.

In Tony's even more expansive moments, one was met at Nice-Côte-d'Azur and conducted quickly through passport control to another plane, a light, single-engine charter job. The pilot flew low and dramatically along the Riviera coastline, so we could have a good peer through villa windows and at bronzed bodies on yacht decks. This low flying once nearly ended disastrously when the pilot came in just a little too low for a hedge which I heard brush the wheels, and the plane slewed scarily before we hit the ground. Never was I happier to be back with Jan gunning the Mercedes round the twists and turns of the road to La Garde Freinet.

Tony had a loyal entourage to help entertain the guests. Besides Jean-Pierre, there were his quiet, exquisitely mannered American producer, Neil Hartley; attentive assistant Anna O'Reilly; Grizelda Grimond, mother of his daughter Katherine; not to mention helpful boys and girls *à tout faire*. Tony managed everything and everyone from animals quadruped to biped, from winged to merely high. You either liked the Le Nid du Duc game and played it. Or not – and left.

The staid found it just too decadently Firbankian.

Neither was it for snobs, people with weak livers, envious people, luxury lovers, and people of nervous disposition to whom party games were anathema. It was for children, Sybarites, radicals, beach bums, and anyone prepared to muck in and help make the permanent party go. Sometimes mucking-in could lead to trouble.

'What are you doing, darling?' Tony asked a county lady in that clipped, quiet drawl which could send shock waves down the spine. She was crouched over the steps leading up from her cottage.

'Just weeding the steps,' said the county lady, confident she was being helpful.

'Darling, those are plants!'

The county lady decided to leave that afternoon.

Without their own car, some guests felt trapped. Tony organized treats for everyone – boat trips, outings to St-Tropez, dinners in restaurants – and naturally did not like his home being used as a hotel. Guest participation was expected.

Some guests rebelled against what they saw as this manipulation of their holiday. 'Caligula!' burst out an angry middle-aged actor at dinner. 'Tony's like a Roman emperor here, and we're his slaves.' The astonishing attack, presumably meant to be funny, reduced the table to silence, broken by Tony's somewhat forced laughter.

One sprig of the aristocracy, a typical sponger of that ilk, lumbered her host with a huge telephone and grocery bill while staying in his absence. Other guests were more generous. John Mortimer, another regular, one night provided *filet de boeuf* for thirty, cooking dinner himself with his wife Penny. Impresario Michael White, finding some of the domestic arrangements a little primitive, presented the house with a washing-up machine.

Dirty linen was occasionally washed in public. But if possible, not *devant les enfants* or when the French neighbours dropped by.

These included an Iranian-born composer-writer-painter Serge Rezvani, alias Bassiak, who had written 'Le Tourbillon', the theme song of *Jules et Jim*. He and his wife were neighbours, as was Jeanne Moreau.

Vanessa and Jeanne were both highly domestic actresses. Vanessa made cakes with the children. Jeanne had taken twenty years to fix up her own house at La Mourre. She had a great feeling for Provence – like Colette. Its sensuality embraced and inspired her. She sang her bitter-sweet, highly romantic lyrics as though they had just come into her head.

I translated Bassiak's songs. One of them was used in Tony's *A Sailor from Gibraltar*, and sung by Jeanne Moreau. While staying near by with my family at Bargemon, S dropped me off at Jeanne's *mas* and continued to St-Tropez, the car packed with our nine-year-old twins and five of their friends from the village school. I was to work with Jeanne, then they'd pick me up on the way back from their outing. With unstarry kindness, Jeanne invited the whole gang to swim and tea. It was a cold, late January day and the sight of steam rising off a heated pool was strange to us all. The children stripped and plunged in, yelling and laughing like cherubs gone wild in a Turkish bath. Camilla and Carey were thrilled to meet the singer of 'Le Tourbillon', one of their all-time favourites. Jeanne gave them raspberry drinks and cakes; and sent S and me away with a tin of truffles and a bottle of champagne to cook them in.

At Le Nid du Duc, consumption of champagne fluctuated with Tony's fortunes. One visit, aware of a drought, I hastened out for a bottle of brut. 'Our only bottle of the summer,' Tony commented with typical hyperbole, as he popped the cork.

Anywhere in the world, it is tactless to beat one's host at bridge or tennis. And Le Nid du Duc was no exception. Luckily my tennis was rough and I never played bridge except once when Tony mistakenly tried to teach me. 'Do you want a drink?' he said eventually, eager to get my hands on anything but the cards. And I gratefully left the table.

With the who's-for-tennis-and-bridge syndrome, Tony had not moved a centimetre to the right as some people mistakenly thought. He just didn't believe politics played any part in Le Nid du Duc. Except when they occurred in sessions of charades.

On my slip of paper, I read with some dismay: 'Czechoslovakia is a faraway country of which we know nothing.' Prime Minister Neville Chamberlain's pre-war statement on Hitler's invasion of Czechslovakia was still apposite after the Russians' 1968 repeat performance. But how to act it? The evening before, I'd been given the one-word title of Jane Austen's novel *Persuasion* which was dead easy. Now I lost precious seconds counting the words, while Tony's foot twitched as it always did when he became impatient. 'Split a word!' he hissed in my ear. 'Do "country"!' I hesitated. 'Cunt – tree.' My team guessed extremely quickly.

Games and drama were the spice of Le Nid du Duc life.

'There's been a drama,' was another of Tony's greetings when one arrived. Apart from lethal mushrooms in the woods, the odd poisonous snake, missed planes, lost dogs, sprained ligaments, strained relations and stressed-out lovers, there was the Near-Drowning drama.

American producer Bob Register and I were bringing Tony's speedboat back from Pampelonne Beach to its mooring at St-Tropez after water-skiing. The engine had been playing up, so it was with some relief that we made it to the mouth of the harbour where it promptly stalled – irrevocably.

In normal circumstances we could easily have picked up a tow. These were not normal circumstances. Bob yelled: 'Holy shit!' I looked up from trying to get us started. The Ste-Maxime ferry was navigating a course straight through our stalled position, without any attempt to avoid us. Its prow loomed, the hooter gave sharp, fierce blasts.

'Abandon ship!' Bob yelled. I went first, headlong into the sewagey, oil-slicked water of one of the world's highest-priced moorings. I heard my shipmate follow with much gurgling and spitting, then a desperate shout of fury.

'Fuck you, you *emmerdeur!*' Bob yelled at the ferryboat's captain, and got a mouthful of sewage for his pains. As for me, I couldn't swim away fast enough, imagining myself being sucked into the ferryboat's wash, losing both legs or being undertowed to a watery grave.

I heard a final blast of the ferry's hooter and a thud. Realising I at least was safe, I turned and saw the struck speedboat turned turtle, Bob in the water, face already red from the sun now puce with rage, giving an up-yours in the direction of the departing ferry. Somehow we righted the capsized speedboat, and had ourselves towed in, clinging to our craft till we could climb on to dry land by harbour ladder. My arm muscles felt like jellyfish.

Stinking and sopping, we joined Tony and the others waiting for us at Senequier, the waterfront bar.

'It's very odd,' Tony teased. 'I mean – to borrow someone's boat and abandon it!' Foot twitching. 'I suppose all you two care about is being alive.' Lizard eyes darting to see the effect it was having on the others. 'You smell disgusting. I expect we'll be asked to leave. Do you want a drink?'

Dramas came and went like the endless flow of houseguests. The occasional tragedy was far outnumbered by the comedies – of manners, farcical, or black.

The Le Nid du Duc I remember was a place of laughter and nightingales, not to mention peacocks. It was a never-to-be-repeated experience. It belongs to a special era, pre-Thatcher, pre-Reagan, pre-Mitterrand, pre-Gorbachev; the playground of a few radicals in the arts seems somehow remote from today's world problems. As Tony himself often said, 'Oh, that's the past!'

But what a past.

12

Villerey-sur-Loire, 1976

The snow began at Montélimar.

'The méteo got it right for once,' S observed as we drove north. The first snowflakes fluttered on to a windscreen warm from our Mediterranean glow, and melted instantly. We sniffed our bunch of mimosa and felt better.

'Oh, it's nothing,' I said confidently. 'The weather always changes at Montélimar. For the better, going south. For the worse, going north. It's normal.'

'I've never known snow before – in either direction. I hope we're doing the right thing.'

Certainly, we were doing the right thing. An old friend, a wise antique dealer much travelled in France, had confirmed it over a farewell dinner at La Garde Freinet: we'd find much cheaper houses in the Loire Valley. Prettier, too. The whole St-Trop' area was over, kaput, finito in any house-hunter's language.

By the time we reached Burgundy, the snow was no longer melting on the windscreen. The wipers barely functioned with the load. After an overnight stop at Moulins, I squirted defrosters, scraped windows and brushed bodywork till I nearly came down with frostbite. Lunch at Romarantin: S jettisoned the dead mimosa, which lay sadly on the grubby snow of the restaurant's car park.

To protect the people and the village which now follow, I have changed names, so you will not find Villerey-sur-Loire on the map. Should you happen upon it, however, it will be recognisable.

We arrived there under two feet of snow, a blizzard off the Beauce, that flat, monotonous countryside north of the Loire Valley.

'Why did French kings want to build châteaux in these godfor-saken parts?' I moaned.

'I hope François Premier had long-johns.'

'Fuck François Premier,' I said. 'How about us?'

The chilliest oubliettes of Amboise, the iciest towers of Chambord, the bleakest boudoirs of Chenonceaux could not have been more petrified by cold than the house we had rented for two months from some English people called Brown. The English, we had so often heard in France, were amazingly good at making cosy miracles out of peasant ruins.

Well . . .

We called for the keys, as instructed, at the Reynaud farm. Wild, mangy dogs flew snarling at me in the snow-covered farm-yard, to be yanked mercifully to a gurgling standstill by the chains round their necks. A bleaker farmhouse I have seldom seen, nor a less welcoming farmyard. Rickety ladders led up to rotting attics, bits of rusty machinery poked out of the snow. Madame Reynaud, cheeks glowing, shawl-wrapped, didn't belong to such cold com-fort. She exuded warmth. As she opened her ill-fitting front door, a fug of onion-and-garlic cooking inspired hope; from the gloom behind her came what sounded like a pig being slaughtered but turned out to be Père Reynaud, Madame's father-in-law, cough-ing.

'We have the public telephone here,' she informed us. And there it was, tucked away in a dark corner of the kitchen, with no privacy. 'You wish to make a call to London even, that's fine. Come up whenever you like.' What – brave those bloody dogs? I glanced doubtfully at S: so that was the telephone number we'd given everyone – the Reynaud farm's public telephone!

The Brown house, as it was known locally, was just down the lane from the farm, across a main road, carry on towards the River Loire – at least four minutes' fast run across a skating-rink for those calls from our daughters, literary agents, house agents, bank man-agers. We were, after all, not on holiday. I was writing a book, S had business in Paris and London, we were trying to sell a home in England and buy one in France.

'I think,' S said. 'We may have done the wrong thing.'

'Don't speak too soon. The house looks charming.'

The perfect cottage for Hansel and Gretel – in summer – with long, steep roofs, gables, dormer windows, and tall chimneys. 'The oldest house in the village,' said Madame Reynaud, blue fingers protruding from her mittens as she unlocked the stable-style front door. Must be nice, I thought, to have the top half open on a hot day, pretty view of the front garden. Today not even a horse would have appreciated it.

Inside, the house quickly revealed itself as a do-it-yourself disaster: electrical wiring like an intricate moment of open-heart surgery performed by a ten-year-old; old car seats covered with blankets; and a medieval kitchen corner. It was apparently being converted piecemeal. A fine antique table and château-sized, hooded fireplace were deceptive; the kitchen-cum-living room led into a freezing, clobber-filled barn which we had to scuttle through to reach the rest of the house. From an unrendered, concrete-walled lobby, we braved a spartan corridor, lined with wine racks, to reach the bathroom. This was the warmest room in the house, and S was to spend hours sitting on the loo, reading.

Far away, up creaking stairs was a master bedroom large enough for a Valois monarch and his entire court; we could have done with them to keep warm. Snow had blizzarded through the closed windows and formed a little unmelting drift on the tiled floor.

Give the Browns their due, they had made the house a museum of heating methods: in the kitchen, metre-long logs for the open fire and coal stove for cooking; in the bathroom, gas heater; oil-burning heater of diabolic complication and fumes in the bedroom; and explosive, pilot-light-failing water heaters in bathroom and kitchen. Two hours a day were spent maintaining this museum in working order.

'Shall we leave?' S proposed.

'Leave for where?' I said, pulling the cork out of an icy bottle of our own red Saumur. Monsieur Brown, a wine buff, had left a fierce note: 'Please do not tamper with the wine.' And another: 'Do not touch the old Rolls, or any part thereof.' Besides rare vintages, he was into rare vintage cars: a superb old French-registered Rolls-Royce shooting-brake stood romantically in the garage; I imagined it in use for the stag-hunt at nearby Cheverny, the delivery deep into the forest of some exquisite *déjeuner sur l'herbe* – cold Sologne pheasant, Vineuil asparagus, and chilled Sancerre or Vouvray. I shivered at the thought.

S opened a tin of cassoulet. We were ravenous. The log fire began to blaze. The needy parts of the house, we were astonished to find, heated up quite quickly; one just had to run the gauntlet of the icy wastes between. By now another blizzard had started. Darkest February night had long since fallen. The wind rumbled in the chimney. And . . .

Inevitably came the knocking on the door. A lost traveller caught in the blizzard? 'M'sieur More!' I recognised Madame Reynaud's voice. '*Téléphone!*'

I threw on my anorak and flung myself, Oates-fashion, into the white night. Only I was not alone. Gallant Madame Reynaud had biked down to fetch me, and now, head bent into the driving snow, I followed her. Crossing the Blois-Amboise main road, I skidded in slush, lost my balance and nearly went under an angrily honking car.

In the warmth of the farm kitchen, a friend from Paris was on the line. A matter of life and death: could we have dinner in Paris next Sunday? Yes, I said – if we lived that long.

Over the next weeks, '*Monsieur ou Madame More, téléphone!*' became a well-known cry reverberating down the lane from the moment Madame Reynaud had mounted her bicycle. Farmer Reynaud, with the exemplary kindness of French countrymen, invariably had a warming shot of *eau de vie* for us, when a call to London took its usual several minutes to connect. The chickens came in to peck around and have a listen. So did old Père Reynaud who never coughed during a *communication*, blatantly directing his hearing aid towards our calls, even though they were in English. Except for calls to Monsieur Bousquet, estate agent of Orléans.

Bousquet said he knew exactly what we were looking for and drove us many kilometres to look at dump after dump. A momentary thaw had converted the snowy landscape into a misty Monet; but the master would have rejected beetroot fields in drizzle. And the Sologne hunting country, with its smug timbered mansions in dark pine woods reminded me of Surrey.

We inspected a desirable residence with lake said to be alive with wild duck. It seemed very well appointed. Why was it so cheap? '*Il y a un p'tit inconvénient,*' Monsieur Bousquet admitted. A new road was planned round the lake.

The eighteenth-century *seigneurie* needed a new roof, the Renaissance farmhouse in the Forest of Orléans looked quiet now but, come summer, had hikers tramping through the garden. Everything in the Loire Valley proper was too expensive. And the beguilingly honest Monsieur Bousquet's small inconveniences grew ever bigger.

Now it may seem crazy to house-hunt in one of the coldest winters of the century. But our philosophy was: if you like a house in winter, you'll love it in summer.

'Is the Loire "us", though?' S wondered.

'Of course, it's "us"!' I insisted. 'We just haven't seen the right house.'

After every day's house-hunting, we would return gratefully to Villerey. We would light the great log fire, pop the cork of a Montlouis blanc and begin to spit-roast a farm chicken. Compared to the impossible houses we'd seen with their *p'tits inconvénients*, the Brown house seemed almost luxurious.

Visits from Pipou were always heartening. A pissy wine-maker with yellow cigarette butt, invariably extinct, bouncing on his lower lip, Pipou would deliver his truly terrible wine by horse-and-cart. He would say he couldn't stop, his wife would give him hell, dinner would spoil . . . *eh bien!* . . . perhaps just one, quick little glass, not to be unsociable. An hour-and-a-half later, Pipou had begun dancing: the only thing his wife and he enjoyed together, he said, was the tango. He demonstrated around the kitchen with S. He also sang. Not for nothing were we in Rabelais country, as his raucous, heart-warming voice belted out bawdy verses about how different nationalities made love:

> *Les français, dans le placard,*
> *N'importe quoi . . .*

After the French doing it in a cupboard no matter what, we egged him on. 'Now the English, Pipou.'

'Tomorrow.' He got unsteadily to his feet.

'Come on,' S said, filling his glass. 'How do the English do it?'

> *Les Anglais sur le tapis,*
> *N'importe qui . . .*

And with the English doing it on the carpet no matter who, Pipou finished his drink abruptly and left. Like a good performer he always left us wanting more – if not of his wine, his company.

We made other good friends in Villerey. Later, when the daughter of one of them got married, we were invited to the wedding, a lyrical all-day June event of the French countryside, starting with a luncheon of courses numberless to man and ending with fireworks while *cousins et cousines* did it in the cupboards no matter what. The bride arrived at the church in Pipou's cart which was decorated with armfuls of wild flowers; his black horse, Chéri, had roses behind its ears, and Pipou himself wore a grey topper and frock coat.

Villerey was a long, straggly village and our adjoining hamlet of Labaroche was a good mile from church, post office, shops, and the one hotel-restaurant. Walks along the slushy main road to the Relais de Villerey were both healthy and destructive.

Drinking sessions with the proprietors warmed the blood and beat up the liver. Cliquette was a comtesse, Roland a marquis. Cliquette's family name was Garonne, and as much liquid went down her as ever did that mighty river. Likewise, Roland. She was tall, gaunt and masculine, a former UNESCO secretary with accentless English; he, some fifteen years her junior, built like a Breton bullock, with freckles and sandy hair.

Roland and Cliquette sober were sociable, kind, and amusing. When drunk . . . here self-censorship brings me up short, however much their exploits might increase sales of this book. Let's just say, there were scenes – and the scenes played to full houses, for the bar was always packed that perishing winter.

Cliquette also did a little hazardous cooking for her clients. Astonishingly, she never caught fire.

'Do you like tripes?' she asked in her upper-class English.

I hesitated.

'Offal is awful, as Nanny used to say. But I do *tripes à la mode de Caen*. It's on tomorrow's menu.'

We lunched at the Relais. S reckoned Cliquette secretly had her old English nanny cooking out back there. And we never ate tripes again.

Our food at the Brown house came from the Sunday market at Amboise where, to save unnecessary journeys on skiddy roads, we did the shopping for the week. It was fabulously situated, its stalls running along the banks of the Loire, selling a mishmash of wares: vegetables between wine and cheap luggage, brioche next to broderie, patisserie by leather jackets. Pitchmen pitched tools and household gadgets at bargain prices, an old craftsman recaned chairs on the pavement. There was even a man who sold accordions – button, keyboard, electronic; photos of France's star players Aimable and Louis Cochiea were pinned up behind; bright *bal musette* music clashed with rock 'n roll from a jeans stall next door.

At Amboise, too, we began to combine the obligatory Loire château visits with house-hunting. 'I think', I said, looking at our schedules, 'we can just fit Amboise in before the ruin at Montlouis.'

There was solace to be gained from the sadness ingrained in its wintry stones. I thought: 'Better the Cold War than the Wars of Religion.'

After the Huguenots of Brittany had failed to persuade François II to let them practise Protestantism, their Conspiracy of 1560 came to a savage and bitter end at Amboise. As we looked down towards the Loire, 'Imagine being hung by your feet from these battlements,' S said. 'Or being cut into quarters.'

'Or chucked into that icy river in a sack!'

'Good old days?'

'Hm.'

We had a couple of hours between the watermill at Candé-sur-Beuvron and the windmill at Coulanges. Just time for the château of Blois.

'It says', S was already into her Michelin, 'the Duke of Guise was assassinated here by Henri III whom he was conspiring to depose.'

'Conspiracies, conspiracies.'

'And Henri III himself got a dagger in his back eight months later.'

'Nice people.'

Chenonceau, it turned out, was conveniently close to the cottage at Chisseaux. So we had a quick whip round.

'And Henri's widow, Louise, retired to Chenonceau where she put on white mourning and lived for the rest of her days. She was known as Louise the Inconsolable.'

'I've got nothing against Louise,' I said. 'But doesn't it strike you these French royals were just a little over-housed around here? And we can't find anything halfway liveable-in! No wonder there was a Revolution.'

'Still, it wasn't all cake being royal,' S reminded me. 'Especially for the mistresses. When Henri II, lover of Diane de Poitiers, died, she was kicked out of Chenonceau, bag and baggage. Too bad, when you've got used to the first indoor staircase in France.'

'In this weather, she would have needed it.'

Time to move on. We had a ruined gatehouse to see near the château of Chaumont.

'Poor Diane de Poitiers,' S continued, trying to make me feel better, 'Henri's widow, Catherine de Medici, not content with booting her out of Chenonceau, humiliated her by offering her this puny little château.'

'I wish someone would buy me this puny little château,' I protested. A chill blast, worse than anything in the Brown house, whistled through the Council Room, and the Sicilian majolica tiles nearly froze my feet off. 'Forget it.'

Then S, totally discouraged by the discomfort and bleakness of Loire real estate of any dimensions, said: 'Let's buy a flat in Paris.'

So we did.

In the mean time, we grew quite fond of the Brown house; fond even of the sound of thick walls contracting with the cold – crackle-crack in the depths of the night. After disturbed nights, I would get up at five-thirty and arm myself with a box of matches. I would light the oil stove in our bedroom, turning it low so as not to asphyxiate S who rose later, go down and light the gas stove and water heater in the bathroom. Then I would bring in metre-length logs for the kitchen fire and light that, and the pilot light of the explosive hot water heater, risking singed eyebrows, prior to electrocution by kettle. Finally, after a well earned café au lait, I'd settle down to my typewriter in front of a roaring log fire.

After breakfast one morning, I took a walk by the Loire. Misty sun penetrated tall poplars, where bunches of mistletoe glistened with frost. Frozen snow crackled beneath my feet. I stopped. I listened to the vibrations of the silence, broken only by a distant express passing on the Tours-Paris line. The river was entirely frozen over, tempting in its broad expanse of flat whiteness.

We had begun our stay at Villerey cursing the cold. And here I was, confidently crossing the Loire on foot, with thick, strong ice beneath me.

Fourteen years later, I crossed the Loire again at precisely the same spot, still on foot, but rather differently.

In hot October sunshine, after a year of drought, the water lapped warmly against my thighs. From the sandy north bank, with vivid blue sky behind, I half expected the US cavalry to pound over the top, horses splashing through the shallows to where I waded, showering me as they disappeared off-camera. It was a western landscape, parched and arid.

I took my favourite walk along the river bank. I once met Pipou somewhere about here, on his wine rounds. He called his horse-and-cart *mon bar ambulant*, and from it I received a glass of bitingly chilled wine. I wondered what had happened to him.

When I asked an old man at the river for news of Pipou, he was evasive. But he certainly remembered that winter.

'I was a gravedigger then,' he told me. 'It took us three days to dig a grave in that whore of a ground. We kept breaking shovels. Lucky it was so cold. Otherwise, the corpses might have gone off, waiting to be buried.'

The drought was worse, though. Retired now, he had had a few sheep on short rations for the past three months. The cattle were starving. No maize, no hay for winter. 'Never seen it this bad, never.'

I left him staring gloomily at the Loire. Soon I was passing a field of unharvested dead sunflowers.

Beneath the shade of a weeping willow, an old couple sat contentedly on folding chairs, unconcerned about the greenhouse effect. He had one eye and a gentle smile; she, white curly hair, and a kitchen apron over a summer dress. Turned eighty, they told me, and proud to have bicycled from Villerey. 'We're fine,' he said, single eye twinkling. 'You'd say it was still summer, wouldn't you?'

The stillness and oldness of everyone and everything, the burnt-up countryside and the shallow river gave my walk a certain uneasiness. As did the floodmark half-way up the building of a riverside pottery: 3 June 1856. Today it seemed to stand on top of a thirty-foot drop. Could the water really have risen so high? On a village house, too, the high watermark confirmed that same flood.

Villerey itself seemed dead. The Mairie, operational centre of village life, announced on its notice board various community activities: a boule competition, Sangria evening, Paella and Sauerkraut dinners. Who would show up, I wondered? Stuck on to the phone box was an ad for Club Retro Le Charleston at Montlivault. Was the whole village off charlestoning at three o'clock on a Saturday afternoon?

The church, where our friend's daughter had been married, was locked against burglars. Shops had gone, their windows bare; the hairdresser had departed, too. Only the *charcuterie* remained, but there was nobody in it.

I tried the Relais de Villerey. *Ici on joue au billard* said a notice in the window. It had, apparently, become the typical French village pool-cum-juke-box joint where you only went for cigarettes and the newspapers, never to drink sociably. I was wrong. The new management was every bit as affable as the old.

'Roland and Cliquette?!' la patronne laughed. 'Oh, they gave up the bar years ago. But they're still in town.'

If the French aristocracy had survived the guillotine, they could survive anything – even a life-style as hazardous as Roland and Cliquette's.

La patronne gave me an update, aided by her two afternoon customers who liked a good gossip. One had a sharp, weasely look about him; the other said little but chuckled frequently into his pastis.

'Roland and Cliquette are folklore,' said la patronne.

Weasel imitated Cliquette: 'Monsieur Le Marquis, she says to Roland, you drank five litres of wine yesterday.'

La patronne played Roland: 'And you, Madame la Marquise, consumed two bottles of Scotch.'

'Tell M'sieur about the breathalyser!' put in Chuckler, chuckling too much to tell me himself.

'La patronne', said Weasel, 'knows a sergeant at the Gendarmerie. The sergeant lent her a breathalyser so Roland can blow into it, to see if he's fit to walk home.'

Home was a hundred yards down the main street.

'Or sometimes he comes on horseback,' la patronne said.

'And comes off,' added Weasel.

Throughout, Chuckler had punctuated his chuckling with that eloquent gesture of drunkenness, a barely clenched fist giving a little twist in front of the nose.

On my way up the main street, I stopped at Roland and Cliquette's village house. The garage was dangerously placed; once Roland, unused to the automatic gearshift of his new car, had backed straight across the street into a neighbour's garden. Today they were not at home. In a way, I was quite relieved – I had driving to do myself. But I was happy they were still together, and evidently unaffected by the drought.

The Reynauds, now retired, had too small a farm to have suffered from it, either. No cows needing grass, just a few chickens. They greeted me at the gate with its sign *Attention aux chiens*. Where curs on rusty chains once leapt at me, one mild hen was laying an egg in the dust. Invisible doves murmured, and beyond the dilapidated front door I heard a familiar phone bell. 'Yes, we still have the public phone,' said Madame Reynaud gaily. 'But I couldn't cycle down to the Brown house these days, snow or no snow, not with my hip.'

The Brown house was unoccupied. Its red bricks reflecting low autumnal sunshine made it actually welcoming. Almost like home, dammit. Padlocked iron gates had smartly painted black-and-white spikes. Wisteria tumbled over the brick wall. I peeked through a crack in the garage: the old Rolls had gone.

A neighbour told me the Browns planned to come here often now they'd retired, and were having an architect make the place more suitable for paying guests. An architect, finally? A paying guest last August had apparently shared her bedroom with a bat; being a bat fancier, she was concerned that a ceiling planned by the architect might chase the bat out. In which case, no rental next August. The Browns must specialise in wacky tenants; the bat fancier was no more eccentric than S and I braving that gruesome winter.

I reminisced about fraught times and people with an old Villerey friend still in residence. Over the years, they had become more fraught.

The priest who married our friend's daughter had been defrocked: the lady who cleaned various second homes in the village had, for a long time, been carrying on a raging affair with the priest. She would leave him billets-doux in her missal at the church after Mass, to confirm or postpone a rendezvous. One day, another communicant took her missal by mistake, found one of the notes, and tipped off the bishop whose heavies caught the ill-starred lovers *in flagrante delicto*.

That was not the end of the church's participation in the affair. The cleaning lady had a son – not by the priest, but by another man long before. The son lived with a woman for two years, and they in turn had a child. On the same day, in the church of Villerey, the couple were married and the child baptised. Who could say the Church wasn't adapting to modern morality?

Other scandals? Well, there was now near by a château of ill repute. Advertising itself as a Bed & Breakfast, the rooms were abnormally high-priced. The double-beds came fully furnished they told me, *avec tout confort*.

And what of Pipou? He had developed an ulcer, and was put off drink. At retirement age, when a *vigneron* must either sell or rent out his vineyard to another, Pipou had no other interest in life. He began to drink again. Home was hell: wife and mother-in-law and Pipou made life impossible for each other. One of them had to go.

Pipou decided, after too many years of misery, it should be him. So one night, he just went – into his barn where he once made our wine – and hanged himself.

My uneasiness on that Loire walk had not been for nothing. My friend told other sad tales of death, drunkenness, and madness. I left Villerey-sur-Loire pleased to have renewed old acquaintances. But there was a fragility about French village life nowadays, and my happiness was tempered with melancholy.

13

Paris 14ème, 1976

'Got a load here for Mrs More,' said the cockney removal man, arriving a day early with our furniture from London.

Mademoiselle Fringue, front lady of 'Pariprop', the property developers, sleek as a mannequin, sharp as an eaglet, teetered about on perilously high heels, inspecting the last-minute paintwork and making frantic calls about absent wall-to-wall carpeting. The flat in Paris 14ème was not yet ours, the final cheque to be handed over next day, and here was a load for Mrs More.

'Bloody awful street to park in!' said our friend.

'You may be there till tomorrow,' I warned.

'I bloody won't, you know.'

The removal man, who slept in his van and cooked his own food on a primus stove ('you can't get a decent bloody meal in France'), was headed for the Dordogne with other stuff for other Brits. He was dumping ours right now – or else.

'*Pas de problème*,' said Mlle Fringue. The French are very obliging about minor illegalities, like leaving a load for Mrs More in a flat she doesn't yet own.

Mlle Fringue was more concerned – and so were we – as to why the builder had made the entrance into our open-plan kitchen so narrow one could only negotiate it sideways. I didn't fancy doing a kind of jig step every time I made a cup of coffee. The French, said Mlle Fringue apologetically, were not used to *cuisines Américaines* as open-plan kitchens are called. Well, S replied, some Americans are keen cooks and like to enter their kitchens boldly, not slither into them furtively. Some Brits, too.

Meanwhile, the removal man and his mate heaved our sofa through a window with much sweating and cursing. It was the long, sizzling summer of 1976; in July, a pig of a job. I went out and bought litres of iced Kronenbourg beer; I might have known it would be trouble. 'Anyone know where we can get a decent beer around here?' was their parting putdown.

Au revoir, England.

S and I had made a drastic decision. On 18 January 1975, a date as memorable to us as 3 August 1492 to Christopher Columbus, we had left England for France.

A middle-aged madness had us in its grip. We needed a change. Not of air or job; a change of country. And where else but France which, by now, we knew well enough to be in tune with both its discords and sweeter harmonies? We were not total innocents abroad – or so we imagined. Still in our mid-forties, we could do it; play an active part in French life; reduce possessions, increase mobility. So much for the theory. As anyone who has tried it knows, nothing is more complicated than the simple life.

It took us eighteen months to find a home.

During this peripatetic time we gypsied around in our old red Audi, loaded to the roof; stayed at Peter and Natasha Brook's near Versailles; headed for Edward and Christiane Behr's at Ramatuelle; changed tracks to Malta and my mother, now eighty-five and unwell, staying nine months to look after her; returned to an autumnal La Garde Freinet and looked after Tony Richardson's animals; looked after ourselves in a wintry Loire Valley; and, finally, came to our senses and Paris.

As driver for our Paris home-hunt, S became an intrepid tigress at the wheel of the Audi which, despite many thousands of kilometres on the clock, could still storm the Bastille and charge the Étoile: when in Paris, drive as the Parisians do. With *Le Figaro*, the house-hunter's bible, on one knee, Paris street-map on the other, I would guide us as early in the day as possible to follow up new flat ads. We zoomed into back-streets to avoid rush hour on the boulevards. We burped breakfast croissants-and-café-au-lait as garbage trucks blocked our way. We cursed and honked like civilised Parisians.

Being late has always panicked me. In Paris it worries no one. The estate agent you're meeting has fixed five rendezvous in the hour, including you, because he knows at least three will be irrevocably detained in a *périphérique* snarl-up.

'Paris is like New York,' S observed. 'The day you feel less than a hundred-per-cent, you're dead. Better not go out of the front door.'

'That's if you have a front door to go out of!'

We searched the Marais where we first encountered a ritual called the *Sur Place*. In *Le Figaro*, those magic words meant prospective purchasers were invited to view the flat between specific hours. Imagine the cocktail party crush – and without drinks. Enchanted by 'our' sixth floor terrace with the Paris rooftop view we'd dreamed about, I shoved my way through to the *marchand de biens*, the middleman in charge, flashing my French cheque-book. 'Ah, a French cheque-book, yes, but it's a foreign account,' he said doubtfully. 'I believe you, if you say you have the money, M'sieur, oh certainly, but how do I know for certain? The Bank of England . . .' An eloquent, apologetic smile and shrug. Sterling had never been so low, exchange control never so tight.

We were doing things strictly by the book, with no sneaky cache of crisp notes about the Audi's person. And, as a result, missed flat after flat, sheerly from the current bad reputation of the British reneging on deals.

French property dealers were as sharp as any. When it came to foreigners, they reckoned wealthy Lebanese refugees with a stash of hot francs were a far better choice than us.

From vertiginous perches in the fifth arrondissement to convertible rag-trade warehouses in the second we hurtled. *Poutres apparentes* and *plein sud sur vert* were the big come-ons; nothing with beams facing south over gardens emerged. Most flats were dark, some were damp, one in Rue de Verneuil had no windows at all. If they were ever just what we wanted, like the eighteenth-century marvel in Les Halles or the charming, what-could-be-the-problem snip on Quai des Grands Augustins, somebody always pipped us to the *compromis*, that first magical document which binds vendor and purchaser to the sale, no gazumping and no backing out.

After one particularly fraught day of failing to find parking spaces, missing rendezvous with agents, losing the perfect flat by seconds, we drove the car on to the pavement of Rue Lalande in the Fourteenth, fed up and not giving a damn if we got a ticket. S put her head in her hands and wept, uncontrollably, for London. A moment of unbearable homesickness, missing our daughters, friends, Branston Pickle, and the *Evening Standard*.

'What are we doing here?' S wailed.

'Starting a new life,' I said bitterly.

'We left England more than a year ago!'

'Let's go back.'

We decided to look at just one more flat. It turned out to be the one.

In the Fourteenth, a very mixed south Paris arrondissement, which includes Montparnasse, the apartment comprised a bedroom and living-room altogether about the size of our old drawing-room in London. Remember those witty Roy Brooks house ads in London? 'Hardly room to swing a dwarf.' This was us. We just had no idea how Parisians lived: every square metre was carefully measured and had its astronomical price. From five floors in NW1 we'd settled for sixty square metres in the Fourteenth. A *pot de confiture* as Parisians called it.

Funds were not only limited by exchange control; from the sale of our house, we also had to buy a London apartment for our daughters, just starting careers of their own.

But we loved our jampot.

We looked out on to the second courtyard of what used to be a *maison de passe* now converted into three apartment blocks. Ours was in an elegant three-storey Directoire building with a slate-tiled roof and *oeil de boeuf*. We occupied the whole middle floor. The small courtyard was planted with young shrubs and trees, where sparrows soon found a perch and began singing. No sound of traffic penetrated it. Opposite, maghrébin workmen were painting the middle building; the summer's intense heat, the dazzling whiteness of the façade's paint, the rich blue of the shutters and the bursts of Arabic quarter-tone singing made us feel we were in Sidi Bou Said.

Nothing could have been more Parisian than the neighbourhood, however. Nor the people who lived in it. One of our first calls was from Jacques Démy, director of *The Umbrellas of Cherbourg*. I had first encountered the Fourteenth working with Jacques in the Seventies. But I was so wedded to my much-loved Hôtel d'Alsace in Rue des Beaux-Arts that the charms of the Hôtel Daguerre eluded me, and I quickly moved – from the very quartier I would one day come to live in!

Jacques and his wife, Agnès Varda, occupied a house (scarce in central Paris) a few blocks from us up Rue Daguerre. I had spent good times there. The house was cosy with cats and children playing and the smell of cooking, while across the back-yard was the cutting-room of husband and wife, both movie directors. I have several times experienced this close (but far from closed) 'family' feeling in the French movie business. Agnès considered auditioning me for the part of a shitty London adman who has an affair with a young Paris student. Then she decided against it: 'You are not quite shitty enough, Julian,' she said in all seriousness. This was *cinéma vérité* time, and I wondered what I could do to prove her wrong. Punch a clochard? Kick a poodle? Rob a nun? It was the 'enough' that rankled.

Friends from New York and London were in shock at the smallness of our flat, and our car, a Renault 5. It was hard for them to understand that living and motoring space were not status symbols; well-to-do Parisians often lived in and drove the tiniest for convenience. You hardly ever got to see their homes, let alone drive in their cars. Entertaining was mostly in restaurants, travel by cab or Métro – safe by New York's standards, clean by London's.

On the rare occasion a hostess did her stuff, it was crystal and dazzling white and the family silver out, probably an outside cook, and the hostess would pretend she'd totally forgotten the menu. 'Ah – duck with peaches!' she'd exclaim as this familiar stand-by made yet another appearance. At eleven o'clock prompt, the uniformed rent-a-maid entered with *le jus d'orange 'foutez-le-camp!'* (the piss-off orange juice), and the guests duly pissed off. Food and wine could be delicious or disastrous, but was served as though the President himself were expected.

We entertained at home but less grandly – like Londoners. Maximum six guests sitting down to chicken roasted with forty cloves of garlic, or twenty balancing plates of Persian lamb polo on their knees. Rich fish terrines, succulent oysters, and fresh home-made pasta from the Daguerre market around the corner meant meals were simple to put together. Guests invariably arrived with gifts of wine or champagne, flowers, or a Lenôtre gâteau. It was a charming Paris habit.

S and I were rejuvenated by the Fourteenth. There was a glori-ous sense of irresponsibility about our *pot de confiture* – like being students again. And students we became. We signed on for a French phonetics course at the Sorbonne with Natasha Parry who, for acting parts in France, also wanted to improve her accent. The best thing about it was our student cards which got us reduced prices at the movies. Once, when we went with Peter Brook, Natasha's husband, I found myself asking for 'Three students and an adult, please'.

The trouble is, you improve your French accent without the vocabulary and grammar to go with it, and Parisians machine-gun you with words, unable to understand why you're struck dumb. In any case I soon lost that elusive *u* again and my *é* invariably came out *eh*.

Parisian friends with good English seemed reluctant to talk it in France, which was good for our French. Most couldn't understand our move: 'Don't you miss that marvellous cheap lamb?' they asked. 'Don't you pine for pedestrian crossings where the cars actually stop?' 'Aren't you fed up with the rudeness and negativity, everyone saying *Non* before they grant you a grudging *C'est possible?*'

'*Non*,' was our answer to all of them.

Even bureaucrats could be surprisingly civilised. A French friend told us the reason: governments may come and go, but the admin-istration is the backbone of the country. Want a bridge built or a high-speed Métro? No problem. Want a new law drafted? Tomorrow, Monsieur le Ministre de Justice. In France, parents actually *want* their children to be civil servants; and the colleges that elevate them to the mighty status of *haut fonctionnaire* are every bit as prestigious as Oxford or Yale. The Olympian, cultivated dis-tinction of the top echelons filters down to the rank and file. At the most forbiddingly bureaucratic office, a sourpuss will suddenly become wreathed in smiles.

'Oh, you're a writer!' beamed one at the Préfecture when I

grappled with my first foreign resident's permit. *Cartes de séjour* were not given lightly, not even to members of the European Community. At that time, one was required to queue up outside Paris police HQ on the Ile de la Cité, then wait interminably with the rest of the Third World in drab waiting-rooms, praying one had the right certificates of good health and financial stability and had filled in the forms in correct French. One slip of a gender, and you're back at the end of the line.

So I was pleased to find myself deemed a desirable alien. In England, admit to being a writer and they say: 'Yes, but what do you do for a living?' She loved writers, she said. She loved literature, and '*la comédie musicale, c'est super. J'adore Gene Killy . . .*' Further discussion of Gene Killy was interrupted by one of her colleagues shouting at a mild, bespectacled black man who had failed to comprehend some finer point of French hospitality. To my surprise, the black man yelled back. I wouldn't have dared. In France everyone knows their rights and exercises them even when palpably in the wrong.

'*Ah, c'est pas facile, notre boulot,*' sighed my friend. 'People give us a hard time.'

'Which nationality gives you the hardest?'

'Guess.'

'The Lebanese?' The refugees were often rich so, I imagined, would expect privileged treatment.

'No – the British and Americans. They believe we should give them a *carte de séjour* – just like that, and no questions asked.'

I crept away gratefully with my permit's progress in good hands.

Foreign resident's permits had to be renewed yearly. Then, if you'd been a good resident, three-yearly. And then ten-yearly. Once I forgot to renew mine. I imagined myself in prison waiting to be charged. Instead, I learned another useful aspect of the administration and a phrase to go with it: *faire jouer le piston* – to use clout. This was indeed possible, because I just happened to be working on a musical, *Roza*, with French composer Gilbert Bécaud. And one of Gilbert's lyric writers just happened to be Louis Amade who also happened to be Préfet of Paris. Only in France could a chief of justice also be a distinguished poet.

This time I was greeted at the Préfecture rather differently, making a most stately progress. From a saluting sergeant at the gate to a receptionist; from the receptionist to a grander receptionist; from the grander receptionist to a kind of butler in operetta uniform; from the butler to a secretary; from the secretary to Monsieur Le Préfet in his tricolour sash whom I remembered not to call 'Louis'; from Monsieur Le Préfet back to his secretary and thence downwards, bearing my valuable papers.

Some French problems seem insoluble by any method. Neither clout, bribes, nor kissing the President's feet would have helped sort out the hassles with our apartment.

Pariprop had won a prize for 1974's best conversion of an old Paris building, and Mlle Fringue's suave demeanour inspired confidence. The team of Israeli electricians, Arab builders, and Portuguese plumbers were hard at it completing the other apartments until one day . . . they vanished. No more cheery singing. Just the birds.

Later, Mlle Fringue arrived with the architect, Monsieur Foutu, who wore a bottle-green velvet jacket and floppy, artistic hat to make himself look interesting. They came teetering over the open drains to tell us that the *chef d'entreprise* had gone bankrupt.

'Does this often happen?' I asked.

'*C'est pas normal*,' Monsieur Foutu assured me. Which signified it was happening every day.

'Well,' said S, 'it's not much fun traipsing through a building site every time we go out.'

'Do not worry yourself, Madame,' Mlle Fringue gushed. 'I'm doing my best to find other builders.'

'We'd certainly appreciate that,' I said.

'*C'est normal*.'

Which meant it would instantly go to the bottom of her priority list. But at least we'd learned the nuances of *C'est pas normal* and *C'est normal*. Useful phrases which we quickly put into practice.

For our troubles were only beginning. We later found Monsieur Foutu had forgotten the sound-proofing of the lift and the damp-proofing of the building. Our walls, impeccable at first, gradually became damper and damper, until they ended up positively dripping.

'*C'est pas normal*,' I told Monsieur Foutu. Which meant I knew this happened every time he put pen to architect's paper.

Monsieur Foutu did not look in the least bit worried. He had just come back from receiving an award in Cannes. Mlle Fringue was going yachting with a top politician next day, and already wore a sailor suit with a nautical cap.

'We will put everything in order,' she cooed.

'*C'est normal*,' S cooed back. Which meant she knew Mlle Fringue would do fuck all but lie on the poopdeck bronzing her body at St-Trop' for the next two months.

We and the other flat owners sued Pariprop. Whole bevies of experts of both parties went through our apartments, endlessly taking measurements and pushing humidity-meters into walls, murmuring 'How can you live in such conditions, Madame!' or 'What a charming conversion!' depending on whose side they were.

After a chain of buck-passing, the lawsuit began. It was, we discovered, a yawningly common event. Eighty per cent of Paris apartment-owners are in litigation at one time or another, and our case with its mind-boggling complications was won, everyone agreed, astonishingly quickly. It took eleven years.

'Do you still like living in Paris?' our friends asked, a shade maliciously and with increasing incredulity as we kept saying 'Yes'. Each time a little less convincingly.

At dodgy moments, nothing cured homesickness like a visit to La Coupole, ten minutes' walk down Boulevard Raspail. Strange, because Paris is a city with American cultural associations, not British. And nowhere more so than the bright lights of the Fourteenth's border with the Sixth – the Boulevard Montparnasse, and its café-restaurants with the ghosts of Scott and Zelda partying, Henry rumbustious and Gertrude queening it; Le Select, Le Dôme, and La Closerie des Lilas where a steak named after Ernest Hemingway is still served.

In early summer, when the lime-blossom defeats the most potent carbon-monoxide, how joyous was that walk to La Coupole. Everywhere shades of Paris past: Kiki, the artist's model, friend of the Japanese painter Foujita and the American photographer Man Ray said, 'All the peoples on earth have pitched their tent here, and yet it's like one big family.'

And they still seemed to congregate at La Coupole. S and I felt totally at home. Its noise and vigour, its vast, seedy space and comedy to get a table were part of the fun; no reservations, you just had to stand in line. Officially, that is; in fact, a dapper, grey pin-striped Maitre d' would respond to a note slipped into his hand and seek us out in the bar when our table was ready.

When the food finally came, the waiters more or less flung it at us. But they were invariably good-humoured and once S was presented with a complete table setting – plates, knives and forks – as a souvenir.

Our spirits restored by *céleri remoulade* and *steak au poivre* among the ghosts of the famous, we would repair to the gravestones of the famous. A place of peace and quiet, when the hassle of Paris became too much, was the Montparnasse Cemetery.

Just round the corner, it was our nearest spot of greenery. S and I strolled down alleys shaded by maples, judas trees and sycamores, eyes skimming the names. Some were on noble family tombs like miniature houses – Classical, Gothic, or Renaissance; others, more famous but less ostentatious, had simple slabs – like the Montparnasse locals, sculptor Zadkine, painter Soutine, and Dadaist poet Tristan Zara.

One grave was itself a work of art. Brancusi's own 1910 funerary stele entitled 'The Kiss' commemorates him in sculpture surprisingly erotic for a cemetery.

Charles Baudelaire, too, had a fitting monument. Superbly decadent, a stone corpse lies shrouded up to the neck. Atop a plinth, Baudelaire rises symbolically from the dead, hollow-eyed, shock-haired, gazing wearily into the future. 'I have more memories than if I were a thousand years old,' wrote the poet in *Spleen*. One could believe it.

Since we came to the Fourteenth, another grave has been added to the list of the dead and famous. Or rather two in one: in 1980 Jean-Paul Sartre was buried beneath a simple stone slab, to be joined six years later by his lifelong companion, Simone de Beauvoir. In life, her feminism decreed they live separately, only to be together in death.

S and I had been touched by the popular magnitude of Sartre's funeral. Along Avenue Général Leclerc, totally cleared of cars, the cortège slowly moved towards Boulevard Raspail. Where the Liberation Army had once drawn cheers, now the cortège moved in silence, thousands of people following to the cemetery. I felt a sudden link with the past; Sartre had seemed outdated, upstaged by more recent fashionable philosophers, yet here he was drawing the crowds again, many his former students, some with their children or grandchildren on their shoulders.

Generations of French thinkers have come and gone – from Pascal and Descartes to Bernard-Henri Levy and André Glucksmann. Behind one thinker, another lurks – with but a single thought: how to destroy his rival. Public polemic between philosophers fuels the regenerative process. The trouble is, today's philosopher must be media conscious: if you can't sell your philosophy on a TV book show, forget it. Hence a slight dampening of French intellectual ardour where the image counts more than the word.

But France is about fashion, and fashions change. Philosophers surely will have star funerals again. In other countries, it is only the royals and generals and political leaders who get the red-carpet exit; France respects its thinkers at least as much as its great chefs and couturiers. It is part of La France's inherently feminine drive: *La Pensée, La Cuisine, La Mode*. The thinkers, chefs and couturiers may be men, but the fashion is made by women. Marianne, the national symbol of France, is a woman, and Frenchmen even at their most macho would have no other. While John Bull and Uncle Sam are unequivocally male.

The Fourteenth seemed to us an eclectic microcosm of the best Paris had to offer. It infected us with its vitality. Though we could never again use 'Gay' Paree to mean what it used to, the Rue de la Gaîté spoke for the quartier's origins.

In the seventeenth century, mean Queen Margot booted university students from their equivalent of the Cambridge 'Backs', down by the Seine at Clerk's Meadow, where they improvised verse, drank too much, and rampaged randily. So they headed south, up the hill which they called Mount Parnassus after Apollo's mountain, and found space and peace to continue improvising verse, drinking too much, and rampaging randily – with no pig of a queen to interfere with their human rights.

Many lodged in windmills; the ruins of one can still be seen in the cemetery. Taverns, bawdy-houses, and dance-halls proliferated. The cancan and polka originated there. Puccini based *La Bohème* on life in the quartier. In 1824, the official opening of the cemetery drew protests from the neighbouring Rue de la Gaîté, its inhabitants afraid of a killjoy backlash. Quite the reverse. After paying their respects to the dead, mourners could have a good old wake in the wild street next door.

Since we came to the Fourteenth in 1976, things have changed in some parts, in others hardly at all. Many narrow, dark, crumbling streets of great atmosphere and dubious salubrity have been bulldozed to make way for the Maine-Montparnasse development. Over Rue de la Gaîté looms Paris's one eccentric skyscraper, La Tour Montparnasse, and the monolithic railway station block for the TGV-Atlantique. In the 1980s, Parisian yuppies fought for apartments in Spanish architect Bofill's neo-classical complex – two crescents, all smoked glass and colonnades with a valuable space of green grass (rare in Paris) for the children.

As rents rose, artists and writers and trendsetters fled to the upcoming Bastille area, and are probably ready to move on again from there. Small shops closed. The once thriving Breton community round Gare Montparnasse has all but gone, their friendly *crêperies* giving way to le fast-food.

And Jacques Démy, another familiar Breton of the quartier has also gone – a victim of leukaemia. Agnès Varda, living separately from him for several years, had been working on a film about his wartime childhood *Jacquot de Nantes* which was a popular success in 1991 and featured Jacques playing himself shortly before his death. Faced with his own mortality and memories of the terrible Nantes air-raids, Jacques speaks simply and directly to the camera: 'I hate violence.' Only in France, I believe, could a wife pay tribute to her husband on film, the way she knew best. It is a most touching epitaph.

Also disappeared from our street is Madame Germaine, the concierge next door. A particular friend, like all good concierges (and not all are good, some even spying on their employers for the police or tax inspectors), Madame Germaine knew everyone, and had a most enchanting smile. In her dressing-gown in the street or from her ground-floor bedroom window as her legs got worse, she would greet us. Then quite suddenly, the windows were permanently shuttered.

Old Parisian ladies are known for their fierce determination to squeeze the last drop out of life. There is, however, a pecking order. '*Excusez-moi*,' hissed the old lady, pushing past S at the Uniprix checkout. 'I have priority. I am seventy-nine.' Whereupon another old lady, spry as a bird, hopped to the head of the queue croaking 'But, Madame, I am eighty-five!'

Come hell and high-rise, the landmarks of the Fourteenth survive: the mighty Lion of Belfort's statue still graces Place Denfert-Rochereau; a tree-lined avenue leads to the eighteenth-century Hôpital Rochefoucauld; we can walk the paths of the Parc Montsouris with its Belle Époque pavilions and cedars of Lebanon, the wide, welcoming pavements of Boulevard Raspail, and across Place Mouton Duvenet where old men play *boules* whatever the weather.

The Fourteenth is certainly cleaner. Thanks to Jacques Chirac, the city's mayor, ingenious municipal motorised pooper-scoopers clean the dog-shit from the pavements. The French have even more pets per capita than the British, so provision is made for their rights by politicians and restaurateurs alike. Like all French, they know their rights. Paris dogs still eat at table in certain restaurants, but they have never much taken to Baron Haussmann's well-watered gutters.

From our more or less shit-free doorstep, we now have half a dozen good new eating places, five minutes' walk away; some forty cinemas, fifteen minutes' walk away; and Roissy airport check-in for trips to London and the States, sixty minutes by high-speed Métro.

'Is there anything you miss?' I asked S.

'I do sometimes miss tea.'

'You can get Earl Grey.'

'I mean', S continued, 'at the Albanian bookshop.'

Astonishingly, this was once the only place we knew of with a photocopier. S used to go there, and the proprietor would give her a cup of tea while he laboriously copied on a machine which was primitive enough to be Albanian. The communist tracts were totally unbrowsable, so S was glad of her tea and conversation with the proprietor.

'Just been doing my tax returns,' S said.

'Ah, Madame, none of us is spared,' the proprietor sighed, puffing philosophically on his pipe. Long before the demise of European communism he went out of business. It was a portent.

In a neighbourhood like ours, few things and people seem permanent. Like Paris itself, where eighty-five per cent of the population is from elsewhere, the Fourteenth was a good stop-over for a couple of nights or a couple of generations. Then move on . . .

Of our original apartment neighbours, only the Carons remain. Alain used to be cultural attaché at the French embassy in Mexico City. Exceptionally for Paris neighbours whom you very seldom get to know, he and his wife Mylène entertained us royally on a visit to Mexico in 1977. Mylène drove us everywhere, showed us everything, and invited us to accompany them on a visit to Oaxaca where we were guests of the Alliance Française. Now Alain has the Quebec desk at Quai d'Orsay, and looks a little greyer, a little more distinguished, when we meet him buying fish in the market.

Making friends of all kinds, we cherished a pleasant illusion of France's classlessness. Away from the Jockey Club, miniskirted ninety-year-old duchesses and the powerhouse meritocracy, nobody cares what school you went to as long as what you do and think and say interests them. For the first time in my life, my accent did not mark me; it was just a bad French one. And what S and I missed of British eccentricity, we appreciated in French individuality.

We made a new friend.

Sylvain is an habitué of Le Vin des Rues, one of the many new bistrots that have appeared over the years. Must try that, we kept saying, and didn't. Well, thanks to Sylvain, finally we did. You won't find it in Patricia Wells or Gault-Millau. Le patron, Jean Chanrion, prefers it that way – a rubicund bear of a man with a bristling red moustache who cooks, delivers your plate, and cuts off the mildest complaint with an amiable riposte on the lines of 'If you don't like it, get lost.'

Monsieur Chanrion refers to himself modestly as a *cafetier* – café owner. There the modesty ends. He was awarded the Cup for the Best Jug, 1989. And his reputation for good, cheap wine had already reached us.

S and I, passing by one day, watched him meticulously chalking up his dishes of the day, preceded by a few words of apposite history. 'Today we celebrate St-Eloi, patron saint of gourmets, who has two saint's days a year' heralded *Tripes Provençales* and *Saucissons chauds aux pommes de terre à l'huile* on the blackboard.

Service does not begin till one. How could we guess that? Everywhere else it begins at twelve. It was twelve-twenty. Clearly one could not reserve. As we stood by the bar debating what to do, I had the uneasy feeling of being in a club of which one is not a member.

A 'member' perched on a bar stool nearest the bar, monitoring our quandary, said in English: 'Why not stay and have a drink with me till lunchtime?' Sylvain was a Fourteenth man: grey beard, eyes matching his flush which matched the small glass jug of wine on the marble-topped counter, a miniature dog peering at us with big eyes from the jacket of his blue denim suit.

'A *chien de race* – how do you say that in English?'

'Pedigree.'

'Twelve years old . . .'

'Must be a female,' S said, pointing to the dog's diamante-bound topknot.

'A female?! Madame, this is a *fille!*' Sylvain could have meant daughter, girlfriend or tart – anyway, no mere female.

Sylvain was surprised we were English; our casual clothes looked American, he thought. When I said they *were* American, he nearly fell off his bar stool. Even the brightest Frenchmen still believe an Englishman should wear a bowler and carry a rolled umbrella. Especially to the club.

Who were the other 'members', I asked? A dozen were propping up the bar. Were they waiting for lunch, too? No, they were just the serious drinkers like him. Sylvain pointed out a dentist and surgeon. Getting themselves good and primed for an afternoon of tooth extraction and organ transplant, no doubt.

'That's what I like about this place,' Sylvain said. 'It's a mixture

of people.' He pointed out a Welsh jailbird at the far end of the
bar.

In no time, Sylvain had 'proposed' us to le patron and we were
elected without a seconder. Contrary to expectations, a reservation
card with our name was put on one of the tiny tables. When we
asked Sylvain to join us, he declined: 'A waste of good drinking
time.'

The table was so small, the communal terrine dish straddled the
gap between ours and our neighbours' to the right; our bottle of
much-needed Badoit was on our neighbour's table to the left. This
necessitated clubability. London friends had their Groucho or
Garrick, we had Le Vin des Rues. None was famous for its food.
But, ah, the chilled red wine of the Lyonnais! Jean Chanrion certainly deserved his award for that.

The Fourteenth is no place for the thin-skinned or weak-
fleshed. Shopping at the Rue Daguerre market could be as much
of a challenge as Le Vin des Rues. Parisian street vendors, when
quality or price is questioned, can come on with the droll riposte
or black impatience. Mostly, it's merely a tease but a tough one to
take if you're a novice. At first, S used to ask for things at the
wrong stall, and earn ironic rebukes like, '*Mais non, Madame, nous
ne sommes pas une maison à gingembre!*' The lugubrious bloodhound
of a herb-lady looked at us with the same chilly contempt, winter
and summer: how could we possibly imagine a stall selling fresh
coriander and lemons was a 'ginger-shop'?

Ears ringing with the raucous chorus of street cries, arms aching
from laden shopping baskets, we would take our very small
remaining change to an outside table of Le Rallye. Huge barrels
adorn the street: it is one of the few genuine old wine bars left in
Paris. (*Spécialité vin de propriété depuis 1910.*)

Bernard Péret and family run this market meeting place of Le
Tout Daguerre, among whom we now include ourselves. Here
you don't have to be a 'member'. Just devoted to the brown-bread
sandwiches of country ham and a choice of hard-to-find really
good Beaujolais. Péret's Morgon and Chiroubles are my
favourites; S, who only drinks white, goes for a Loire Quincy; and
we sit watching our world, once strange, now familiar, go by.

One figure in the landscape is disturbingly motionless.

On the paving stones opposite sits a young man of about twenty, head lowered. *J'AI FAIM* says the sign in front of the lad, able-bodied, with the numb expression of the long unemployed. Among Rue Daguerre's abundance, his hunger has a special resonance of sadness.

Luckier are those who play an instrument; good street musicians can scrape together a living of sorts, for Parisians are generous to talent. A girl accordionist enlivens our Métro station with *bal musette* tunes, and her cap jingles with falling coins.

The street cries of the market vendors join with the music. Paraguayan flutes and drums vying with jazz saxophones and nostalgic Barbary organs playing '*Sous les Toits de Paris*' and (especially for us?) '*Avec Les Anges*' from *Irma La Douce*. And then a Piaf song, unaccompanied, the gutsy girl's voice rising above the other music in a blood-warming crescendo.

No, no regrets . . .

14

Enclave des Papes, 1979

Man is like a tree in the land where the mistral blows: putting down roots is more than just digging your hole. There are the elements of nature and the gods to contend with. And never before living in the Midi had I been so exposed to their assault course of the senses.

It was dawn. The lizards were up before me. So were the mice. And some unidentifiable beast was clogdancing on the roof tiles.

'Could that be a badger?' S suggested.

'Sounds bigger,' I yawned. It was a very short yawn. Suddenly I had become an early riser, flinging the shutters wide to let in the perfumes of that first summer – genista and wild thyme and sun-scorched grass.

Another cloudless day. We were far from blasé about it. A cool freshness accompanied the light show on the horizon – indigo, pink, orange, gold; we relished the stillness and the morning shock of our big distances before the heat haze obscured them; across the valley of the Ouvèze and the jagged silhouette of the Dentelles hills.

The creature on the roof stopped dancing. And S identified the bird singing in the silence as the nightingale which continues long after the rising of the sun, sometimes in harmony with the cuckoo. It sang on all through breakfast on the terrace.

Terrace? Hardly, yet. A patch of beaten earth on the edge of a scrubby, burned-up meadow alive with wild flowers and poppies, on which an old white table held our café au lait, toast, and peaches. We lazed in canvas chairs, indolent as the lizard which slipped in and out of a crack in the wall.

'D'you think that crack's dangerous?' S asked.

'I like it,' I said.

'So does the lizard. Let's leave it like that.'

It was our justification for not spending a franc too much on the old house. It had, for us, the right romantic dilapidation, its stone covered in worn buff ochre plaster. The ochre comes from deposits on Mont Ventoux, so that buildings blend with the surrounding land, in our case Côtes-du-Rhône vineyard slopes. We decided not to strip that traditional plaster to reveal the stones, as was the fashion in second homes. Overdone restoration had begun to chi-chi the character out of country and village house to conform with the *Maison et Jardin* idea of the simple life. Hence a desperate rivalry between owners as to whose house could look the most simple most expensively.

The house itself, facing south, with no windows on its northern, mistral-facing side, was nothing special — a classic Midi farmhouse with few refinements. It had once contained two families — plus animals which kept them warm in winter, when temperatures could plummet to $-15°C$. But the view . . . Across the Rhône Valley to the mountains of the Ardèche, down over Avignon to the Alpilles hills, from the bottom of the garden to Mont Ventoux, from the ridge behind the house to the Midi's northern borders with the rest of France. We were, literally, on top of the world.

From this perch, we could see our village below, nestling perfectly between a V of wooded slopes. Our spur became a hog's-back and continued rising, so there we were at the very beginning of the Alps; the land did not become flat again till the northern Italian plains.

The Italians have a good word, *campenilismo*, which describes how a village decides who is a foreigner and who is a local: if you can't see his place of origin from the church bell-tower, he's a foreigner. Our village church has a delicate wrought-iron structure round its bell, to let the wind howl through unimpeded, like other villages of the Enclave des Papes. The popes, at first foreigners themselves, had brought with them the spirit of *campenilismo*.

In 1309 Pope Clement V had decamped from Rome, owing to

rival factions which made life in the Vatican too hazardous; popes remained in Avignon till 1377. And no body, in its peregrinations around the world, is more adept at putting together a nice folio of real estate than the Catholic Church. Our nearest market town, Valréas, and the surrounding villages had been sold to the Papal Court as a cool summer resort by the Dauphin, much to the annoyance of his father, King Charles of France. The Italian poet-in-residence, Petrarch, never one to mince his words, called Avignon 'a sewer which collects all the garbage of the universe'; exhausted by too much Châteauneuf-du-Pape and wild, wild women and the gruelling heat of an Avignon summer, Church dignitaries would dry out with the lighter wines and peasant girls of the Enclave des Papes. To this day, in our village, fine houses once inhabited by cardinals adorn Rue des Nobles.

France did not get the Enclave des Papes back until 1791, following post-Revolution unification of its territories. In the new departmental structure it remained part of Vaucluse which incorporated the former papal lands. So on the map there's this tiny island of Vaucluse plonked down in the Drôme – and anyone from outside it is an *étranger*. Stranger and foreigner are the same word in French.

We felt better about that. Our plumber from Tulette, Drôme, a few kilometres away was a foreigner, too.

It wasn't that our village was intentionally closed, and certainly not hostile; it was a prosperous Côtes-du-Rhône village, efficiently run by a Communist mayor who was also a school-teacher. It did not need tourists except a passing trade of wine-buyers in the Cave Coopérative, nor foreigners except maghrébin labourers for the vineyards, augmented by Spanish harvesters at the *vendange*. The maghrébins kept very much to themselves and as the village's only Brits, so did we.

We had come here not knowing a soul, just mysteriously drawn to the Enclave by happenstance.

In that first winter our solitude seemed not to matter. After all, this was a second home; we came as often as possible from Paris, braving death by Autoroute du Soleil or seven hours' train journey to Orange. Fixing the place up took all our time; bruised fingers from badly aimed hammers could not have coped with dinner parties. Now, in summer, we felt like sharing our idyll with more than just our lizards and clogdancing badger.

Midi novelist Henri Bosco wrote, encouragingly: 'There is no solitude when the earth is full of gods.'

And we were never lonely. Now the winter hibernation was over and people emerged from their battened-down state, the visits of neighbours became more frequent. We knew not to push it; nothing is more unwelcome than the hearty foreigner going native and trying to be one of the boys in the local bar. Meridionals, though far from dour, are reserved. René, our nearest neighbour, put out feelers, paying tentative calls. Then one day he demolished half a bottle of pastis with me before lunch and laid down the law about how to plant vines to shade our future terrace. We were in.

'Never buy vines from Jannot!' he advised. 'He's a bandit!'

We agreed. Jannot had already sold us a beautiful full-grown parasol pine with a massive root-ball but failed to secure it sufficiently against the wind. We had dreamed of the soughing of a gentle breeze in the green needles and the smell of resin. We arrived home one day to find it wrenched from the ground, its guy-ropes snapped. It had been our first planting of roots and augured badly.

The friendship of René and his wife, Sylvie, restored our confidence. By the end of the summer, René had established himself as unofficial guardian of the house, firing his hunting gun over the heads of trespassers; hikers caught sunbathing naked in our meadow disappeared bare-bottomed into the vines as the shots rang out.

Other neighbours, also vineyard owners, appeared.

One was Benoit who sold us a stack of green firewood which had to be coaxed into flame with doses of paraffin. Benoit was a communist millionaire who ploughed back his agricultural profits into comfortable modern villas to rent out, while he and his family lived in a spartan decor of hard chairs, lino and plastic. His only son jumped off his tractor to greet us, smiling loopily and scratching his balls regardless of the company. Madame Benoit would kill a rabbit in front of us with her bare hands and skin it still warm. One Sunday, she paid us a social call wearing a flowery dress but no stockings. I shall never forget the sight of her hairy legs emerging from a brand new Citroën Pallas; one would have thought a faun was coming to tea.

Another neighbour, Monsieur Castelli, greeted us most amiably with a casual discussion of the summer's dryness. This led to most disquieting news. Our well, he said, was only eleven metres deep. Yes, we saïd, we knew that. Eleven metres, Monsieur Castelli warned, was not deep enough. Not where we lived.

'So we could run out of water?' S asked, braver than me at hearing the worst.

'*Pardi!*' Castelli exclaimed as though it were a fait accompli. He also warned us about the dangers of the track to our house with its steep bank down to the vineyard below. Then, quite suddenly he fell into his own thoughts, speaking half to himself, barely concerned about the presence of strangers, 'and he came off the track, *le pauvre*. He had lost an eye and had no perspective.'

A tractor, we discovered, had toppled over the edge; its driver had been crushed to death. It was hard to imagine such a fate on our glorious lane lined with genista bushes. The tractor-driver had been a close friend of Castelli's.

Gradually, we awoke from the romantic dream foreigners have of the Midi, and began to touch the reality of its emotions – as strong and intense as its sunlight.

Further up the hill lived the Duvals, a family of *pieds noirs*, once prosperous French farmers in Algeria. After Independence, they had left their lands with hardly time to pack one small suitcase each. Later, arriving in the Enclave des Papes, they scraped together enough to buy a parcel of land which they planted with vines – and started again from zero. Max Duval, who had left Algeria aged seventeen, was still bitter. 'Don't get him started on that!' warned his tall, blonde wife Adrienne. He spoke four languages including Arabic, and saw in us a safety-valve, other foreigners to talk to. 'We thought we were French. But when we moved here after Independence, we soon found out differently. At school, my French schoolmates joked that we ate Arab babies. The first thing I learned in France was to use my fists.'

Max, like René, was always forthcoming with a tractor or stronger arm than mine to dig a drain or plant a tree. Other

étrangers emerged. No one was more foreign in the Midi than a
Parisian, and Parisians of British origin like us were on a par with a
Parisian of Madagascan origin like Bruno. Bruno had dropped out
of a colonial background to be a landscape gardener, while his wife
Isabelle set up as the region's youngest and most attractive lawyer.
A Portia in the Midi can come in handy, especially when a squab-
ble about property or water clouds the halcyon scene. Bruno and
Isabelle were the new-style French couple, both looking after the
children, she going out to work, he cooking for the *Maître*'s return
from Assizes in Valence.

Bruno and S spent much time planning the transformation of
our wilderness into a garden. A tall cypress hedge would protect us
from the mistral. There would be the classic dry garden plants –
santolina, rosemary, lavender, every imaginable herb, oleander,
buddleia, cistus, plumbago, euphorbia. Roses and virginia creeper
would cover the tattier spaces of our façade, bees and butterflies
dance around the plants. New tastes for the table, new perfumes
for the air would be ours. And, wonder of wonders, a water-
sprinkled lawn planted with mulberry and maple and olive trees
around a pool invisible from the house.

But all these marvels were far, far in the future. Hadn't
Monsieur Castelli warned us about the inadequacy of our well?

The strange experiences began.

In Valréas, S happened upon an eighty-year-old carpenter prepared to take us on, '*Mes Parisiens*,' Monsieur Eydoux called us
affectionately. I used to love the woody smell of his workshop, his
slow, methodical pace, an old craftsman's preservation of energy
for the job in hand. And we badly needed a stairway to our bedroom.

Not too hot on priorities, Monsieur Eydoux first made us a
balustrade for the living-room mezzanine. I collected it and him
and his tools at his workshop. He thought nothing of sitting astride
the balustrade in the back of our Renault 5, his birdlike body balancing it for the journey. He worked with me as his apprentice the
whole day long, installing the balustrade, chipping away at stone,
drilling, hammering, and generally exhausting himself. 'Never do
that again!' his family reprimanded him. 'Not even for your
Parisians!'

So next time, with the wooden stairway finally complete in his workshop, I was on my own. Monsieur Eydoux lent me his tools and told me to get on with it. 'You will install it,' he said calmly. 'With no trouble.' I am, on the whole, a cack-handed handyman. Under Monsieur Eydoux's guidance, something inspired me, and I installed the stairway with the old man's tools, with neither swearing nor visible signs of stress.

'What happened to you?' S asked in amazement.

'I don't know,' I said. 'It was like someone else was doing the work.'

It did not happen again. But new other-worldly feelings began to manifest themselves. Our living-room, which had been the barn for a couple of oxen until well into the Fifties, had a magnificent stone manger. We took it out to make more space, but it belonged to the house. To jettison it would have been to upset the household gods. So it became a garden seat – a seat which always emanates a sense of tranquillity.

Then came an unusual guardian of the house.

One day, S went to get the car out of the garage and returned, her tan reduced to a pasty dun of terror.

'There's the most enormous . . .' Words failed her. She stammered a hissing sound, and it didn't take much to guess. From the wood stacked at the end of the garage had emerged a snake, several metres long, lifting up its head as though indignantly sniffing the car fumes. This was its domain, and we found every excuse not to use the car for the next few days. Until neighbours started telling us how fortuitous was its presence: the grass snake was harmless and, what's more, lived on mice.

'Leave him be,' they said. 'A snake is good luck.'

So we let him have his domain. And neither the car nor the firewood was stolen. Nor did we ever have a mouse in the house.

The *genius loci* was very powerful – and, on the whole, benevolent. When the moon was full, I walked along the ridge behind the house; there had once been a Roman encampment and burial ground above the vineyards where René, with his tractor, turned up shards of broken waterpipe identified as Roman. As I approached, a buzzing in my ears began; it did not come from the dark side of the moon, the vibrations were resonant of a life going

on in that fertile earth, passing on its continuity like the seasons of
the year in their cycle of birth-life-death. From Roman soldiers to
me, walking there on that still, bright night.

Our children felt the pull too. Camilla and Carey were regular
visitors – with lovers, husbands, and children as the years went by.
Camilla had always been sure she would be an actress. Carey was
now a photographer, and the variety of light and landscape at our
new family home inspired a stack of photos. She and I had an idea
to do a book together, based on our experiences of the Midi. With
Views from a French Farmhouse, published in 1985, began a father
and daughter collaboration – like some of the most fruitful ventures, entirely unpremeditated.

Life in the Midi was never predictable, and whatever happened
had its own intensity. I loved the contrasts of climate and the habits
that went with them: listening to music round an open fire fuelled
by vinestocks; walking in the exhilaration of wind off snowy
mountains; dining long into a summer night of moths and glow-
worms and the song of frogs, with the *guinguette* string of coloured
light bulbs on our terrace making a permanent fiesta; sleeping
through a sun-throbbing July afternoon, in a shuttered room, cool
and protected by thick, strong walls.

Only rarely did the gods turn angry. And when they did, we
certainly knew it. The relentless summer heat built up electricity,
and suddenly the great dog-day storms would explode. Twice on
July 16, with a year's grace between, we were struck by a thunderbolt. Why July 16? Twice? Each time thousands of francs worth
of damage were laid on our insurance company. Power points
leaped from the wall, timeclocks were charred wrecks. It was
apocalyptic – like a scene from *Ghostbusters*. After one of the big
bangs, fearing the nuclear power station at Pierrelatte had finally
done a number, I saw René and son dashing in terror from their
work in the vineyards, as though answering the call of the last
trump. A thunderbolt had hit the field. Seconds after that, a ball of
fire rolled past us in the living-room, to the horror of a barefoot
houseguest who was making a phone call: he could have been
electrocuted.

The contradictions of the Midi are always there. Rains can belt
in August – to the joy mainly of the Richerenches truffle growers,

for summer rains mean winter riches from a good harvest of their 'black gold'. Opera singers at the Orange festival can have their high-notes carried away on the mistral, while audiences are wrapped in scarves and duvets. Grey clouds can loom over the pagan vinestock paraded in lieu of a patron saint's effigy at our village wine festival.

Even Midsummer Night can be chilly for the Enclave's most touching festival, also combining pagan and Christian rites, La Nuit du Petit St-Jean.

From Italy with the popes came the iconography of St John the Baptist as a child and companion of the young Jesus. The town of Valréas has evolved something entirely special, a mixture of legend, superstition and religious belief.

The Valréassiens choose a five-year-old child from a poor family to be 'king' for a year. The ceremony of his 'crowning' is a purely local affair, not bruited abroad or in any way touristic. No trashy souvenir or commercial hype; no visitor is asked for a sou. During the year, it imbues the town with a sense of community; neighbours and their children help each other make the magnificent, authentic medieval costumes for the pageant.

As twilight deepens outside the romanesque Church of Notre-Dame on 24 June, candles are lit one by one in the tall surrounding houses, till the whole square seems illuminated by a hundred fireflies. Trumpets sound. The doors of the dark church open, and a white horse emerges in a sudden blaze of light – to the astonished gasps of people like S and me who had not seen the ceremony before. On the horse, held by a young rider in the medieval costume of Pontifical Captain-at-Arms, comes last year's Petit St-Jean, holding the cross of the Lamb of God. Followed by standard-bearers, halberdiers, and torch-carriers in their hand-made costumes, they proceed to the Château de Simiane in the town centre where this year's Petit St-Jean, clad only in a sheepskin, waits on his throne.

There the main ceremony begins. The old 'king' hands over his office to the new, the two tiny boys performing the coronation ritual with great seriousness. Then a grand procession follows, the cortège supplemented by the King of the Cowherds and the Chariot of Agriculture pulled by two oxen; beating the bounds of

the town, they return to the centre and end with the singing of a
mighty anthem in praise of the Lamb of God and Petit St-Jean.
And everyone repairs to the bars to celebrate.

Another festival, much more modest, marked our first summer.
Perhaps festival is too wild a claim. It was our own contribution to
the summer festivity, and more of a *soirée sur l'herbe*. Except there
was no grass to hold it on; we threw carpets over the burnt-up,
dusty stubble of our meadow, amid the poppies and wild flowers
which somehow survived the heat. I lit the barbecue, and prepared
for the arrival of the twenty or so guests.

Helmut, a young German guitarist who was to provide the
music, arrived first. Enjoying a summer of one-night stands, camp-
ing out in his BMW, Helmut was bronzed as a Camargue gypsy.
But he wished to wash his hair before the concert.

'My hair is not concert-ripe,' he informed S.

'Well, don't use too much water, please, Helmut.'

'No, no, just a dropping of.'

We heard him sloshing about in the shower for about half an
hour. But he looked doubly dashing with concert-ripe hair.

It was an idyllic evening. Taking a culinary hint from Colette
who knew about these things, I made a herb brush of laurel,
thyme, sage, and mint; dipped it in a mix of olive oil, wine vinegar
and pounded garlic and brushed it over the Drôme lamb chops.
The braise of sweet-scented vinestocks added their fragrance to the
evening air.

Reclining like odalisks or Roman emperors on the carpets,
propped up on fat cushions, our guests ate their al fresco dinner
and drank much Côtes-du-Rhône made from grapes of the vineyards surrounding them. Helmut drank rather more than most.
But the mood was uncritical. We could forgive the odd fumble in
a Villa-Lobos Étude or a Bach lute suite running away with itself,
while we watched the twilight deepen and the sliver of a new
moon appear and shooting stars dance across the night sky.

Helmut played many encores till he, too, fell silent. Finding the
village auberge long since locked up for the night, he returned to
us. We had a full house, so he took his bedroll from the BMW and
dossed down on the living-room floor.

I was awoken early by running water: Helmut taking a shower

before leaving. And Monsieur Castelli's prophecy came true: the
well ran dry that very same day.

Snow, in the Midi, is a rare enough event, and when you are praying for it, even rarer. Our prayers had been answered. Where else
could mists rise from white vineyards, come swirling up through
the pine trees and, as the sun broke through, fade insubstantially
away like a curtain rising on a strange scene? The wide Rhône
Valley covered in snow!

To replace our well, we had long since drilled 150 metres down
for water. And our supply depended on melted snow from the
Alps replenishing the water table. The mild, snowless winter of
1990 was followed by a long dry summer. In normal years, our
supply was abundant for drip-watering new trees, water sprinklers,
and topping up the swimming pool which was also a firefighting
reserve on our hill. That year, we once again told guests to limit
showers to a brief splash.

At least, we didn't have cattle to feed and dying sunflowers. The
nearby towns of Taulignan and Beaumes-de-Venise had no water
at all.

Then the trouble began. Too much sand seemed to be coming
up with our water. Our pump started to gurgle and gasp omi-
nously, as though some devil were down there in the bowels of the
earth. Falling water table? Hole in the pipe? Everyone had a
different theory; Monsieur Castelli had five. No solution but to
have the tubing up – maybe all 150 metres of it! A huge piece of
equipment with what looked like an oil-drilling team arrived; up,
up came the tubing and finally the water pump to reveal . . . one
very tiny grain of sand blocking a vital part of the pump's action. A
very, very expensive grain of sand, that.

Water can make friends or enemies in the Midi. It is highly val-
ued in barter. In exchange for our use of a piece of René's land, he
has the right to fill his swimming pool once a year from our supply.

So now, depending on melted snow as we do, we blessed its
unusual abundance and beauty.

The lawn would be green next summer, the cypresses unflecked with the sickly brown of drought, and morning glories blossoming daily beneath the hanging grapes of our arbour. And the cedars, bohemian olives, fig-trees, and that loveliest of Midi trees the *mico-coulier*, planted for our grandchildren, would continue to strengthen their young roots.

Our own had dug deeper. S's green fingers had made a miracle of a garden from the inhospitable clay and stone. The house had become our home, the Paris flat relegated to a useful pied-à-terre.

The change had begun, psychologically, the moment the TGV made Paris-Lyons in two hours in 1981; not much later Montélimar, our station, in three hours, fifteen minutes. And soon, as the high-speed line extends through the Midi, less than three.

The sooner we get there, the quicker we slow down.

From 180 m.p.h. to 5 m.p.h., suddenly we're back to the pace of walks along deserted forest tracks and over stark hills and through herb-fragrant garrigue. About three in the afternoon, I take the same walk every day – up the lane and along the ridge. The experience is never the same.

Each day is a new shock to the senses – in the changes of season, of light, of nature. Today S and I crunch along in crisply frozen snow; the sun melts the white snow which drips from russet, not-yet-fallen oak leaves. Tomorrow the thaw will be nearly complete, snow only on the edges of the lane, and when Mont Ventoux wears its grey cloudcap instead of the glistening white, a landscape of eerie mists hangs in the valleys between us and it. A fragrance of damp pine needles floats on the air.

In spring, Mont Ventoux's summit is still white. Now with shale not snow. In the forest-filled distance, over a few days, a transform-ation takes place. The persistent russet oak leaves, protecting the young buds beneath, fall away in the last chill breeze. Then a warmer breath permeates the cold earth, and suddenly the land explodes with green. Buds are burgeoning on the vines. Already the velvety ochres and earthy umbers of winter are swamped by the ris-ing tide of green.

In summer, walks are only possible very early or very late in the day. Afternoon shade temperatures pushing the hundred mark make us good for nothing but sleep. Now there are purple patches of lavender field amid the greens and golds, a heat haze enveloping the hills of the Drôme.

Autumn is the most crowded season. I might even see a couple of cars, meet a few mushroomers who know the secret places for orange-fleshed *sanguins*, or hunters complaining of animal's inhumanity to man by not being around when he wants to kill it.

The Midi never stands still. No more can we, lopping the trees, clipping the hedges, sweeping the terrace, making the bonfires, getting in the firewood, bottling the wine, and pulling the corks. It's February, so I'm pruning the vines of our *tonelle*, while dreaming of a long, lazy summer lunch, shaded from the mad dog heat, when I reach up and pick my own dessert – a choice of plump, sweet Italia or Muscat grapes.

At one such lunch, an unexpected compliment was paid us by a guest. Emile Garcin, a real-estate agent, had come with Argentinian friends from St-Rémy; on his books were some of the fanciest estates in the south, some of the most photographed village houses done up by international designers. Comment on ours seemed unlikely.

'How lovely', he said with genuine feeling, 'to see an unrestored house!' (It was probably years since he'd seen one!) 'Keep it that way.'

Our low profile, we hoped, would discourage burglars.

Burglaries in the Enclave were on everyone's lips. Up till now it was outsiders who committed them. Then, horror of horrors, one day a gang from Valréas did our village, reviving an old feud between the two communes. And imagine the embarrassment of Valréas when the gang was found to include scions of local dignitaries. No one wanted to believe it. *Voyous* and *drogués* in the Enclave? And of good families, too? *Pas possible!*

There were scandals closer to home. René had fallen out with both his neighbours. His son, Gérard, out shooting thrush had downed a brace on the Duvals' vineyard. Adrienne happened to be 'green', and objected strongly. So Max complained to René, who reckoned the Duvals were exaggerating and had acted in an unneighbourly manner.

René's anger was more justifiable in his falling out with Benoit. To the Midi male, a hunting dog is a treasured companion. One of

René's beagles was found by Benoit sniffing round his rabbit hutches. So Benoit shot it, and buried it in the woods. René's other dogs picked up its scent, and led him to the dead dog which – worst offence of all – had had its collar removed. '*Le salaud!*' he roared at this, the ultimate insult. 'I shall take Père Benoit to court!' But he didn't. Often the common interests of Midi countrymen are stronger than their differences.

The Midi blows hot and cold. Its emotions are mercurial, its vendettas resolved over a drink or a grave. One minute foreigners are responsible for all its ills, the next they are seen as vital to the economy.

At present, *campenilismo* seems to be on the way out. The Mayor, whose power is absolute, decided our village should have a stand at the Foire d'Orange, the region's biggest autumn trade fair – to show what the village could do as well as make wine. And foreigners could help.

Françoise, an attractive, go-for-it lady who worked at the post office, summoned a meeting. Imagine my surprise to discover, besides a local born sculptor and gallery owner, there was a Parisian jeweller, a German leather-worker, and an Alsatian potter. Like hibernating animals, we foreigners had emerged from our holes. I didn't quite know what a writer would do at a trade fair among the tractors and local gastronomy. Françoise knew.

'Julian,' she commanded, 'you will be there with your books and Carey. We will make a display of you.'

So they did. And, by a stroke of good luck, I managed to hijack a BBC-TV crew filming in the area and they included our village's stand in their film. The crew were wined and lunched by the fair director and weaved woozily about the Fair immortalising it on film.

When I showed René my video of the programme, he was moved to eulogise things British from mint sauce to Manchester United in a most unFrench manner. Including our presence in the Midi.

'I'm not racist,' he said, 'But better *les anglais* than *les maghrébins*. At least you don't live off our Social Security.'

Give us time.

René was also most approving of my election as an *honoris causa* member of the local wine brotherhood, the Confrérie de Saint-Vincent in 1988. Tante Yvonne, an eighty-one-year-old restaurateur who served our village wines at her Lambesc restaurant, nominated me. And when her husband André died, she presented me with his confrérie black felt hat and beautiful maroon silk cloak.

With the European Community looming larger every day, there is a competitive thrust in the air, a fear that Côtes-du-Rhône may lose out to Rioja or Chianti if it doesn't do a good PR job as well as make good wines. And one chilly March evening, the organisers of the summer Fête des Vins called a council-of-war to sell us villagers on a new attraction to add spice to the festivities and draw the crowds.

Enter La Roumeco.

'The what?' went a ricochet of mumbling round a packed Salle des Fêtes. The Chairperson called us to order and presented Jean-Claude, a dynamic young local designer who would surely be furnishing the Elysées Palace with outrageous chairs within a year or so.

'La Roumeco', he began, eyes misting with poetry, 'is a living legend . . .' He had us in his pocket already. More, more . . . 'La Roumeco is our local monster.'

A gasp of disbelief went up, followed by some irreverent laughter. Jean-Claude held up a hand, his voice dropping an octave. 'I am quite serious.'

La Roumeco was news to me, too. I knew about Le Drac. Le Drac was a river monster who made a Beaucaire girl fall in love with him; this happily bewitched Rhône maiden joined him in the muddy depths, much to the chagrin of her family. And I knew about La Tarasque of Tarascon. Another amphibious horror, La Tarasque swallowed eight of the sixteen lads trying to put it to the sword. Whereupon Saint Martha conveniently turned up from Saintes-Maries in the Camargue and sprinkled it with holy water. La Tarasque instantly stopped chewing up the Tarascon boys and allowed itself to be stoned to death.

Tarascon and Beaucaire have done good business at their festivals ever since, so Jean-Claude knew what he was at.

But where had this Roumeco been suddenly dredged up from?

'He has been lost in the mists of time,' Jean-Claude continued. 'But if you give me the go-ahead to construct a carnival model of him, we will be saving him from extinction!'

And, appreciating its publicity value, we listened to the legend. La Roumeco, a vampire monster with fiery eyes of lust, came into town one night and seized six of the comeliest virgins, spiriting them away from their homes to the dungeons of the Château (where the best wines now mature). We immediately got the symbolism: vampire, virgin, blood, wine. A very appropriate monster for a wine festival, La Roumeco. And bravo the gallant boys who rescued the girls before it could taste one drop of their blood to decide whether it was a good year or not!

We loudly applauded Jean-Claude's telling of the legend which, even if he had made the whole thing up as seemed highly probable, got everyone's vote as a fun addition to the Fête des Vins. Nobody got a straight answer as to why the vampire was La and not Le, and this added further spice. A gay vampire?

When 'he' first made his appearance, La Roumeco turned out to be a combo of bat, pig, wolf, and fish with sharp white teeth and claws and fins like a 1956 Chevrolet. Four sturdy sons of the soil sweated inside his body, trundling him through the narrow streets in a carnival parade. His red eyes flashed lecherously. He was followed – at a safe distance – by six girls in white Grecian tunics, then a posse of their rescuers, medieval knights on horseback.

The village had turned out in force. Max and Adrienne Duval greeted us. How Max had mellowed over the years, his vineyards a success, his place in the village assured. Adrienne was now a highly active member of the Municipal Council which had wisely voted funding of La Roumeco. The new Mayor, smiling his affable, wide, gap-toothed smile, grasped my hand in a strong *vigneron*'s grip.

'Do you guarantee the virginity of those girls, Monsieur Le Maire?' I asked.

'In these days?' he shrugged. '*Que voulez-vous?*'

Somehow, when you can exchange a joke with your Mayor, however corny, there is a feeling of having arrived. It is a good feeling, another step forward.

Like buying the field behind the house, as we had recently

done, from René. And having Bruno shape it up with his baby bulldozer, and plant new trees. And finding Monsieur Bernard, who helps S with the garden, waiting for us as we returned from La Roumeco. La Roumeco didn't mean a lot to Monsieur Bernard: as cemetery gardener, he was used to real vampires; and as a man with thirty-two grandchildren, six virgins more or less gone missing were all in a day's work.

In a few seconds S and Monsieur Bernard were deep into garden talk. 'Well, the mistral's dropped,' he said. 'Just right for trimming the cypress hedge. *Enfin, le temps est propice.*'

Monsieur Bernard always knew what conditions were propitious for what; he was imbued with nature's wisdom. In spring, it had been: 'It's a waxing moon, Madame More. Better get the oleanders planted.'

And in October, it was the prophecy of a hard winter: 'Onion skins are thicker, acorns more plentiful. That's a sure sign. Maybe we should leave the planting of the conifers till spring. A cold snap in November and they'll be done for.'

But our own tree was well and truly planted. The roots had taken. And now, if anyone asks 'Aren't you ever homesick?', the answer is simple: 'Only when we leave home.'

Peter Mayle
Toujours Provence £5.99

The magnificent sequel to *A Year in Provence*

'The days pass slowly but the weeks rush by. We now measure the year in ways that have little to do with diaries and dates. *Merci Provence* . . .'

A Year in Provence has passed . . . yet the dream lives on.

And Peter Mayle, now known throughout the Luberon as 'The English *Écrevisse*', slowly begins to turn native in the old stone farmhouse at the foot of the mountains between Avignon and Aix.

Toujours Provence finds him skulking through British Customs with a suitcase full of truffles, tracking down a man whose ambition is to make toads sing the 'Marseillaise', taking *pastis* lessons and looking nervously over his shoulder at forest fires.

From vantage points as varied as the Cannes Film Festival, the *caves* at Chateauneuf-de-Pape and the Ménerbes Dog Show, Peter Mayle hilariously and memorably recounts the pleasures and pitfalls of the Provençal paradise – for today and for ever.

'Splendidly amusing . . . filled with things which will help you to understand, at least in part, the glory of this wonderful place.'
DIRK BOGARDE, WEEKEND TELEGRAPH

'Peter Mayle has achieved every Briton's dream . . . a delightful sequel.'
DAILY EXPRESS

'Peter Mayle's first book was about losing his virginity in southern France; his second is a frank confession of the joys of intimacy with it. This collection of anecdotes and anniversary waltzes is a chatty adieu in which smugness is kept at bay by likeable enthusiasm.'
FREDERIC RAPHAEL, THE SUNDAY TIMES

Peter Mayle
A Year in Provence £5.99

'Among the vines stood an old stone farmhouse, weathered by wind and sun to a colour somewhere between honey and pale grey. In the afternoon sun, with the wooden shutters half closed like sleepy eyelids, it was irresistible . . .'

First, a dream of a life in the South of France . . . and then a home to match the dream. Moving into an old farmhouse, at the foot of the Luberon Mountains between Avignon and Aix, was the beginning of an exotic and bewildering new life for Peter Mayle and his wife – the beginning of *A Year in Provence*.

It was a year that began with lunch. By its end they had survived the buffetings of both the Mistral and the soupy accent of the native Provençal, overseen the planting of a new vineyard, risen above invasion by builders and guests, and eaten and drunk the best that France had to offer.

A Year in Provence is Peter Mayle's hilarious description of their pleasurable and occasionally frustrating experiences – an account that attempts to answer the question: What is it *really* like to live in the South of France?

'Stylish, witty and delightfully readable. The style is high comedy and Mayle is bitingly funny about local rural *mores*. But the jokeyness only partly obscures Mayle's warm enthusiasm for local life and landscape. He writes vividly . . . and throws himself with infectious gusto into Provençal sensuality.' THE SUNDAY TIMES

'An engaging diary . . . Peter Mayle's idyllic portrait makes you almost taste the wonderful food and wine, feel the sun and balmy breezes, and take part in the games of boules and goat races.' SUNDAY EXPRESS

'Anyone with any feel for the land and the people who lead their lives close to it will be enchanted.' YORKSHIRE EVENING POST

Miles Turner
Paupers' Paris £7.99
Revised 1992–93 Edition

The classic guide to getting the most of Paris for the fewest francs . . .

Ten years since its first publication *Paupers' Paris* still has as much freshness and charm as the city itself.

Whether you're planning a quick weekend break or a longer spell of Left Bank living, *Paupers' Paris* is an invaluable guide, with up-to-date information on the best value shops, restaurants and hotels, as well as vital advice on tipping, manners, clothing sizes, baby sitters, dry cleaning, public loos and generally how to achieve Paris *savoir-faire*.

Perfect for anyone with more taste than money, *Paupers' Paris* shows how to enjoy a real holiday in the world's greatest romantic city.

'Reams of advice and information. It's clear that he loves Paris dearly.'
THE OBSERVER

Arthur Eperon
Burgundy £6.99

Burgundy is a land of gentle hills and dense forests, of restful waterways and tranquil old towns and villages. Once a powerful dukedom, its great abbeys the wellspring of European Christianity, Burgundy is rich in history, art and architecture, from the Romanesque basilica at Vézelay and the Renaissance château at Tantay and Ancy-le-Franc to the beautiful old buildings of Dijon. Best known for its wine, Burgundy is equally proud of its cuisine.

Arthur Eperon offers you his own recommendations for discovering this charming area. Whether you are cruising on the canals, exploring Mâcon or Beaune, touring the wine villages or sampling the local family-run restaurant, you will find them all described here, with anecdotes and hints to inspire the seasoned as well as the first-time traveller.

France has been Eperon territory for over forty years. Sharing his experiences of the most varied and beautiful country in Europe, *Eperon's French Regional Guides* are at once authoritative *and* uniquely personal, covering all of the popular and some of the lesser-known regions of France.

Arthur Eperon
The Loire £6.99

The Loire Valley, with its majestic river, has been justly famed for centuries.
Attracting Roman, Norman and English invaders, it was to become a
second home to the French court. The Loire runs through lush meadows
and hills covered with vines, and is fed by beautiful rivers like the Cher and
Indre. Romantic châteaux and historic towns add to the region's *embarras
de richesses*, luring visitors back time and time again.

Arthur Eperon offers you his own recommendations for discovering the
Loire, from riverside sunbathing to the splendours of the château of
Chenonceau – where Diane de Poitiers and Catherine de Medici laid out
the gardens; from the hilly vineyard country west of Sancerre to the
evocative city of Amboise. All are described here with anecdotes and hints
to inspire the seasoned as well as the first-time traveller.

All Pan books are available at your local bookshop or newsagent, or can be ordered direct from the publisher. Indicate the number of copies required and fill in the form below.

Send to: Pan C. S. Dept
              Macmillan Distribution Ltd
              Houndmills Basingstoke RG21 2XS
or phone: 0256 29242, quoting title, author and Credit Card number.

Please enclose a remittance* to the value of the cover price plus: £1.00 for the first book plus 50p per copy for each additional book ordered.

*Payment may be made in sterling by UK personal cheque, postal order, sterling draft or international money order, made payable to Pan Books Ltd.

Alternatively by Barclaycard/Access/Amex/Diners

Card No. ☐☐☐☐☐☐☐☐☐☐☐☐☐☐☐☐☐☐

Expiry Date ☐☐☐☐☐☐

Signature:

Applicable only in the UK and BFPO addresses

While every effort is made to keep prices low, it is sometimes necessary to increase prices at short notice. Pan Books reserve the right to show on covers and charge new retail prices which may differ from those advertised in the text or elsewhere.

NAME AND ADDRESS IN BLOCK LETTERS PLEASE:

....

Name _____

Address _____

_____

_____

_____

6/92